UNACCOMPANIED WOMEN

RANDOM HOUSE

unaccompanied women

late-life adventures in love, sex, and real estate

jane juska

WITHDRAWN

Chatto & Windus
LONDON

Names and significant details have been changed to protect
the privacy of those whose generosity and good humor have
enriched my life.

Published by Chatto & Windus 2006

First published in the United States by Villard Books in 2006

2 4 6 8 10 9 7 5 3

Copyright © 2006 by Jane Juska

Jane Juska has asserted her right under the
Copyright, Designs and Patents Act 1988 to
be identified as the author of this work

First published in Great Britain in 2006 by
Chatto & Windus
Random House, 20 Vauxhall Bridge Road,
London SW1V 2SA

Random House Australia (Pty) Limited
20 Alfred Street, Milsons Point, Sydney,
New South Wales 2061, Australia

Random House New Zealand Limited
18 Poland Road, Glenfield,
Auckland 10, New Zealand

Random House (Pty) Limited
Isle of Houghton, Corner of Boundary Road & Carse O'Gowrie,
Houghton 2198, South Africa

The Random House Group Limited Reg. No. 954009
www.randomhouse.co.uk

A CIP catalogue record for this book is available from the British Library

ISBN 0 7011 7804 3
EAN 9780701178043 (from Jan 07)

Printed in Great Britain by
Clays Ltd, St Ives plc

Book design by Victoria Wong

contents

unaccompanied women

puzzle pieces

When I was thirty-seven years old, I met the man of my dreams. He was a tall man, of course—Who would dream up a short one?—and slim with bright blue eyes that sparkled with the fun of life. He was funny, clever, witty, and occasionally profound. He was smart. He was cultured. He was single. His name was Dan. The year was 1970, when all things were possible.

Not long before Dan and I met, I left my brief and unhappy marriage and, with a five-year-old son to support in all ways, never thought about male companionship; indeed, I needed fewer not more complications, and life had taught me that adding a man to one's life was just asking for trouble. Everything was simpler without a man, and that included sex, which I had taught myself to do, thereby freeing me from the emotional trappings that came along with another person. No need to ask "Was it good for you?" No need to wonder if he'd call. No need to worry that you weren't pretty or clever or imaginative enough in bed to ensure a repeat engagement. No need to heap blame on yourself when your husband turned away from you, no need to wonder what an orgasm felt like. Do-it-yourself sex was the answer to a lifetime of insecurities and unmet needs. It was, after all, the seventies, when hedonism was in and your mother's admonitions were out. Besides, it was boys, not girls, who went blind.

In the seventies the California high school in which Dan and I taught English was wild. Built for fifteen hundred kids, it housed almost three thousand teenagers, and in the seventies a lot of them were stoned a good deal of the time. Like, hey man, why not? So were some of the teachers. Everyone smoked something, and during our fifteen-minute morning break the faculty lounge, a cloudy haze, looked like a cocktail party with bad furniture. The talk, though, was great. We were all young and smart and funny and occasionally profound. One day as I stared out the window onto the quad where hordes of kids jostled each other or held each other up, Dan came up behind me, put his arm around my shoulders, pointed to the theatre of the absurd going on outside, and said, "Someday, my son, this will all be yours." I collapsed with laughter, and we became fast friends.

Dan taught me to love opera, black-and-white movies, and, on Sunday afternoons, champagne. Accompanied by the glories of *La Traviata* played at top volume on his fine stereo, we toasted each other, celebrating our like-mindedness on books and music and people, very few of whom escaped our often malicious judgment. From opposite sides of the room we drank to our superiority.

Dan lived alone in a tiny redwood cottage high in the hills, at the end of a long path that wound up through madrone and live oak from the street below; it was the most romantic place I could have imagined. On the evening of my undoing, Dan, in his Levi's and sweater, relieved me of the bottle of champagne I had brought; from inside the cottage I heard Tosca lamenting her lover's fate. Overhead the stars were beginning to shine; inside, a fire burned brightly in the fireplace. Was this a night made in heaven? Without a drop of champagne, I was tiddly on the promises implicit in the evening before me.

I don't remember dinner, though I can safely say that it was wonderful, for Dan, along with everything else, was a wonderful cook. He seemed to do it easily, as easily as he gardened, as easily as he selected the perfect concerts for the two of us to attend, as easily as he shushed those in the movie audience who whispered

little street, around the corner from the post office and the bank and the movie theatre and restaurants Italian and Chinese and French and Middle Eastern and Mexican and Indian as well as, if you felt like American, a soda fountain—malts, lime rickeys, the works. My neighbors said "Good morning," and so did I; we were friendly and at the same time respectful of one another's privacy. Unlike me, who was a renter, most of them had lived in their houses for many years. So when a single man, young, no more than thirty, bought the modest house next door to me for nine hundred thousand dollars, we raised our eyebrows in wonder: My neighbors had become millionaires almost overnight. My cottage, too, shot up in value, and I began to worry that my landlords might raise the rent accordingly. The fear of being ousted, of being unable to pay increased rents, is endemic to renters; deep down we know that nothing is really ours, that, except for the protection of a few good laws, we live at the mercy of those who own the property we pretend is ours. So we try not to think about those very real possibilities, which resurface every so often, against our will, in the middle of the night. I put myself back to sleep by reassuring myself that, someday, I would be able to buy a small place, not for pride of ownership but in the interest of getting a good night's sleep.

In the meantime I went about the business of the retired person: Being Busy. Instead of rising every morning at five A.M. to prepare myself for the onslaught of one hundred sixty hormonal teenagers, I sang in a choir, taught a class in writing at San Quentin State Prison, taught a few classes at a nearby college, and every Thursday morning escorted women into Planned Parenthood for abortions they had chosen to have, no matter the calls and the hoots of the self-righteous, who thought the choice belonged to them and not to the women who walked beside me. I was one of those newly retired people who say, "Oh, I'm so busy I hardly have time to catch a breath!" Being Busy, like Staying Active, is not only the American way and so commendable in and of itself; being and staying busy—a full-time job—is useful for keeping at bay those deep-seated emotions that threaten stability, that can turn a plain and simple life into anything but.

Well, I failed at retirement, at keeping busy, and my punishment was that "anything but . . ." happened to me. A deep-seated emotion—desire—unseated itself, rose up and began to knock insistently at the door of my sexuality. I wanted to invite a man into my life. The problem was that, despite senior hikes, senior birdwatching, senior mixers, even a couple of senior dances at a church the doors of which I had not darkened in over fifty years, I couldn't find one. I took classes at night; everybody in them was either married or thirty-two or both. I went to a reception for college alumni; everybody there was married or one hundred and seven, so I just gave up; celibacy was better than this eternal hunt, and not nearly so humiliating. Then suddenly one autumn evening as I walked home from the movies, genius struck, albeit briefly, and there plopped into my mind what it was I wanted and how I would get it. By the time I got home, a personal ad, fully formed, was ready to go: "Before I turn 67, I would like to have sex with a man I like. If you want to talk first, Trollope works for me."

No use in trying for busy any longer, the cat was out of the bag. I could no longer suppress my need not just for sex but for touching, for intimacy, for a man right next to me or on top of me or underneath, whatever we found that was to our liking. I wanted a full life and had to admit that I didn't have one. I was greedy, needy, ready, and determined. Next day, I went to the library, just down the block, where I searched *The New York Review of Books* for instructions on how to submit what it was I wanted and whose results I was prepared to live with. Or so I thought. Holy cow and Lord A-mighty.

The New York Review is a highly regarded publication full of long essays on everything—politics, literature, art, science—with a back page devoted to ads—real estate, seminars abroad, employment oppportunities, and, occupying the most space of all, two, sometimes three columns of personal ads. It seemed to me that men who read such an august journal would be a cut above the men who read ads in a regular newspaper; I expected the *Review* to provide a filter, leaving the dregs for those who weren't me. I expected to get a little class out of all this. What I got were sixty-three-and-counting responses to my little ad and a new life I barely recognized as my own. Never again was my life plain and never ever simple. Did I get what I wanted? Yes, I got exactly what my ad asked for, along with a life that got tossed around like a shoestring in a windstorm, that got twisted into knots, until it freed itself only to be buffeted about again by forces beyond my control.

At times my life seemed not to belong to me at all; it dizzied and upset me at the same time it filled every nook and cranny of me with men, some of whom I came to love, some of whom loved me back . . . or not. To keep my sanity—truly, to quiet the din in my head, the roar in my ears—I wrote voluminously in my journal. In the end I made the journal into a book called *A Round-Heeled Woman.* As Mark Twain says in *The Adventures of Huckleberry Finn,* "You don't know about me without you have read a book by the name of . . ." Then he goes on to create his richest character ever, Huck, and we forget there ever was a previous book.

Likewise, the publication of *A Round-Heeled Woman* brought with it another new life. So, as Mark Twain claims he did in *The Adventures of Tom Sawyer:* "told the truth, mainly," I will, too. I will tell you about my lives, so various and new, and about the people in it now as well as then. Along the way, if I learned anything—and I did—I will tell you that, too.

I know right this very minute that I'm different from the person I was before I went after what I wanted. During my late-life adventures I gave away myself, sometimes bit by bit, sometimes wholly. Fortunately, I got most of the pieces back, though not in the same order. I think what I'm after now is making the pieces of me fit, smoothing the edges so they don't rub up against one another and hurt. Have I given up the passionate life? I'm still deciding. Maybe writing this book will help me find out.

had tried sex and drugs and alcohol, and every one of them had satisfied me, so Jesus was unnecessary; instead I replied, "I'm hanging up now." And I did, but not before he screamed, "You're a fucking whore!" Ten minutes later the phone rang again, but this time I let the machine get it: "Jane," said Denny, "if you had a relationship with the one who created you, you wouldn't have killed all those babies." I unplugged the phone and went to bed.

Denny is not the first to charge me with promiscuity and godlessness, although usually the language is less direct. Usually the callers and letter-writers feel sorry for me: "I can only say I am saddened by the downturns your life has taken" followed by "I am not being judgmental" followed by "Go see *The Passion of the Christ.*" Christians in Milwaukee, a whole congregation of them, I am told, pray for me weekly. I would not be surprised to learn that church people everywhere are wringing their hands, for my book details behavior utterly contrary to religious teachings. However, it is not only Christians who feel sorry for me.

Joseph Epstein was an intellectual hero to me for many years; I looked forward to the sound thinking and wise humor he brought to his column in *The American Scholar* and was saddened by his departure as the journal's editor and by the rumor that Mr. Epstein's politics had shifted radically rightward. When PBS in Boston called me and asked me to be one side of a conversation with Mr. Epstein, I was flattered and agreed immediately. I prepared for our talk by buying—in hardcover—his new book, *Fabulous Small Jews,* which I read with great pleasure. Off I went early one Saturday morning to a studio on the Berkeley campus, nervous as could be: I was going to have a conversation with a man I had long admired. From the studio in Boston, Mr. Epstein trumpeted monogamy, underscoring his own long marriage as the example for us all. In the end, he said, referring to my book, he couldn't help but feel sorry that I would never experience the joys of growing old with just one man. I cried into the microphone, "Oh, Mr. Epstein! I'm so disappointed in you!" What disappointed me was that my intellectual hero seemed to have lost the latitude necessary for true thought. I had admired him over the years for the wide range of his thoughtfulness, which now, beamed to me from somewhere in Boston, seemed like a narrow stream of single-mindedness: My Way Is the Right Way. This was not the first time I had heard or read Mr. Epstein on the virtues of his particular marriage, but this was the first time I wondered why we have never heard from Mrs. Epstein.

The *National Review,* a journal by and for neoconservatives, felt sorry for me, too. In an article that appeared shortly after my book came out, the writer expressed her sorrow that, in the end, I will have no one to cut my grass. Let me tell you, if I had any grass, there would be no shortage of volunteers to cut it.

In *The New York Times,* none other than the op-ed columnist, the estimable David Brooks, took my "lifestyle," if that's what you want to call it, to task: Although he didn't address me directly in his column "The Power of Marriage," he warned me and others like me of "spiritual suicide." He announced that anyone who has "several sexual partners in a year" is in trouble, and warned against finding oneself "in an assembly line of selfish sensations," which translated, I'm guessing, means multiple orgasms. Way to go, David. This way of thinking, this certainty, this absoluteness, is something I had believed Mr. Brooks too smart to be a victim of. But I have found that all too often intellect shuts off when people talk about sex and marriage; suddenly their childhoods kick in, their Sunday schools, their parents' finger-wagging; suddenly, according to Mr. Brooks, it's trouble for anyone who has "several sexual partners in a year." What he offers is a formula for all of us: One man plus one woman equals one marriage forever and ever, amen. I am, therefore, behaving in a manner certain to bring a self-induced end to my spiritual self. Again, I wonder what his wife might have to say. I think Mrs. Brooks would agree with her husband; he's so cute.

"Oh, Mr. Epstein!" I cried near the end of our conversation.

"Don't put me in a box!" A box with a lid on it. I won't go. Let me tell you: "Selfish sensations," when ignored, are a deathblow. "Selfish sensations"—that pleasure most profound and most natural of two people together, the pleasure called sex—when resisted, when denied, lead to spiritual—and sometimes virtual—suicide and murder. Messrs. Epstein and Brooks would offer marriage as a solution, as the only solution, despite the gloomy statistic that more than half of all marriages in this country fail. Still, in the absence of a more workable substitute we cling to marriage as our strongest institution for holding back social chaos.

Shall we think for a moment about fundamentalist Islam? Where virgins are promised on the other side as the reward for murder and mayhem committed by young men on this side? What if we gave them female companionship on this side? Remember the Berlin airlift of 1948 and '49, where, from our Douglas C-47 Dakota airplanes we dropped the necessities of life into a city sealed off by Communist Russia and became heroes to the rest of the world? Well, if sex isn't a necessity of life, what is it? I believe that the deprivation of "selfish sensations" in the name of religion is responsible for most of the upheaval that has been a sordid part of human history. By some accounts, throughout history Christians, in the name of rectitude, have been responsible for as many as one hundred million deaths. Let's put an end to this. Let's give young men of Christ and Allah a way of venting frustration and bloodlust before it reaches explosive dimensions; let's offer them women, or, better yet, let women offer themselves. Couldn't young men be encouraged just to date? Walking side by side along the river or on a street—a man and a woman together—cannot be a bad thing. How simply the urge to violence could be dispelled.

In the meantime, all you fundamentalists of whatever stripe you are, stay out of my life. I plan to read your books just to keep track of your wrong-headedness, but you don't have to read mine.

On the other hand a lot of people liked *A Round-Heeled Woman.* They called me on the phone, they wrote me letters, they crowded into the bookstores where I did readings and signed books. They cheered what they called my courage and thanked me for restoring hope.

"DO YOU THINK you're a nymphomaniac?" So began *A Round-Heeled Woman*. Bill, at sixty-one, good-looking, attentive, and outspoken, was the speaker of that first sentence. He had not read my book, for it was yet to be written; unwittingly, however, he had begun it. I tucked his question away for use another day: Midnight, sitting close together, didn't seem to be the time or place to bring up my writing plans. But he had heard about me, and my ad, from my friend Ilse, and now he seemed interested in me. In the weeks following he sent flowers; he brought me books; for Valentine's Day he gave me my own subscription to *The New York Review*. He invited me to bed.

The last sentence of the book is "Paint your wagon, I'm coming." It was said to me before I had any intention of writing a book. It came from Graham, tall, slim, funny, kind, terribly bright, and thirty-two years old. His letter in response to my ad in *The New York Review* was the last letter I answered. "Not quite Harold and Maude," he wrote of what the two of us might become, "but close." Full of qualms and curiosity, I answered, and a few months later we met. He was damned near perfect. "Do you agree that Melville's 'Bartleby' is the most perfect story ever written?" he asked. I did. "Tell me the name of your favorite poem." I did, and he recited The General Prologue of "The Canterbury Tales," of course in Middle English. "Why is it," he asked rhetorically, "that on a Chinese menu you have to get to at least number fifteen before anything gets interesting?" And very late, in a room high above Central Park, "Why are you wearing all those clothes?" And then I wasn't. He was my heart's delight, and I was his. But before Graham there was Meredith. And there was loss.

Friendships among women are tricky things. We are inclined

to take them for granted since they happen so naturally, since they are born of common interests, since, unlike friendships with men, they seem easy to come by and easy to live with. Or so we believe. My long friendship with Meredith would prove me wrong, would show me that tact, understanding, and nurturing were as essential to women's friendships as to any relationship I might have with a man. I took Meredith for granted and paid the price.

In the summer of 1999, some few months before I conceived the notion of placing an ad, Meredith and I spent a fine week at a lake edged with tall pines, a lake reflecting snowcapped mountains. Meredith and I had a lovely lot of talk, much laughter. We went to the county fair, we enjoyed each other's company. Why not do it again the following summer? Yes, we agreed, we would.

But then came Graham. I chose the coward's way to tell Meredith: e-mail.

Dear Meredith,

I feel absolutely terrible about this, but I am going to do it anyway. I have to disinvite you to the lake. On a whim, I invited Graham, believing that of course he wouldn't come. But he's coming, and I want to see him. I don't expect you to accept my apologies or do anything but be angry with me. But I will continue to hope for forgiveness sometime.

Meredith and I became friends in 1955, a long, long time ago, in San Francisco. Me from Ohio, Meredith from Detroit, we followed the rule: gloves and heels in downtown San Francisco. Hats were voluntary by this time, though women our mothers' ages still wore them in Union Square. For Christmas, Meredith and I gave each other elbow-length leather gloves and compacts, pretty and round and containing face powder I never knew where to put or how much, so I didn't. Still, I tried to be a lady, or at least lady-like. Meredith, tall and slim as a model, did much better. As ladies, we never talked about sex, especially our own.

It is our generation—Meredith's and mine—the one that grew up in the fifties, that is silent about sex. Like girls of our time, we never even mentioned sex except obliquely, and Meredith was very good at oblique. She was a great literary gossip: She knew all the dirt of the literati, such as that Simone de Beauvoir shacked up with Nelson Algren in Chicago, then returned to her celibate life with Sartre. And she did it more than once, sort of like going to camp in the summer. I listened intently as Meredith told me that on his wedding night John Ruskin screamed in horror at the sight of his wife's naked body, and that Dante Gabriel Rossetti dug up his wife's body to reclaim the poems he had put into her coffin on her death. And that Tennessee Williams was gay. "He is not," I said. "Look at all those manly men in his plays, look at Stanley Kowalski!" "Oh, Jane," sighed Meredith, exasperated over my stubborn naïveté, "only a writer in love with other men could create those characters." We giggled over the gossip and the people who lived in it, but we were careful never ever to connect anything they did to our own lives; we never explored what they did, we just guessed and kept our guesses to ourselves. For Meredith and me it was as if we weren't having sex, though both of us were, Meredith with a married man, I with Jack, both relationships headed for disaster. Not talking about certain things ensured our friendship; we understood the taboos against intimacy of all sorts; we honored our mothers' code.

One time, our mothers notwithstanding, sex interfered. It reared its ugly head and would not go away. Before the pill, before *Roe v. Wade,* pregnancy loomed at every turn. Birth control was available by way of a diaphragm, that little round thing that, once inserted, popped open and screened (almost always) the sperm. Meredith and I never talked about the diaphragm, whether or not we used one or where to get one if we wanted to or how to get the damn thing in or out if we got one. Meredith clearly did not get one. She got pregnant by way of a man who, as a husband and a father of two, could not marry her. So in order to keep her job, she needed an abortion. Unwed mothers then were fired if their disreputable state became known, and pregnancy being what it is, it could remain hidden only for so long. So Meredith needed an abortion, illegal and dangerous though it was, and Tijuana was where others we had heard of went to do the dastardly deed. At the time Meredith had no money, so I gave her money, some mine, the rest borrowed from friends, and off she went, the father of the unborn child along with her, no doubt to make sure the job got done. Meredith returned, the father went to jail for nonpayment of child support, and I listened to Meredith recount the bloody tale of pain and humiliation she'd endured south of the border. Twenty minutes of a real-life story was enough for us. We were relieved to return to ignorance and the safety thereof.

Meredith went on to spend her nights at law school; I spent mine in North Beach. I was fascinated by the 1950s' renegades, the girls who went to Greenwich Village in New York or North Beach in San Francisco and became beatniks, which meant, at least to me, that they had a lot of sex. When I wasn't wearing gloves and heels on my way to lunch with Meredith, I tried to become a beatnik. I grew my hair long, and hung out in bars. But I never had sex. I never even got asked to have sex. The closest I got was one night at a bar called The Place on Grant Street in North Beach. The Place was small, dark, and probably dirty, though there was never enough light to find out for sure. The one waitress in The Place—Sheila was her name—appeared magically out of the darkness, holding pitchers and trays handed to her by some sorcerer in the alley out back. No bartender was ever seen. Every Monday night was Blabbermouth Night: Anyone who wanted to could take the grungy little stage and harangue or sing or recite their poems or do magic tricks, whatever they felt like, the only requirement being a sincere attempt at being outrageous. No girls went up there, of course; we sat in the back and drank beer and wished we hadn't worn kneesocks and sneakers.

One night Dirty-Talking Charles, as he was known to all of North Beach, strode up—"weaved" is more accurate—to the stage, turned to the audience, and began to chant, "Sex is the answer, sex is the answer." On he went, never varying, never pausing, never ever ending, it seemed to me. Finally, many beers within me, I called out, "So what is the question?" Dirty-Talking Charles, without missing a beat, said, "Will you?" In 1956 that was a showstopper.

That's as close as I ever got to talking about sex or having some for far too many years to follow. I also failed to become a beatnik; I could never figure out what to wear on my feet, and the long braid I wore down my back gave me headaches.

Meredith stayed away from The Place and the other hangouts in North Beach, earning her law degree in record time. My yearnings remained mine alone, unspoken to anyone, rumbling around my insides like those steel balls in a pinball machine.

Sexism was not a word then, only a practice. The boys and men who read their poetry on the stage of The Place and up and down the California coast, in bars and on street corners, claimed the company of women to serve them food, admiration, and sex. I suppose I should have been grateful to be excluded, but I wasn't. I wanted like anything to go with them, to do whatever they asked just for the adventure, the fabulousness of it all. But there were no takers. I needed to be bolder, to ask outrageous questions, to offer clever answers; I needed to be prettier, but all I was was afraid, and so I went back to work as a secretary to wait for the right man to come along. The waiting seemed endless. Always available for witty conversation, much of it about books, never about sex, Meredith was a friend indeed. Together we avoided the unmentionable; we were a team.

Now, some forty years later, I hoped she would understand that I could not pass up an opportunity to make love in the afternoon, evening, morning, noon, night with this wonderful man. Surely she would understand eventually that this was unusual, a onetime thing, likely never to happen again. She didn't. She wrote back, *"It is my belief that e-mail is a poor way to communicate anything important."* What the hell did that mean? So I called her on the telephone. "I am so sorry, but I've told you about Graham. How . . . can you . . . ?" Click.

Graham came to the lake, and we went to bed. Before and after, we canoed, went to the county fair, talked endlessly about everything, and Graham skipped stones—one, two, three, four, five, fifteen! skips—far out into the lake. He wore a sarong. "It's from Kenya," he explained. "It slips off rather easily." Afterward he read Proust aloud to me while outside our window the sun went down into the lake far away on the other side. Sometimes I lay on my side and just looked at him. The sunset paled.

In October, some six weeks after Graham's visit, Meredith phoned and said, "Let's have lunch and get this elephant out of the living room." I agreed.

I was early. And I was anxious. I did wrong. Yes, I did. Did I do wrong and right? I didn't know. Yes, I probably did them both and at the same time. One thing I was certain of was this: I was being called to account and I was scared. I have always avoided confrontation. My mind grows fuzzy at the mere thought of it, although, my long life having provided extensive experience in heartbreak and healing, I am better at it than when I was twenty-five or even twenty-six. I am more capable of standing outside my feelings, my feelings are not as vulnerable to hurt. Who was I kidding?

Café Claude in San Francisco was Meredith's and my favorite restaurant. It is in a little alley in downtown San Francisco; you have to know about it to find it, or be French, because French people run it and, I'm sure, French people cook the food. "'Allo, 'allo," says the maître d'.

No longer burdened with gloves and heels, Meredith and I were dressed much more casually, but at sixty-six Meredith was as elegant as she was when we first met, perhaps more so. She made more money, for one thing, and lived alone in a three-story Queen Anne in Noe Valley, one of San Francisco's most desirable neighborhoods. When she heard I had sold my house in Orinda and was moving into a cottage sans washer and dryer, that I would *wheel my dirty clothes* to the laundromat in a little cart *in public,* she inhaled sharply and said, "Just don't do it when I'm around." Indeed, she never saw my cottage. Safer that way. To irritate her for the hell of it, when I visited her in her Queen Anne, I would wear my Birkenstocks. Once, in a department store, she caught me in them and said, "I'm going up to Better Shoes, please don't follow me." We both laughed, hers more of a sputter.

But it was true: Her shoes and clothes were expensive; she bought nothing on sale. She had never entered a discount store; a mall was her idea of hell. Wary of Macy's appeal to the common herd, she had never been to its first floor, where cosmetics promise new life to the bourgeoisie. Instead she entered on Geary Street and took the elevator directly to the designer floors. Once she was there her eyes narrowed and her focus became as intense as that of any athlete about to take the field. She would raise her head, sniff delicately the air around her, and glide among the racks and tables, smoothing her hand along the fabrics as she did. She would find what she had come for. She had no use for the new look, tight-fitting industrial fabrics stretched over bodies meant to be hidden, not flaunted. Like the rest of the country, San Francisco has exchanged elegance for discomfort and show. Style now is loud. Meredith's style was as appropriate, as beautiful, in the year 2000 as it was in 1955. It is Ralph Lauren with imagination. Whoever dyed her hair should have gotten an award.

There she was, earlier even than I, seated at a corner table, back to the wall so that she could look me over as I entered, her hair a gleaming black, pulled back sleek into a chignon suitable for every century. I don't remember what I was wearing, something that made me wish October weren't so warm, that instead an autumnal chill had settled in, calling for a cover-up, like a coat, full-length.

Though I couldn't see them without peering underneath the table, I knew her shoes were of calf leather, medium-heeled, the toe rounded just a bit, a design of some sort—a scroll, a feather, a sweet bow—etched into the vamp by an underpaid Italian still living with his mother. She wore trousers, men's trousers to fit her slim hips, tailored to accept the slight but determinedly female tummy. I knew that when she rose, her trousers would fall into just the right break, skimming to good effect her long and limber legs, covering just enough but not all of the Italian shoes. God, if I looked like that in pants, I'd pay all that money, too. My trousers come from CP Shades, where all pants are made with elastic waistbands.

I decided to take the plunge, deliberately choosing courtroom language: "So, what's on the docket?"

Meredith was quick to answer, "Why did you do it?"

I stalled. "Do what?"

"Invite someone else when you'd already invited me." Boy, did she have eye contact. I was feeling just a bit pierced.

"Because it was Graham. Because he could come that week, and if we were ever going to see each—" Meredith's face made it clear that pleading my case would do no good, but I stumbled on. "I regret making you angry; you have every right to be angry, but . . ." Hell, I was not going to lick her Italian boots. "I do not regret the week with—"

Meredith cut me off. "I don't think I was so angry. I was more hurt. I still am."

Get over it, I wanted to say but didn't. "I'm sorry. Graham is special. The circumstances—"

"And I'm not?"

Oh, please. "Yes, you are special but in a different way." Meredith looked skeptical, and I wanted to shout, For crissake, Meredith, can't you see how you and Graham are different and special, both of you at the same time? I wanted to say but didn't, Listen hard, Meredith, great fucking beats great shopping all to hell.

"I guess our systems of friendships are different," Meredith said. Her salad remained untouched, her eyes were still glued to my face. I could feel my cheeks melting.

"Systems are vulnerable to blips," I argued, "and Graham is a very big blip. Graham is a goddam meteor shower!" My voice rose, and Meredith's mouth made a moue, her way of reminding me of her distaste for crude language and loud voices. I persisted, albeit quietly. "In fact, I don't have a system of friendship; I have friends."

Meredith gazed down into her soup. "Well, then, . . ."

One last try. I leaned across the table and almost whispered, "I regret hurting your feelings, but it seems to me that a long friendship like ours ought to include forgiveness. I had hoped that with the passing of time your hurt would ease."

"It hasn't."

Meredith's soup bowl was empty. She had managed to eat it all—spoon pushed away, not toward—without spilling a drop. Shreds of my Niçoise decorated my bosom. I was bespattered with egg yolk, tuna, several lettuces, and an olive. *La salade, c'est moi.*

Outside the café I said, "Talk to you soon." Meredith was silent, and I knew that my friendship with this prickly, sensitive, funny, smart woman was at an end. I had been found guilty before the court convened. Throwing myself on the mercy of the judge, admitting that I had willfully and with callousness aforethought brought hurt to my friend, then asking forgiveness, had wrought only stern silence.

"You're a lot of fun," Meredith told me at the corner of Grant and Pine, "but you are undependable, unpredictable, and irresponsible."

The elephant in our living room was, of course, sex. Months after our failure even to budge it, when instead we had succeeded in making the elephant even bigger, when it grew and grew until it had no choice but to stomp to bits all the furniture in the joint, I concluded that my real crime against Meredith was that I had broken my promise—implicit but integral to our friendship—to remain celibate in our later years. She had spoken briefly, years before, of a man she had met on her trek to Nepal, a man she loved, she thought, but who left and married another. Since that betrayal, she wanted nothing to do with men. I had joined her there—we were alone together—and now look what I had gone and done. I had done a very serious and unforgivable thing, just as the men in her life—the married man, the trekker in Nepal—had done.

There is, among women, an unwritten rule: Never dump a woman for a man. Men have no such rule. Why do we? Perhaps it serves as protection for women against the greater power of men; it ensures that we will not be left unguarded and alone and in the lurch whenever a man strides by. Of course, this rule is broken all the time, but when I did it, I knew full well that I was going against the code of my gender. I also knew that breaking rules, whether or not they are stupid, has consequences and results in punishment. Way down deep, beneath the desire, beneath the joy in Graham's visit, a doubt niggled. Graham was long gone, back in New York; and whenever I forced myself to be realistic, I saw no future with him. Who, then, would I talk to, shop with, laugh with? At the rate I was going I would have no one, only memories.

The Feather River Canyon, where Graham and I spent our week, is quite possibly the most beautiful place on earth. The water sparkles as it rushes down mountains, cuts through rock, ripples through meadow. The sunlight through the trees dapples everything, and the sound of the water cools even in the late summer. I knew then that when things got tough, the memory of that time at the lake would rise clear and sweet and set itself against hurt and loss. It would soften despair; it would restore hope.

It was the same for Graham. In an e-mail he wrote, *"The week we spent in the Sierra remains dearer to me than almost any other time of my life. It has a rare perfection to it. It rises up so easily in memory and it is perfectly polished, radiant, and it always makes me happy."*

Meredith, you are wrong: E-mail *can* convey things important and beautiful.

In the end, hard as it is to believe even for me, it is Graham who will fit Byron's description of friendship. He will see me through hard times and good times; he will pluck me from the slough of despond more than once, he will insist that I can write and that I must. He will be, in Byron's words, "often tried and never found wanting."

But oh, Meredith, I miss you.

After the book came out, almost two years after our fateful and final meeting, I looked for her at every reading I did. Surely she would show up at one of them, surely she would send a note. But of course not. She must have been terribly offended, not just at what I had gone and done but that I had written about it. Where were my manners?

In January of 2004 my telephone rang with news of Meredith's death from liver cancer. She died at home, leaving no family behind. At her bedside, at her request, was her fellow trekker, a man who had left her for another. I wonder who got her house.

CHAPTER 3

betrayal

Remember me when I am gone away,
  Gone far away into the silent land;
  When you can no more hold me by the hand,
  Nor I half turn to go yet turning stay.

—from "Remember," CHRISTINA ROSSETTI

ouse. *2 bdrm, 1 bath, eat-in kitchen, garage, front and backyard, view, $137,000.* That was 1973, when my son and I lived in that little house. Today the same house would sell easily for eight hundred thousand dollars, and I couldn't afford to buy it. Actually, I couldn't afford to buy it even then, and so my dad, like all good dads with money, promised to provide me with the down payment. He was a surgeon then, and on the day the actual check was to be handed over, he was practicing his profession in the operating room at the hospital way back in Ohio. I phoned. The hospital operator, hearing my name, said, "Oh hi, Jane, I'll connect you," and into the operating room I went over a loudspeaker. My dad said hi, as did his nurses and the anesthesiologist. I explained the situation—I needed real money now, and was he going to give it to me? Some murmurs among the operating team, and then my father said, "You can close now." "I can?" I cried. "Thank you, thank you!" Everyone in the operating room twenty-five hundred miles away erupted into laughter, all except, I'm pretty sure, the patient. A jollier morning in the OR was never had. As a surgeon's daughter I should have realized my father meant for his assistants to go ahead and sew up the patient, but at that particular moment I was not a daughter or a woman or a mother or a teacher; I was a person about to go into escrow, a role that obliterated common sense, practicality, and all aspects of reality that did not include home ownership. My dad was true to his word—the money got to me, I loved him even more; and for some happy years my son and I shared this little house with our little gray cat, Bessie, who relieved herself in all corners of the house save the one that held her cat box, and our mongrel dog, Tear, so named because he tore everything up. For short we called him Terrible.

From 1976 until 1997 I owned and lived in another, rather grander house made of redwood and glass, decks front and back looking out onto two acres of live oaks and madrone, where wild irises and forget-me-nots bloomed in profusion each spring. A house that, as the years went by, needed work. I didn't have the money to do it, so I sold the house and, with my son happy and successful in his own life, moved cheerily to my rental cottage in Berkeley. It was small, three hundred fifty square feet, but boundlessly charming: It had its own flagstone patio, apple tree, and rose bushes, and two sets of French doors that opened onto all this loveliness. I learned early on not to notice my landlord's house only a few yards away, on the other side of the garden, and in the spring and summer the leaves on the apple tree, and the wisteria that wound itself around the trellis that marked my patio, all but hid "the big house." At Christmas I strung lights along the trellis. It was pretty. A friend who came to visit every so often from her four-thousand-square-foot house in the suburbs said, "You're living my life." On no occasion, however, did she suggest a house exchange.

The original plan was to move into this darling little place, put what money I had made on the sale of my house into the market, watch it grow, and then buy a house, smaller and in Berkeley instead of in the suburb where my son and I had, more or less, grown up. A sensible plan; lots of people have made this plan and lots of people have made it work. Not me. Changing times, changing real estate markets, made my plan no longer feasible. Not long ago at a reading, and not for the first time, someone in the audience asked, "How has your life changed?" My answer is always the same: "I still live in three hundred fifty square feet, and I still go to the laundromat every week. In all other respects my life is unrecognizable from what it was only a short time ago."

Renting's okay, most of the time. Home owning has never held any appeal for me. I know lots of people who dream of standing on the deck or roof garden or front stoop of their very own home, master of all they survey, ignorant of problems to come: leaking roof, rotting moldings, broken sewer pipes, warped floors, god it never ends. Nope, not for me. Neither has owning a car been of any importance to me. So I am content to drive a twelve-year-old Honda; and even though I don't care about it all that much, it is mine, fully paid for, and no one can kick me out of it. My cottage is a different matter: I could get kicked out, I could be found an undesirable tenant; more realistically, new owners could buy and boot me, replacing me with an odious mother-in-law. They could also raise the rent. Both are legal possibilities.

When I placed my life-changing ad in *The New York Review,* I had reason to worry. What if someone answered and came to call, pushed his way through the wooden gate into the garden and to my cottage on the other side of it? My landlord, though not at all nosy, wouldn't be able to *not* notice that the caller was male. And what if I had sex and emitted screams? Or groans? Well, I just had to take my chances.

Young Graham came, strode through the gate, and fitted his six feet quite comfortably onto my futon, with room to spare for me, though not at his feet. Apparently my sounds of ecstasy did not travel beyond my patio, for no one, not my landlord, not my neighbors, took notice, except to avert their eyes and bid a good morning as we took a morning walk.

Alas, Graham went home and, though he wrote and called, oh my goodness I missed the feel of him. In his e-mails, sometimes two or three in a day, he was curious about my life and sympathetic to the problems that came my way or that, perhaps, I brought upon myself. Sometimes he would give advice: *"Human company is a campfire . . . a small flickering ward against darkness, but you only want to get close enough to toast marshmallows. Any closer, and you get that unpleasant smell of burning hair."* Always he signed his notes *"Love, much love and more."*

So my life was not exactly manless. John, my New England recluse, did not die as we both had feared he would. He, too, had answered my ad and, despite my misgivings over the photograph he sent—he looked like a fugitive in a witness protection program— I had taken my life in my hands and driven the country roads to his cabin in the woods. Kind, funny, and a great reader, John turned out to be wonderful in and out of bed. At the end of my visit John readied himself to go to the hospital for tests of his one remaining kidney, hence my fear that we might never meet again. But his kidney turned out to be healthy, and John and I became fast friends. He wrote, he phoned, he visited, and once he had squeezed his long frame into my cottage and onto my futon, he stopped apologizing for the smallness of his cabin in the woods.

Sidney the Outrageous, another of my New York men, a man who on our first meeting and in full view of everyone ordered me to put my (sweatered) breasts on the table—in the café of the Morgan Library, of all places!—I came to value for his lifelong love of musical theatre, his lifelong residence in New York City, and his lifelong compassion for the poor, those left to the mercy of local and national politicians. Sidney called me religiously, once a week, and we talked on and on about world events, about the theatre, about whether or not now was the right time to have our cataracts removed.

Matt called, too. Matt was the man who got away, the man whose letters were funny and informative and full of learning, the man who refused my offer to come visit him in the frozen wilds of Wisconsin, the man I never expect to meet. He'd call, always late at night, and we'd have a party, me on wine, Matt on his marijuana and manhattans. "Jane," he'd say at some point in every phone call, "we've got to meet. We both love New York, we both admire Margaret Fuller, you're almost as funny as I am; we'll make some kind of plan soon." Once my book was published, Matt had a wonderful idea: "You know," he told me round about midnight, "if your book does well, we could afford a pied-à-terre in New York." We talked on and on about where, about how much we could afford. What a glorious fantasy! Suddenly it came to me: "But, Matt," I warned, "if we shared an apartment, we might have to meet!" "Well now, Jane," he said, quick as a bunny, "we wouldn't be there at the same time." Oh.

So I was not pining away for want of male attention. But I was pining, less and less, I hoped, for Robert, the very first to answer my ad, the first to call, the first to write, the first to invite me to live with him in his apartment in New York overlooking Central Park, the man with whom I fell in love, the man who didn't love me back. I did live with Robert on several occasions, the first for more than three weeks. We talked about books constantly, books we bought from a sidewalk vendor, books that lined the walls of his apartment; and when we grew tired of the sound of our own voices, we roamed the bookstores, went to the movies, to the ballet, to the opera. Retired from his position as a professor of medicine and as skillful a lover as I had known up to that time—there had been three in sixty-seven years, none of them anything to write home about—Robert did his best, I suppose, to make the reality of me fit the fantasy the two of us had created in our late-night phone calls, in our e-mails. But despite our best efforts at pretending, and my stubborn refusal to let go, finally I had to get the hell out of there and salvage what remained of my life. It is a most painful experience to watch love turn to like, turn to disinterest, and finally turn to dislike. I watched the man I loved do exactly this, until, as blind as I tried to keep myself, I finally saw what I needed to do. "I'm leaving tomorrow," I said to Robert. "It's clear I'm no longer welcome." Robert nodded in agreement and next morning said to me, "I just want to remind you that you said you were leaving today." I began to throw my clothes into my suitcase. "Have you decided on a time?" he asked. "Now," I said. "But wait!" he cried. "We were going to the movies at four! Can't you wait until after that?" If I had had any doubts about the wisdom of clearing out, "movies at four" dispelled them. I left. But leaving is not forgetting. Would I never be free of this man I had so loved? Ilse, my new best friend, promised to help.

Unlike Meredith, Ilse—born and reared in Sweden, where sex is considered a normal activity available to everyone—talked about sex easily, and I talked back. Ilse was fifty-two when we became close friends; I was sixty-six. Ilse was six feet tall. I wasn't. Every Friday morning we walked the hills behind Berkeley. On our walks Ilse customarily wore a burgundy leather skirt, skinned onto her until just above the knee, a black turtleneck pasted onto her torso, and, on her fingers and wrist and neck and ears, a full set of jewelry, gold, how much of it real I couldn't tell you, but some, I'll bet. On her hiking feet she wore an old beat-up pair of docksiders.

Keeping up with Ilse was not easy, and not just on the trail. She read widely and spoke quickly and authoritatively; she expected you to answer back. Her knowledge of music was wide ranging, her love for it deep. She was a wonderful cook, a gorgeous gardener. And something else: We were both renters, Ilse having left her house, in return for a sizable alimony, in the care of her husband and his mistress.

Often our walks made it necessary to climb a fence. Some private landowners had taken it upon themselves to try to keep us out by means of a chain-link fence, a locked gate, barbed wire, that sort of nonsense. When we encountered such an obstacle, we overcame it differently: Ilse stepped up to the fence, hiked up her leather skirt, threw one long leg over the top, swung the other one over, *et voilà,* she was on the other side. I, in contrast, lay down on the ground near a spot where there was adequate space between the barbed wire and the dirt below. Pushing the wire up, I slid myself underneath and rolled to the other side. Once there I brushed my sweatshirt and Levi's free of dirt and weeds, *et voilà.* Then we were off cross-country, onto the fire trails and the cow paths, through the manzanita and live oaks, pausing every so often to gaze at the crystal-clear reservoirs sparkling below.

Having grown up properly in Sweden, where talking about sex was as normal as having it, Ilse found herself nonetheless amidst a nasty divorce, her husband a chronic drinker and womanizer. I was launching myself into the world of sexuality Ilse had just left, though, as you will discover, she was not gone for long.

"I think what you are doing is great," said Ilse in her husky accented English when I told her on one of our walks about placing my ad in the personals. "This Robert fellow, tell me about him." She tossed one long leg over the fence and, once settled on the other side, watched amusedly as I scuttled beneath it. "You have feelings for him?"

I had a lot of feelings for Robert. And lots of regrets. I told Ilse about Robert's impotence, his back ailments, his stomach upsets, his Viagra, his . . . his . . . I told Ilse I loved him, he didn't love me, he had brought me to life, he had canceled it, he was my friend, I missed him.

"Do you have to be lovers? Couldn't you be just friends?" Ilse asked.

"I'll try." And I did. I wrote to Robert: *"I need your friendship and your caring about me even if there's nothing beyond that."*

"I can't imagine your spending your birthday anywhere but in New York and with me," he wrote back. I went.

"How did it go?" Ilse asked on my return, ten days later.

"It's harder to be friends than it is to be lovers," I said grimly.

"You should give me Robert's e-mail address," she said.

I did.

In my absence Ilse had been busy. She had gone to Sweden to visit her family. "Sit me next to a sexy man," she had told the flight attendant. The flight attendant did. At the end of the long flight Ilse and Lars left the plane together and headed for a week's retreat on a nearby island. "I am not in love," said Ilse purposefully on her return. "I do not make mistakes like that. It was purely sexual." She was telling me how to do it. She went on to describe a marathon of lovemaking or sex-having—"Twelve hours, twelve hours, and he didn't come"—that left me openmouthed and gasping.

"Was there something wrong with him?" I wanted to know.

"No, no, no, he did not permit himself to ejaculate."

"What about you?"

"Yes, yes, yes, I came over and over again."

A thought struck me. "Ilse, I think you had tantric sex."

"And what is that?"

I wasn't sure. I knew only that it had something to do with postponing orgasm, only I wasn't sure if both people had to postpone before it could be tantric, or just one and then they could take turns, or what. Also, from what I had read, in tantric sex there is a lot of breathing and staring. Ilse seemed to have benefited from both. She was radiant.

"All the sex I have ever had is nothing compared with Lars, and I cannot imagine having anything like it in the future," she told me. "I told this to my friend Bill, who said, 'Nonsense,' but I am right." While Ilse was my only confidante in matters of sex, love, and betrayal, I was not hers; she confided also in Bill during the daily phone call he made to her.

Ilse and Bill, a colleague of Ilse's husband at the university, had met each other during the early years of their respective marriages. They became friends and remained friends as their respective marriages unraveled and ended in divorce. "Only friends," Ilse insisted.

"I do not like the idea of sex with my good friend Bill." I suspected that Bill thought otherwise.

"Yes," said Ilse, as we puffed our way uphill. "Call it what you will—tantric sounds fine, though what's in a name . . ." Lars had come again, so to speak, on his way to a conference in Los Angeles. Her voice trailed away as she breathed deeply and stared up into the clouds above.

"What does your friend Bill say about all this?"

"He says there is satisfaction closer to home, not really such a comfort to me, I don't think."

But Lars had come and gone back to Sweden, leaving Ilse with a taste for the good life. So Ilse went online. She sent off a photograph of herself standing in a field of daisies—where the hell she found all those flowers, I'll never know, Sweden maybe—her long blond hair blown back, her long legs splayed, barefoot, into the grasses, her skirt hiked up to midthigh. She looked sensational.

Ilse was off and running, lots of dinner dates, a few sleepovers, but nothing, nothing to compare with the Lars who never came back. Our Friday morning walks continued, taking on a new urgency.

"Do you still have feelings for Robert?" she asked one morning.

"I'm getting better," I said. "I think I can do a friendship with him soon."

"I am sure he would like that," she said.

And so I wrote Robert about the difficulties of writing my book, though really what I wrote about were the difficulties of being me without him: *"Right now I am so in need of your common sense, your intelligence, your clarity; you are the only person I have known who listens to me in just the right way."*

As you can see, this was not a letter of friendship; it was a letter of pleading. I was nowhere close to being able to be a friend to Robert. Damn, it was almost two years since Robert and I began the tarantella, and I was still spinning.

And so on our Friday walks I talked to Ilse about Robert, and she told me about Lars and about Bill and now, with her amazing success online, about Ted and Clifford and Arthur and James and George. Finally, fed up with my whimpering, she decided on a bold stroke. "I am going to introduce you to my friend Bill. He has had enough bimbos; it's time he met somebody with brains."

I was hopeful. After all, three thousand miles and many dollars were significant hurdles. Though my East Coast lovers had offered to help me with plane fare and hotel costs, I turned them down: It didn't seem right to accept Sidney's offer and then scamper off to see Graham—or vice versa. So now, hell, I was broke. I had to stay home! I was just about where I had been at the beginning—celibate and sad.

Ilse, Bill, and I went out to dinner, just the three of us. I sat on one side of the table; Bill and Ilse sat on the other. It was clear who belonged with whom. I remarked on this to Ilse on our next walk. "Don't be foolish, he will call."

> *When devils will the blackest sins put on,*
> *They do suggest at first with heavenly shows,*
> *As I do now*
> —Iago, in *Othello*

Bill called and proceeded to put on a heavenly show. We went to concerts. Bill gave me presents, Bill called me frequently on the telephone, which, given his daily habit with Ilse, must have interfered with his normal life, which had something to do with mathematics and NATO. I didn't care; it was nice to receive his kind of attention from someone close by, someone whose phone number was, like him, toll free. One evening as we sat on my couch, Bill said what became the first sentence of my first book: "Do you think you're a nymphomaniac?" That night we went to bed.

Now, why did I do that? I wasn't in love with him. I liked him well enough: He was amusing, smart, educated, rich, and a good kisser. Well, why not do that? Seemed the natural thing to do, he seemed to want to—more than I did, and—Jesus, when will I learn that one doesn't have to sleep with someone just because that person has been nice to one? Maybe I *am* a nymphomaniac, except I don't believe there is such a thing. I think that word was made up by men who use it to keep control of their women. So I'm not one, though self-control has not been my forte for some time now. But I learned a lesson by way of Bill: I needn't give myself away out of politeness or gratitude. At least I thought I had learned this lesson, and certainly should have, for that night with Bill was A Long Night's Journey into Day, a loveless, exhausting, seemingly endless conjoining that ended when both of us finally fell asleep, neither one satisfied, only mystified. Next morning, like the dutiful nymphomaniac I wasn't, I fixed eggs. He ate them, then walked down my garden path without a word.

Time and Bill passed. I did not lament his passing, but I was puzzled: Why would he put himself (and me) through such a night without at least giving himself (if not me) the satisfaction of release? Finally it came to me: Bill wanted to perform, not for me but for Ilse. Bill wanted me to tell Ilse that, like Lars, he had staying power, he could be tantric as all get-out. Bill wanted me to pimp for him.

Ilse called. "How was your evening with Bill?" she asked, as if she had been prompted by someone known to both of us. "Okay," I said, and shut my mouth. My revenge on Bill would be silence.

And so I returned to missing Robert and reading Graham's letters and talking to Sidney on the telephone, and John, too. But by god, I was determined to be a good friend to Robert and not spoil everything with goopy love talk he could not return. So we wrote and wrote. One day Robert sent an e-mail: *"Now that we are friends, perhaps you can advise a foolish old man who has fallen in love with a beautiful woman almost half his age."*

Robert and his e-mail. Robert and his long-distance courting. Robert and his falling in love—again. Can you guess who this "beautiful woman almost half his age" might be? No wonder

Robert had sold his house in Aspen and written me his thoughts about moving farther west. Clearly he had moved west, or Ilse had moved east; clearly they had met and . . . I got drunk. I phoned Ilse and screamed, "Who else do you want? Graham? John?"

"Oh, Jane," she answered. "I am so sorry. Nothing is more important than our friendship."

"Bullshit!" I screamed, and hung up. I wrote to Graham, not for the first time or the last, one of what he came to call my dui's— "discoursing under the influence." They looked something like this: *"Dear Grwahm, I asm miseroiabike."*

Some weeks later, in what would be his last e-mail, Robert wrote, *"Never have I felt so betrayed as to have been introduced to Ilse. I know you have no interest in that or in me. But I felt I should tell you that."*

So I am to blame. Robert is miserable, and it's my fault. I am delighted. I am so delighted over the misfortune of the man who couldn't love me and the woman who took him from me that I do not answer his e-mail. I am cured. Gee, in only two years.

The person I still miss is Ilse. Finally I had a friend with whom I could talk about sex and intimacy and being in love and getting hurt—all the things I would never have dared bring up in Meredith's presence. Ilse was levelheaded and funny and straightforward and . . . selfish and greedy and . . . how can one person be all these things? 'Twas a man who did it. Maybe Meredith was right; maybe life is easier, nicer, without men in it. Well, it's too late now; I can't go back.

IT WOULD BE almost two years before I saw Ilse again. Ilse is nothing if not persistent: She e-mailed and phoned. I was unresponsive to both. Then, one day she called and before I could hang up told me that Robert was dying from a brain tumor. "He would very much like to see you," she said. I felt sad that he was dying, but I felt no responsibility to make his death easier; I felt nothing, really, except a warning deep inside, something like TROUBLE

AHEAD. AVOID ACCIDENTS. SLOW DOWN. So I said to Ilse, "No." "Then come for a walk with me," she said. "Okay." Surely, enough time had passed so that I could pick up again what had been so precious to me—Ilse's friendship.

We walked our usual trail, uphill and downhill, and then back at Ilse's rental, a big high-ceilinged rambling house—*3 bdrms, 2.5 baths, fireplace, decks, washer/dryer*—she handed me the poems Robert had written over the previous two years. She had bound them together, along with photographs he had taken of flowers, pictures that in their sexuality were much like the paintings of Georgia O'Keeffe. Ilse said to me, "I don't know what to do with them, where to send them, even if—I think some of them are very, very good—but how to get them published . . ." So that was it. I looked through the poems quickly; some *were* very good, all were very sexual. Ilse's name appeared throughout. "I know my name comes up often," she explained, "but they're not really about me." Who, then? I wondered. I closed up the poems and the photographs, turned to Ilse, and said, "I want nothing to do with these." Ilse summoned up real tears and said, "He's going to die, and what will I do with these? It is so sad." I answered, "Go to the library; ask the librarian." And, for the last time, I stomped up the wooden railroad ties that formed the steps through her garden and went home to my landlord's garden, where I was safe for a while at least.

AS I THINK BACK, a lot of high school stuff went on: stealing a best friend's boyfriend, trying to patch up a torn and dirty friendship, being sorry, being angry, screaming over the phone, sobbing into the pillow. What's different is that, unlike anguished teenagers, we people in what some idiot named our golden years don't have as much time to get over it. When we are injured, we hurt just as much as we did when we were young, but as we age, we heal much more slowly. The time for picking oneself up and getting on with life gets shorter and shorter; maybe that's the reason so many people in their later years avoid the risk of new relationships; maybe they have learned Sartre's lesson: Hell is other people.

Not all of the other people, though. Throughout all this I wrote to Graham, telling him of tantric sex and love, and he wrote back: *"I have always thought that certain tantra practices were an all too perfect metaphor for the emotional unavailability of so many men."* I wrote him about friendship and betrayal, and he wrote back: *"Perhaps you just mention the bad apples, but some of your friends sound as if they should be demoted."* And without prompting he wrote, *"I like the Jane of the page just as much as the Jane of light and air."*

It is wonderful to have someone on your side, and even more wonderful when that someone is smart and sexy. Graham's e-mails keep me steady and warm. I am not at the end of my wits or my life, as long as he is in it.

CHAPTER 4

in which our heroine
becomes a sexpert

When I lost Ilse, when I lost Robert, when my money ran out and I had to stay home, where once again I felt lonely, where I would do anything for company—even sleep with Bill—I decided to bring everybody back alive. I would write them—all of them—into a book. I would dig through the rubbish of my life and make a rose, a star, an apple beyond compare, and I would call it *A Round-Heeled Woman,* a phrase Robert had used when we were still talking, a phrase I tucked far back in my mind where no senior moment could touch it. So when Robert turned away, when Graham stayed forever young, when Sidney pulled up the drawbridge whenever I got too close, I heard a voice, insistent and persistent: "I can write about this." When the wonders of New York threatened to overwhelm me, I listened to that voice and I wrote. My journals were full of writing, along with tears of happiness, of wonder, and of pain. So now, Jane, I'm pretty sure I said to myself, let's sort through this mess, see if we can make some sense of it. Suddenly, closer to seventy than sixty, I was no longer retired. I had a brand-new profession: I was a writer. I had given up one impossible profession, teaching, for another impossible profession, writing. Good Lord, would I never learn?

Writing, however, failed me in the wake of 9/11. Sidney, from his apartment in midtown, got through on the telephone and assured me he was safe. No word from Graham, none at all, no e-mail, no phone call, silence. I paced the floor and drank too much wine and phoned him at his office and at his home and wrote e-mail upon e-mail to him, and after two weeks of this, two weeks after 9/11, I flew to New York to find him, certain that if I looked in just the right place he would be there safe and sound. What was I thinking?

I could not write, even with my journal open and my pen touching its paper, what I saw at Ground Zero. I had trusted writing to lift the heavy darkness within me, but when I read the words I put on the page, I was ashamed at so paltry a rendering of what I was seeing, smoke and flame still rising from the bowels of hell. Writers have compared Ground Zero to Dante's Inferno, but it was worse, for in New York, unlike in Dante's hell, there was no poet to lead us up into the sunlight. I closed my journal and cried. Surely the end of the world had come.

Late that night in my hotel room, my pillow sodden with tears, my cell phone rang. It was Graham. "I'm all right," he said. And then I really cried.

Next day we met for lunch. I was overjoyed to see him alive, though clearly he was not well. Having been on the sidewalk only a few blocks from the Trade Center at the time of the explosions, his face was the color of the ash that had filled the air. He coughed throughout lunch; and while he proclaimed that soon he would be his old self again, now he was distracted, jumpy, and ill at ease. Nothing I said could help calm him or amuse him or interest him. He remained polite and distant. Lunch was short and sad. What was I to do? There seemed to be no reason to prolong my stay in New York; Graham was in no mood for a picnic in Battery Park, for a walk along the water's edge; indeed, taking pleasure in anything at all seemed out of place, trivial, inappropriate. He was in no mood for me either, and I feared that in some important way I had lost him. I had come to New York to raise him from the dead if need be, and here he was, a ghost of his former self. In the months to come I would learn that the root of his distractedness lay beyond 9/11. It would wreak its own kind of devastation on me.

Like people everywhere in the world after the cataclysm that was September 11, I was awash in feelings of hopelessness, uselessness, despair. And so, on my return to Berkeley I walked the few blocks from my cottage to the American Red Cross center to give blood. There were many of us there; all the chairs were occupied, the technicians busy. When I finally got a technician, it was a young Chinese woman. Judging by her accented English, she was undoubtedly new to this country, and heavily made up as if she wanted to be American overnight. Still, beneath the foundation and the blush, the rouge and the lipstick, the eyebrows plucked and the lashes extended, she was pretty. She complimented me on my veins, stuck the needle in one of them, and said to my left hand, "Squeeze," so that my blood would run faster. She left to help others squeeze. Everyone else in the rather large room was reading. For the first time in my entire life I had brought nothing to read. I reached into my purse, praying that my Penguin book, the best deal going today at $.95 USA/$1.49 Canada, was somewhere at the bottom of that mess. It was not. Instead I pulled out my little green notebook, a miniature journal, which leaves my purse only when I'm writing in it. In it are notes for the book I had written, called *A Round-Heeled Woman,* the book I had finished, the book that had yet to find an agent or a publisher, the book that was an albatross in my life. I wouldn't even have opened that little notebook had anything else been available. The technician came to check on me.

"What you read?" she asked.

"Notes I made for a book I wrote."

"You write book?"

"Yes."

"What you write book about?" She pointed at my fist: "Squeeze."

"It's about a woman who sleeps with a lot of men."

She was quick to answer. "Oh! You write book about slut!" She pronounced it "srut," and loudly. The rest of the donors in the room were quick to translate and paused in their reading to do so. My technician made her rounds of the room, saying "Squeeze" to the donors and muttering "slut" beneath her breath. Like all good students she knew that repetition is a key to learning. She was practicing her English.

Ever the teacher, when she returned, I asked her, "What do you call a man who sleeps with a lot of women?"

She was silent for a moment, her brow furrowed in thought, and then the light broke: "No such word!" She paused, then exclaimed, "Not fair! Not right!"

Her orders to us to squeeze were then more militant, so when she returned to my chair, I said, "I'll give you a word for both men and women." She was eager. "It's 'promiscuous,'" I said.

"You say again." I did. "You say slow."

"Pro-mis-cu-ous," I said.

She placed one hand on my throat: "Now say." I did. Only a few inches from my face, she stared intently at my mouth as I repeated "Pro-mis-cu-ous."

She moved her lips as I did, *et voilà!* she got it. "Pro-mis-cu-ous," she said again and again, more and more loudly, her smile broadening with each repetition. And of course by this time everybody in the place was grinning, even me. It was at that moment that I became a sexpert.

I didn't know it then, of course; it would take some time before I took on the mantle of sex guru, even longer—even never—before I wore it comfortably. But it was inevitable, I suppose, and now I am not surprised by questions and comments called out as I walk about my neighborhood: "Hey, Jane, know where I can get a dildo?" By the time that question sailed in from across the street, I did know. If you live in the San Francisco Bay Area, go to a store called Good Vibrations on San Pablo Avenue in Berkeley. I have it on good authority they've got them there, a wide selection, too.

But I erred when I offered my Red Cross technician "promiscuous." I should have qualified it. Not all men and not all women who sleep with a lot of others are promiscuous. "Promiscuous" describes behavior that does not discriminate, that is, sleeping with lots of anyones. That's not me, nor was it me in November of 2001. I discriminated beginning with *The New York Review,* a good filter, I believed, for winnowing the creeps from the shafts. So, Miss Pretty Little Technician, if you read this, remember, not all women who have a lot of sex with men not their legally wedded are sluts. Neither are they nymphomaniacs. Nor, despite what some therapists may say, are they necessarily sex addicts. Naming things and people may be necessary for efficiency's sake, but at the same time naming them tends to limit understanding as well as behavior. Which is why a lot of things get named. As Linnaeus or maybe the Chinese have said, If you name something, you own it.

I left the Red Cross, uncertain whether my technician was richer or poorer for my language lesson, though I chose to believe richer, for I am a firm believer in the power of words, no matter what they are. My little green book tucked into my purse, I returned once again to the library, to the *LMP,* the *Literary Market Place,* and picked out a few agents, all of them in New York, who, I had to believe, would like my book and send it on to a publisher. Taking courage from the knowledge that Thomas Wolfe had submitted *Look Homeward, Angel* more than fifty times, I forged ahead into the vast and uncharted world of publishing. It might come to pass that I would be not just a writer but an author. A dizzying thought.

And it happened: My book found an agent, who found a publisher, and I was free to continue (1) tripping to New York and (2) exploring my new career as an author and sexpert.

It is May of the year 2002, and here I am in New York City, the city that will reclaim itself from the devastation of 9/11 in record time, the best place in the world to be when spring shows up. I am here on business! A bartender will ask me, "Are you here for business or pleasure?" and I will answer with a huge grin, "They're the same thing." Indeed they are, for this very evening I will have dinner with Graham, who in his e-mails and phone calls seems to have done what he claimed he would: become his old self again. And as he did so, he resurrected me. In fact, he became more than his old self; he became my muse. "I thought muses were female," he argued when I announced his new post. "Times have changed," I said. "Gender has become irrelevant to musedom."

Graham became more than an inspiration; he became my backbone, my cheerleader (today men can be cheerleaders, too). "You're a wonderful writer," he insisted. "Of course you can write this book; look at your e-mails to me, they're fine writing, and *A Round-Heeled Woman* is the perfect title." I would protest: "It's too hard; I'm stuck, I can't, I just can't!" Often my tears would reduce me to blubbering; then Graham would say, "Read me the last sentence you wrote." I would, and he would say, "Now, what's the next one?" Incredibly, I would know, and off I'd go once more to string words together in the best way I knew how.

Muses not only inspire; they perform miracles, and my muse, Graham, surely the best in all of musedom, was responsible for my transformation into Author and for the joyful excitement that fills me now. I am about to visit my editor.

Random House has consolidated its offices from around the city into a big, big building at the corner of Broadway and Fifty-fifth. From the outside it's one more skyscraper, its front almost entirely uglified, like many buildings in New York, by scaffolding. Inside, in the lobby, Oh wow!

Whoever saw such a fancy lobby, wood-paneled floor to ceiling? With shelves carved out of the walls for books, like the openings you see in the mesas of New Mexico, where I have never been, the walls of the Random House lobby are beautiful. They look like oak, and while I know they do wonders with particleboard these days, I choose to believe this is the real stuff. So the walls are oak. And all up and down, in the niches carved out for them, are books, first editions published by Random House. There must be thousands. I have read them all. Steinbeck, Hemingway, Fitz-gerald, the literary lions of my youth. William Faulkner, whose *Absalom, Absalom!* almost convinced me to drop out of college, so incomprehensible was it to me on first reading (second and third, too, not so on fourth, and hardly at all just the other day). Sinclair Lewis's *Kingsblood Royal* took me back to the summer of 1952, to the attic beneath the tin roof of Bald Hill Lodge in New Hampshire, where I sweated out my off-hours as a waitress and survived because also in the attic was everything Lewis wrote.

There in the lobby of Random House I clasp my hands together and raise them to chin level, in what I suppose must look like prayer. It is a prayer, I suppose, a prayer of thanksgiving because looking at those shelves and those books is like looking at my life and remembering, with deep pleasure and gratitude, the hours those writers have given me, not to mention all the information I ever got about sex. D. H. Lawrence and sex, veiled but there and dark and bloody; Philip Roth and sex, unveiled and wildly funny, though not until 1969, too late for me to enjoy a healthy adolescence. In between Lawrence and Roth, John Cheever taught me about impolite sex in a polite time, John O'Hara showed me the danger of sex between men and women who strayed from their social classes. By the time Philip Roth appeared in my life when I was thirty-four, I was terrified of sex—my reading had taught me it brought ruination upon the people who practiced it, even if they were married, which I was, and miserable. Roth finally made me laugh out loud over sex, although even in *Portnoy's Complaint* sex between men and women leads to lots and lots of trouble. Therefore, can there be any doubt that Random House was responsible for my growing up a confused but determined virgin? It would take Grove Press to unloose Henry Miller upon the reading world, and my own trip to Europe in 1955, where, banned in this country until 1961, Miller was available to show me, reluctant learner that I was, that sex could be animal rutting, could be had for the pure pleasure of it. My god, the scene in *Tropic of Cancer* where they do it on the kitchen table—and they weren't even engaged!—has stayed with me a very long time, fifty years and growing.

Out of the gutter and into the stars, Camus's *The Stranger* would provide the underpinnings of what I would come to believe about life and how I would live it. Boswell's *Life of Johnson,* the Random House edition, I will be reading until the lights go finally out. No wonder I stand transfixed in this lobby before this literary edition of my life.

From the corner of my eye I see a uniformed man, a security guard I would guess, approaching. He is tall, slim, elegant, with snowy-white hair, a gallant, if you will. His badge names him Albert. He bows from the waist and says, "All those books. Have you chosen the ones you want?"

"I don't want those books. I want my book to be up there."

"Oh, do you have a book?"

I nod, and he continues, "What's your book about?"

Since my experience at the Red Cross I have refined my answer to this question, and I say, "It's about sex over sixty."

He steps away. "*How* old?"

"About our age, yours and mine."

"What's the name of your book?" I tell him. "I'm getting me a copy," he says. Then he looks down at the Random House floor, not nearly so beautiful as its walls, and stammers, "In your book, do you—do you talk about drugs?"

He sees I don't understand and tries to clarify. "You know, drugs that help people, older folks, when things don't . . . don't work the way they want."

I realize he's talking about Viagra. "Yes, a little," I say, remembering that Robert took Viagra occasionally, which did indeed allow him to do what he wanted to do, but made him feel queasy. "Do you mean Viagra?" I ask.

Albert puts a *Shhh* finger over his mouth and whispers, "Yes, yes, that's it." He does a little jig. "Does that medicine work?"

My sexpertise surfaces. "Sometimes it does," I tell him, "but some men suffer side effects."

"Like what?"

"Upset stomach sometimes." I flash once more on Robert claiming dyspepsia as the result of the Viagra, which he decided not to take ever again, or so he said. I have no idea if he told the truth, but, always helpful, I continue my blithesome counsel of Albert. "People need to consult a doctor before they try this sort of thing. Some men do fine with Viagra, some men don't." I reek of false confidence. "Here's my elevator."

An hour or so later I descend to the lobby, and here comes Albert. He stops short of me, bows again, looks down at me, and says, "You know, I've been working for Random House for a long time, so I've seen lots of authors and book people." He leans down even farther and peers into my face. "You aren't Dr. Ruth, by any chance, are you?"

Can't hide forever. The amazing part of this is that, although I don't know it then, in little more than a year I will be invited to share the speakers' platform with Dr. Ruth herself. Just think: I have come from being The Ice Maiden in my adolescence to being One Hot Number in my old age.

I wish Albert a good evening. He bows his gentlemanly bow and holds the door to the street open for me. Outside, I stand stock-still; people bump into me, the light changes, I don't move. I am simply astounded at my life.

Even now I am not entirely at ease, either in my role as a writer, which is as it should be—writers are supposed to stay on edge, so I've read—or in my role as a sexpert. Never mind, people talk to me about sex all the time. Not long ago I met Nora, my new best friend, and her best friend, Alicia, in San Francisco, where the two of them had come for a visit. They are both twenty-six years old. They are fans of my book and of martinis, and so I felt free to ask them if they, the two of them, talk about sex. Lord, yes! And before you know it, we are sharing our views on favorite positions and why. Alicia likes to be on top, so we talk about position and power, about physiology and psychology. Nora champions the missionary position: "Hands down, it's the best." I loved our conversation. Times, for some of us, have changed for the better.

What might Meredith's and my friendship have become if we had read Grove Press books, if we had even heard of Grove Press? What if Erica Jong had written her *Fear of Flying* in 1943 instead of 1973? What if instead of gossipping about Simone de Beauvoir, Meredith and I had read what she wrote in her book, *The Second Sex*; after all, Random House had made it available to us way back in 1952. Would we have talked about sex and its importance in our lives, as so many people seem to be doing today? I can imagine that, had we done so, our friendship would have been stronger; I can also imagine that our friendship would have ended even earlier. Alas, speculation of this sort is fruitless. All I can say for certain is that Meredith and I were women of our decade, and you know what they say about that: You can take the girl out of the fifties, but you can't take the fifties out of the girl. Sometimes, though, you can.

Write about what you know: the first lesson of writing. Well, I did. Write to find out what you know. I did that, too, and the inhibitions of my past lives fell by the wayside. Freedom, no matter if it comes early or late, feels good. Apparently the same is true for some of my readers.

On a bright and sunny morning, too beautiful to stay inside, I stroll my neighborhood, happy to be alive and ambulatory and disguised from my public by a baseball cap and dark glasses. Coming toward me is a woman about my age, her dog close behind. I smile as we pass—I believe in smiling at strangers; can't hurt, and if everybody did it . . . —and suddenly I hear, "Wait! You're the woman who wrote the book!" I turn, am introduced to the dog, Mike, and listen as words spill from Mike's owner, who tells me her name is Jenny: "I loved your book, just loved it, and I want to place an ad, not really, but I know what I would write if

getting a date

It doesn't matter how many people you talk to during the day if you don't have someone waiting who cares about you.

—JEAN ARTHUR in *The Devil and Miss Jones*

est you think me picky, inflexible, overly demanding, let me tell you that from the moment I placed my ad I looked behind me, next door to me, down the block, in restaurants and stores for a man or men who lived nearby. Had I met one, even one, I might have given up all thoughts of New York. But I didn't meet one; I couldn't find anybody, so off I went. Even though I had met wonderful men there, now I had to face the fact that Robert was in my past for good, and Sidney, John, and, especially, Graham were three thousand miles away. Despite the wonders of telecommunications, they were untouchable. I was almost as bad off as I'd been in the beginning, before I placed the ad. This was humiliating: All that work, all that effort, all that money, and I ached—still—for a man's touch. So now I had to stop wringing my hands and gnashing my teeth and start over. It was time to get a date. It was past time; it was 2003 and I had just turned seventy.

A Round-Heeled Woman has not yet been published, but the man who calls me on the telephone tells me he has read the prepublication edition sent to bookstores and critics. He tells me a friend of his lent it to him. He tells me his name is Gerald and that he lives in Berkeley. He would like to meet me. Yes, I will. When?

I love Indian food, so I am happy when Gerald suggests we meet at an Indian restaurant on the other side of town. I love the other side of town. I love that restaurant. I plan to love Gerald.

He is tall. That's good. He stands outside the restaurant waiting, sort of slumped against the wall, and he says to me as I walk toward him, "You don't look like the picture on your book jacket." I sigh, remembering Robert's initial remark as I stepped from the plane three years earlier: "You don't look at all like your photograph." Gerald's comment does not bode well for our future.

Neither does this: Gerald sags. His shoulders droop. The corners of his mouth turn down. The lines in his face fall from his forehead straight down onto his cheeks, which sag into his chin. He looks like Deputy Dawg. I remind myself that I have nothing against Deputy Dawg, So don't draw conclusions so fast, Jane. Not everyone can look like Graham. We order dinner. Immediately Gerald tells me about himself. "I have had an entirely uneventful life—two uninteresting marriages, several dull children grown and gone, thirty years of the same job in the same office in the same town."

I protest: "Your marriages can't have been completely without interest!"

"But they were." His eyes seem to be focused on my left collarbone.

"And your children!"

"I was never fond of babies. They got worse as they grew. I don't see them anymore."

I bet not.

"I'm a nonpracticing Jew," he tells me. "I grew up in Cleveland, had a terrible childhood, just terrible."

I'm damned if I'm going to encourage him to tell me all about it. I look at my watch to get the test results. The test is this: At the beginning of a meeting with a man, I check the time and measure how long it takes him to ask a question or make a statement about me. We are mid-curry—T minus one hour and counting—when Gerald speaks: "You're not at all what I expected."

I want out, and then he says, "You're softer. Are we getting along, do you think?" I decide to stay, though I do not think we are, in fact, getting along. "Of course," he tells me, "what you wanted all along was love, that's what you were looking for." Gerald does not intend this as a topic of conversation, for he does not wait for me to agree or disagree. He says, "In Cleveland I was an only child."

Gerald has drawn conclusions about everything: his childhood, his job, his marriages, his children, even me. There is nothing for him to explore, to learn from; no wonder he droops. The check comes. "We don't have to go," he says as he places a 5 percent tip on the table. "Okay, then, I'll walk you to your car. We might see each other again."

"You don't have to walk me to my car," I say, since no, I am thinking, we will not see each other again.

And then Gerald asks the only truly important question of the evening. He looks into my eyes and says, "Do you ever get lonely?"

I answer quickly, "Why do you think I'm here?" I shrug and walk away into the evening, lonelier than ever.

I am spoiled. What my ad in *The New York Review* had brought me was heartbreak, yes, but also joy and companionship and intellectual stimulation and real, true conversation. Had I met Gerald before my adventures, I would have found him fascinating, scintillating, even inspiring. Oh no, I wouldn't. But maybe I should have tried harder, maybe I should have encouraged him to roll out his childhood. After all, Jane, who do you think you are to cut this sad man off at the knees? A little patience, a little kindness wouldn't kill you. And besides, it is quite possible you are turning your East Coast men into saints, like what happens to some people when they die and their loved ones, left behind, reconstruct them in their memories as perfect. Jesus, am I grieving? Well, kind of.

Hell, I'm going to have to put another ad in! This time I'm going to have to limit the geography to the Bay Area, since I no longer have the money to fly to New York whenever I get horny. Dammit, I know what touching feels like, what kissing feels like, what conversation feels like, and I'm still hungry. But I'm not starving, not yet anyway.

However, first things first: Pinned on the door of my cottage is a note from my landlord: *"Please call in the morning. I need to talk to you."*

My landlord is perfect. Actually, since she is a woman, I suppose she is my land*lady,* though the linguistic distinctions between male and female are fast disappearing: People who strut and fret about the stage are all "actors" now, the term "actress" being what? Demeaning? Because it refers to a female? In the medium of print, gender specification is rare, all subjects referred to by their last names only. I can't figure out why writing a "Ms." or a "Miss" or a "Mrs." in front of the actual name has fallen out of favor. Is calling everybody by only the last name supposed to make everybody equal? Seems to me it just makes everyone confused, which I guess is okay as long as everyone is equally confused. However, I digress. My landlady is named Paula. She is small and pretty and young— somewhere in her early forties—and lives with her second husband on the other side of the garden I have come to think of as mine. Real ownership, of course, negotiated at the end of her first marriage, belongs to Paula. Paula and her new husband are a quiet couple, pleasant. And happy, I believe, to have me living in their backyard and paying a healthy rent. For four years I have been the ideal tenant: quiet, prompt with my monthly check, and careful about recycling—paper in the green tub, cans and bottles in the blue. Every so often my son comes to visit, as do a few friends; no one stays very long, space being limited, and ten P.M. finds me lights out, sound asleep. One would hardly know I'm here.

Until . . . Now, just wait a minute. In my own defense, even with the amazing change in what you might call my lifestyle, no caterwauling whatsoever has gone on in my little rose-covered cottage. The lights are still off by ten, and I recycle with zeal. However, one cannot disguise a six-foot man who stands on the patio in the morning, stretching and yawning at the day ahead. And I suppose that from her window she must have seen that there was more than one—though *not at the same time,* Paula! So far, though, she has said nary a word about the visits of Graham and then John. But this note pinned to my door signals something new, and I am scared. Moral turpitude: Is that in my lease? I scour the document and find nothing that prohibits sleeping around, although right there on page 3, item 16, is *"Quiet Enjoyment: Tenant shall not . . . interfere with the quiet enjoyment of any . . . nearby resident."* Oh boy, how quiet was our enjoyment? I fear I'm about to find out.

That night, all night, I imagine myself once again on trial, found guilty, and sentenced to a life on the streets. So once again, to gain some semblance of control over what will surely be my undoing, I write out my fear and anger. Since I really have no quarrel with Paula or her husband, not until tomorrow anyway, I select as the target of my rage the powers that be in Washington, D.C. Maybe once I write it, I'll be able to get some sleep. The letter I write is about being old with very little money and no place to go. It is about me and who I was before my writing adventures earned some money. But I suspect it's not just about me; it's about other retired people, too.

I am seventy years old and retired. I want you to know how life is for one of us no longer viable in today's economy. It is frightening. Why is my life so uncertain? Why is my future so dark? Why, at age seventy, after forty years of work, am I unable to count on my government to keep me safe from abject poverty, catastrophic illness, and the fear that I will spend my last years living in my car? It is not dying that troubles me; I have known from the beginning of my life that I would die. It is how I will

get to my dying—how cold and how hungry and how sick?—
that keeps me awake at night.

In the morning, in the clear light of day, I read what I have written and send it anyway to the op-ed page of *The New York Times,*
where it doesn't get published. Oh, well, it helped me pass the
time, kept me company in the dark night of my soul, until morning, when there she is, my landlady, sweeping her back steps, and
she is not smiling.

"My husband has taken a position with a firm in Virginia," she
tells me. "I will be putting the house on the market shortly."

So I'm not going to be evicted, not by this landlady, anyway. I
am safe for the moment; I breathe a sigh of relief. But dammit, the
change that is nigh has shattered my illusion of security. God
Almighty, who will buy this place? I can see it now: hordes of
small children climbing and falling out of my apple tree, backyard
barbecues smoking up my French doors, dogs trampling my com-
post heap. Worse, the new owners will have it within their legal
power to toss me out in favor of a blood relative, or at the very
least to raise the rent.

When seen in the light of my midnight letter and the ensuing
notification of my landlady, getting a date, enjoying dinner, agree-
ing on a movie to see, talking and listening to a man, even bed-
ding him, seem frivolous. Well, thank god for frivolous, for it
lifted me, for a time anyway, out of the depths of despair into the
light fantastic: What difference did it make if my money trickled
down to nothing over the years? At least I had a car to move into;
I should be grateful. So I packed my bag and went to New York,
where, as long as I could pay the hotel bill, I was guaranteed a
room and a bath with hot and cold running water. I feel safe in
New York.

CHAPTER 6

other women

come a little further—why be afraid—
here's the earliest star (have you a wish?)

—E. E. CUMMINGS, from Sonnet XLVIII

A martini is a pretty thing, gently lapping the rim of a glass made just for it, silky and shiny, almost transparent. In the steady hand of a pretty woman, a martini can be beautiful. It is and she is, for I am happy. I am in New York.

She has asked the bartender for two olives. She sits at the bar, legs crossed at the knee, twirling the toothpick gently. Then she lifts the toothpick to her mouth and, with a purse of her lips, makes the first olive disappear. She smiles at the bartender, turns to the book that lies open next to her.

I am four seats down. I ask the bartender for a sauvignon blanc, martinis belonging to my past, when I was pregnant and martinis were the only liquids I could keep down, a time long ago when the olives were small. This being the age of huge—hamburgers, cars, athletes, breasts—one oughtn't to be surprised that olives, too, are on steroids. When the bartender brings my wine, I ask how much it costs, thus labeling myself a bumpkin from the country. "Three hundred and fifty dollars," he says, and I say "Good. Let me know when I hit a thousand." I explain to him, but loudly enough so that the pretty woman, now into her second olive, can hear, that I am in competition with a friend back home in California for the title Who Paid the Most for a Glass of Wine on Her Visit to New York City. My friend is ahead: On her last visit she paid fourteen dollars somewhere on the Upper East Side; however, I am still in the race, and this evening, if I can get the bartender to tell me the actual price of this glass of wine, I may zoom ahead.

The woman smiles at my story and closes what looks to be a new book, a book of Renaissance paintings, which suggests she has come from the Metropolitan Museum just across the street. Me too, that's where I've been this blustery winter day, visiting Sargent's *The Wyndham Sisters,* three elegant beauties in a portrait so large it cannot travel. Except for last year, when it went to Boston's MFA, which is okay with me since I was not in New York then and didn't inhale sharply, as I did when, on another visit, it was gone—for purposes of cleaning, it turned out. On every visit I climb the stairs to the American Wing, pull up a chair, and visit Lady Elcho, Mrs. Adeane, and Mrs. Tennant, daughters of the prestigious British family. There they are, posed in their father's library, their mother's portrait on the wall behind, their white silk dresses billowing onto the ivory of the divan on which they sit, shimmering like the peonies that flank them. They are the picture of elegance and grace, and in fact were known in their aristocratic circle as The Three Graces. The expressions on their faces, not entirely inscrutable, allow for viewers like me to make up stories, to ask questions about them, to wonder: Were they happy? Why did the youngest die first? Of what? I sit and wonder and admire.

A guard comes toward me, and I figure I am doing something wrong. "Excuse me," he says, "you're a regular visitor here, aren't you?" I nod. "Are you by any chance related to the Wyndham family?" Me? In my baseball cap and backpack and hiking boots? I shake my head. "I just wondered," he says, clearly disappointed, then continues: "A man, quite elderly, lives in Manhattan, comes

to visit the woman on the left. He says when things get too confusing, he comes here and talks them over with his grandmother.
That's her." He points to Lady Elcho. "And then the one on the
right, Mrs. Tennant, well, her family has been here to visit. They
live in England." Now he wrinkles his brow and points to Mrs.
Adeane, Madeline, seated in the middle, her two older sisters on
either side. "She's the puzzle. Nobody ever visits her, so I thought
maybe you came for her." I shake my head sadly and murmur, "I
wish I were her family." "Well," he says, shrugging his shoulders,
"so do I, because I want to retire. I'm due for retirement, and you
know, I just can't go till somebody comes for her." I assure him
that, after this, I will come especially to see Madeline. "She died
young, you know," I tell him. "She may not have had time to leave
us a family." Reluctantly I exit the American Wing and trudge
across the street to the Stanhope and its fine bar.

The Wyndham Sisters would not have known martinis; it
would take almost fifty years before the martini was invented. If
they had imbibed at all, they would have sipped sherry, and they
never ever would have perched themselves on a bar stool and
talked to strangers. Still, there is a grace and loveliness about this
woman, too, whose glass is now denuded of olives. She smiles at
me and says, "And why are you here in New York?"

"Partly business, partly pleasure. I'm a writer."

"What sorts of things do you write?"

"If I tell you, I'll have to move closer." The bartender hands me
another sauvignon blanc. "You're only up to seven hundred," he
says.

"I'll have another, too," the woman says, "when this is gone."

She moves over, I move over. We introduce ourselves—she is
named Shelley—and I tell her about *A Round-Heeled Woman* and
how New York has provided me an interesting sex life.

"Me, too!" she exclaims. She is brimming over, she is truly on
the edge of her bar stool. She tosses back the last of her martini

and whispers, "I'm a mistress." I am clearly interested, so she continues: "Actually I'm from Florida. I teach art in a magnet school there, and my lover"—she giggles and explains that all this has happened sort of recently, that never before and right out of the blue—"he flies me to New York once or twice a month, and we have wonderful, wonderful sex." And then, "He's married."

"Oh," I say, and add him to the list of married men who cheat on their wives.

"He loves and respects his wife, but they don't have sex."

I add him to the list of married men who claim not to have sex with their wives. This is a very long list. Some of the names appear on both.

"His name's Steven; he's older than I am. I'm fifty-two."

"You look terrific," I tell her.

"Do you like this suit? Steven gave me a thousand dollars and told me I needed a suit. What do you think?"

"It's gorgeous." And it is. Amazing what a thousand bucks can buy. I shift to a more comfortable position on my bar stool and peer at the drinkers seated at the tables behind us. The light is low, the drinkers appear to be interested only in each other; the mood is easy, companionable, discreet. I turn to Shelley and whisper, "Did you buy new underwear when you became a mistress?"

"You bet I did!" *Shhh!* "I marched right into Victoria's Secret and told them to fix me up." She lowers her voice. "I'm wearing a bustier right now, right under this suit."

"Isn't it uncomfortable?" I wonder. Whalebone for corsets has long been out of fashion (that's what Save the Whales was all about). But in the pictures I've seen of bustiers—"How *do* you pronounce it?" I ask her. "Boos-ti-ay."—those corsets that harness the torso are held firm and tight with stays of some sort that aren't made of ribbon—more like steel, probably plastic today—nonbendable stays like those that hold the sails flat on sailboats. Anyway, though in the Victoria's Secret catalogue the model's breasts peep prettily over the top of her bustier, somewhere it's gotta hurt, especially when you sit down. Where does your belly go? Not to mention your hips. Do they peep not so prettily beneath this contraption? Or are they just crushed into silence by stays of steel? And yet, here she sits, dimpling over her second martini. "Actually, it's really comfortable. And look." She slides her skirt up and then down quickly. "Did you see? I never ever wore garters or stockings like this. My god, this is fun!"

And so is she. I ask her how they met. She is a-bubble. "We literally ran into each other in a coffee shop and, and . . . Sex with him is wonderful. He knows what to do—he's sixty-five—and he knows the words to go with it. That's the amazing part; he knows just the right words, and he isn't shy or embarrassed to use them." She looks down at her lap. "He's had many mistresses, you see."

I nod my understanding and agree that she is a lucky woman; after all (and I don't say this aloud), he might have chosen someone younger, probably did at some point, maybe will again. Or maybe he's smart. Maybe he knows Benjamin Franklin's advice to a friend about mistresses: "In all your Amours, you should *prefer old Women to young ones.*" (Italics his.) Franklin, having preferred the sixty-one-year-old Minette to the young lovelies of Paris, explains, "Because when Women cease to be handsome, they study to be good . . . There is hardly such a thing to be found as an old Woman who is not a good Woman." And lest the man be troubled by sags and wrinkles, Franklin advises putting a basket over her head, "the lower Parts continuing to the last as plump as ever."

I doubt Steven puts a basket over this pretty fifty-two-year-old head. She continues: "I was married for twenty-six years, still am legally. My husband was a crook when I married him, though I didn't know it then, and got crookeder and crookeder until they put him in jail, and he still won't give me a divorce, and oh well, we had sex in the beginning, I had orgasms, but it was work! I worked for every one I got!" She smiles dreamily into her glass. "And now it's pleasure, pure pleasure."

"I imagine," I say, "that sometimes it's not easy being the other woman."

"Yes." She nods. "The other night his driver drove his wife to the opera, then came back for me and Steven, and when we got to the restaurant, Steven had to go in first and make sure nobody in the restaurant knew him. Sometimes it's hard." She looks directly and defiantly right at me and says, "But you know what, this is a chance made in heaven and I have decided to take it. My older son thinks it's terrific. My seventeen-year-old daughter is not convinced, but I told her, I'll never get a chance like this again and I'm going for it all."

"Good for you," I say, and watch as she slides off the bar stool and sways a bit as she struggles to get her coat on.

"Bye," she says, "nice meeting you," and totters off. I hope the cold night air will sober her up before Steven's driver comes to collect her, before her bustier loses its grip and takes on a life of its own. Being a mistress can be dangerous.

My own Steven, though I have been prudent and so far refused his oft-repeated entreaties, lives not far from the bar that has provided such comfort for Shelley and me. My Steven and I will have dinner, and yet again he will tell me how wonderful his wife is, how he loves and respects her, how they have not made love since their sons—now in their thirties—were born. "I wouldn't burden her with sex," he has explained. "But you—my god." Then suddenly, "I have a house in Provence. Come with me next summer. Come live with me and be my love."

"The three of us? Your wife, you, and me?" I ask.

"Well, not quite. There's a house nearby I would take for you."

And he could skip in and out, and we could wave at each other from our windows, maybe string a wire from his bedroom to mine and send notes, billets-doux they would be called in Provence. And when his wife was doing the marketing, we could . . . Gee, I've always wanted to star in a French farce. "No, thank you."

Long ago I directed myself never to take up with a married

man, not out of principle but because I knew the ending, me sitting by the phone on Christmas, Thanksgiving, New Year's, Easter, and Halloween, not to mention Veterans Day and all eight days of Hanukkah, willing the phone to ring, never accepting the reality of his marriage. Relationships, sexual relationships, get complicated enough without a saint of a wife hovering overhead. It must be that not having sex with your husband makes you holy or something; in my experience it makes her respected and honored and admired and safe; in my experience an asexual wife gets to live the life of a decent God-fearing American, which, by cracky, appeals more and more to me as I see the possibility of such a life swirling down the drain. Women who don't have sex with their husbands and their husbands love them anyway live the kind of life I assumed, way back in the olden days, I would have, a life in which it was natural to use "we" without stammering. But I never did have that life, which doesn't mean I still want one. Or that I don't.

It's not fair, though. My mother led me to believe that if a husband were not happy at home—she would intone the word "happy" so that I understood it meant "sexually satisfied"—he would of course seek solace elsewhere, and the wife would have only herself to blame. My mother believed in doing one's wifely duty, thereby assuring the longtime success of the marriage. She believed that if a husband strayed, the wife was to blame. One of my favorite movies is *That Hamilton Woman!* (1941) starring Vivien Leigh as the Other Woman and Laurence Olivier as Admiral Lord Nelson. A classic case, my mother would have argued, had she seen the movie, which she did not because in 1941 in our small Ohio town there was no movie theatre. The movie, which years later I rented from my video store, showed Nelson's wife to be cold and undoubtedly frigid and "unwifely," proving my mother right. Of course her husband strayed, I thought. The reason is right there on the screen. I wonder what my mother would have said about recent scholarship that pretty much proves that Nelson's wife of many years was a kind and loving wife. Nelson would be harder to explain—and thus far more interesting. Do husbands who stray have unyielding wives to blame? Not necessarily, though it is convenient for Other Women to think so.

As I watched this sumptuous movie sometime in the seventies, my sympathies were entirely with Emma Hamilton and her married lover. My mother would not have sided with Lady Hamilton, who was married, too, thus doubling her sin. My mother believed that women who prowled after married men were sluts who would eventually get their comeuppances, and she would have pointed to Lady Hamilton's sad end as proof: dead in Calais at age fifty, penniless and alone. I guess we know what my mother would have said about her daughter sitting in a fancy bar in New York City encouraging a once-decent young woman in her participation in adultery and fornication.

I keep Patricia's letter to me close at hand. After *A Round-Heeled Woman* came out, lots of people wrote me. Patricia wrote all the way from London, "My current batch of paramours are all married, which I regret . . . when I want to see a film or attend the theatre, or experience a new restaurant, or show off in public with someone other than a woman friend." I reread Patricia's letter whenever I think, Well, why not? What's the harm in a little affair, so what if he's married? The truth is that there is no such thing as "a little affair." Affairs have a way of growing into big things, like love affairs, and then, boy, you're stuck. Because no way in hell is he going to leave his wife for you, not after all those years, and, in fact, the more you come to know and to love him, the more you don't want him to leave his wife; how could you ever make up for what he would lose? And besides, the way he folds his clothes—like it takes thirty minutes before he's ready for the sack, though, to be fair, there's no room on the floor because that's where your clothes are—sometimes makes you sigh with relief at the thought that Goody, he'll be gone soon. Still, there is, as Patricia points out, "the loneliness factor." And then, too, you love him. Christ, better to stick to your rule: No married men.

All that notwithstanding, here I am in New York City applauding a woman who has let herself be swept off her feet by an irremediably married man. In the soft candlelight from the tables behind her, she looked like a painting in her Renaissance painting book—Raphael's Madonna in a thousand-dollar suit. There is nothing lovelier than a woman newly in love. Not even The Wyndham Sisters, who live just across the street.

auld lang syne

O plunge your hands in water,
Plunge them in up to the wrist;
Stare, stare in the basin
And wonder what you've missed.

—from "As I Walked Out One Evening," W. H. AUDEN

he property is for sale, my landlady tells me. Merry Christmas! Graham got married. Happy New Year!

One dreadful day, from out of the blue, my computer announced an e-mail from Graham. It was one of those instant messages: *"I will be out of the office until the first of the year due to my upcoming marriage and subsequent honeymoon. May the Year 2003 bring you joy and success."*

There went my life. He took it plumb out of me, never even bothered to warn me in person, in bed, in a letter, that he was— What's the expression? Seeing someone, a euphemism for having sex or, worse, making love. Watch out, he could have said, I'm going to break your heart. Oh, Christ. If I'd let myself think at all, I could have guessed that this wonderful man would not lead a celibate life in my absence. How ridiculous. Of course he ought to be married, he's thirty-four, for crissake. He needs a normal life with a probably normal girl, not with a crone who writes him drunken love letters and hides under the covers to make love. But jesus, we had just, just—here's what I wrote him afterward, after he had made a visit to me way out here: *"After you and I made love and you hoisted my backpack, we made our way up to the little park atop Nob Hill. We ate small chicken legs and chocolate chip cookies made by me, and you said all the right things, distracted as you were by things to do with work, and so I went home."* There it was again, his distracted-ness: Something was happening. I made the something be his work because of course I wanted this real-time fantasy to continue for-ever. I really and truly loved him, despite knowing that in doing so I was asking for another broken heart. So? If anybody had won-dered, I would have said—and probably did—that of course he needed to have as close to a normal life as somebody that smart and good-looking and funny and kind is capable of. Well, maybe not kind. Even so, he deserved all the good things and good people of the world and didn't I wish him all the best oh christ. I was dead inside, just absolutely dead. Except when I was angry—not at his marriage but at the way he told me—as if I were a busi-ness acquaintance or less. Oh, tell the truth: You were angry at both. So I sent him a wedding present. Maybe I would take up with a married man after all. Shame on me.

GRAHAM SENT ME no warning, but I'm sending one. If you're thinking of keeping company with a married man, keep this in mind: You can sip all the martinis in New York, you can buy suits and negligees and have delicious sex, but if you are an Other Woman, you will pay a price.

New Year's Eve is a time to try men's souls, and women's, too, and if you are an Other Woman, you're in trouble, because you don't have a legally bonded male (sons and pets don't count) right there next to you, so now you're in for it. New Year's Eve is the day and the night when the social order exacts its revenge on you for failing to follow its rules, for being a maverick, for threatening by your very behavior the stability necessary for its survival. And it's going to hurt because when you're an Other Woman, holidays are when your lover stays home and behaves like the respectable person everyone thinks he is. He makes hot toddies while friends gather to trim the tree, and he goes to dinner with his wife and a few old friends, longtime married couples, and he does nice things for his children, such as drive them to the snow so they can ski. And then on New Year's Eve maybe he sneaks off and calls you from some closet somewhere, his voice muffled by his wife's new down jacket, which he bought her for Christmas.

Forget what science tells us: New Year's Eve is the longest fucking day in the year. And then comes the night. On the stroke of midnight who doesn't get kissed? You. You sit in the darkness of your lonely room, and goddam, you want to be respectable. It's not, Oh god, he's going to sleep with his wife. After all, it's probably the only time they'll do it this year, so what do you care? It's that afterward *they* will get to go to the movies or to brunch—respectable couples have brunch; people like you have coffee—or to old friends, and maybe visit some grandchildren. It's this time of the year that punishes the hell out of you for straying, for ruffling the waters, for committing the ultimate crime—sleeping with another woman's husband—and you're going to feel real pain, for what would the world be if people like you won the day? Chaos is what.

Go read Kafka's "In the Penal Colony"; it's all there, the criminal strapped to the rack, his crime etched slowly by needles into his body. On the sixth hour of his torment comes enlightenment; the convicted man understands—or so the people who once gathered to watch are led to believe—the commandment he has failed to heed: Obey Thy Superiors—and then he dies, though not until the machine goes horribly awry and mutilates him. It is a grisly story of justice gone crazy.

You won't die—adultery is not yet punishable by death—but the twelve days of Christmas are long enough to do a fair bit of sticking it to you to make you understand the price one pays for living on the edge of society. What you're supposed to do, of course, you Other Women, is see the light and break it off so that your lovers can resume their rightful places as bulwarks of the status quo, as the pillars of marriage, that institution created to keep men and women from running amok. If the people who oppose gay marriage had any brains at all, they would see their protesting for the nonsense it is; they would understand, in fact, that their arguments, if that's what they are, run counter to the continuation of a calm and orderly society, for there's nothing like marriage to keep guys off the streets and out of bars. Marriage civilizes, don't you know. Of all social institutions, marriage is the one that can keep a good man down.

And all this secrecy is so American, isn't it? This hypocrisy, this pretense of fidelity, this rage of a wronged wife, the abject apologies of the errant husband: not in France, at least not in Paris. The existence of Other Women is acknowledged, though unspoken, by wives; it is tolerated. The funeral of France's president, François Mitterrand, was attended by both his wife and his mistress. The photograph of both in the gathering of mourners was on the front page. Ménage à trois? French. Never in America, where the Puritan ethic mandates pretense, punishes truthfulness, and allows nothing that is not imprisoned within the cell blocks of civil and religious life.

For me the misery of this long day's journey into night began way back when, when I was twenty-three and hopelessly in love with Jack. I spent the holidays, at the behest of my mother, back in Ohio, leaving Jack to fend for himself in San Francisco. I was miserable the entire week and succeeded in making everyone around me miserable. He didn't call and didn't call, and I couldn't call him; a girl didn't do that in 1956, especially in front of her parents, who, if she did, either rolled their eyes or patted her on the back when he didn't answer. It was just total humiliation to hear the phone calls be for everybody but me.

Almost fifty years later New Year's Eve still sucks. Now there's supposedly this big-deal economic recovery: Who's recovering? A little bunch of people at the top while a whole mass of folks underneath are struggling to keep from drowning. So on this particular New Year's Eve a little bunch of people are paying two thousand dollars to get into the Rainbow Room or, if you're strapped, one thousand for the Waldorf. The rest of us are playing Monopoly with the neighbors or sitting alone watching Walter Cronkite light up the Vienna State Opera Orchestra. Guess who still doesn't have a date. It's not Mrs. Cronkite.

But let's imagine for a minute that I had two thousand dollars to throw away on a gala event, and another two thousand for a dress with all the trimmings—okay, ten thousand. I could get all gussied up and celebrate the advent of the new year . . . where? Where is a single woman, bedecked and bedizened as she might be, welcome on this festive occasion? Not at the Rainbow Room, I'll bet. Unlike single men, who can show up drunk, stoned, solo, or all three and still be met with open arms, single women—albeit sober and dignified—who have the bad taste to appear unescorted are taking their reputations in their hands. Besides, while the single men at these parties have each other for company, women alone are alone.

All this grousing comes from way back, maybe as far back as 1956, when, on the eve of 1957, there I was sniffling away over Jack, until finally my parents, who never went out on New Year's Eve, went out, leaving me with my little brother. Mortification loomed. Poor little guy, just turned ten but really still nine. Everyone loved Terry. From the day he was born he was sunny, funny, and adored by one and all. What punishment to have to spend this holiday with his old sister, whose chief claim to fame was her ability to pout for days at a time. Which she was doing now.

"What's wrong?" he inquired timidly.

"Nothing." I sure as hell wasn't going to share my distress over having been stood up, probably for the rest of my life. I lay on the couch, arms hiding my eyes, which were red and bleary from imagining Jack in the arms of another. Terry crept away softly, probably in the hope that I had fallen asleep and he could go watch television past his bedtime.

Time passed. Here he came, tiptoeing up to the couch. "Happy New Year," I heard him say. I opened one eye, to see him standing next to me holding a tray. On it were baloney sandwiches—on white bread cut into little triangles and without crusts!—and two glasses of milk. "I thought we could have a party, too," he said. And we did. Then we watched Times Square on the television as 1957 came to Ohio. Terry fell asleep leaning against my shoulder, and at the stroke of midnight I leaned over and kissed him on the top of his curly head.

I believed that marriage would protect me from the shame of spending New Year's Eve alone, but, as I would discover, there are all kinds of mortification. Ten years later, on this night of all nights, my husband, Tom, and I would celebrate the coming of the new year with his mistress. I didn't know that then. All I knew was that months had passed since my husband and I had seen a movie or visited friends or walked along the river; all I knew was that there was a growing coldness between us; all I knew was that I was getting fat and couldn't seem to stop eating. And so I begged him for an evening out, for a New Year's Eve out. It didn't matter where, just out. Having perfected my ability to pout over long periods of time, I wasn't surprised when my husband sighed and said, "Okay, we'll go out for a couple of beers. Mind if Lynne comes along?" Lynne was a name I knew from my husband's talk about his job. "I don't mind," I said cheerily. "The more the merrier!"

What would I wear? It was too late to buy a new dress, and besides, we didn't have the money. I would have to wear something dark, something to hide my increasing bulk. Pulling out of the closet a dark blue cotton dress I had worn the previous summer, I hoped my husband wouldn't notice that it was old, though I had nothing to fear, really; my husband hadn't looked at me for a long time. Oh god, clearly this dress had shrunk, hanging there in the closet all fall and half the winter, because dammit, it was tight; still, with some difficulty I zipped it up the back, reminding myself as I did to not exhale. Off we went.

The bar was dark; that was good. It was crowded; that was okay, too. And Lynne and I sat at a table, my husband between us, the three of us slamming down one beer after the other. My husband, having learned from me, was working his way into a sensational sulk (sulk being the masculine form of pout), but I just had another beer and admired Lynne's new dress. As I leaned forward to smooth the velvet of her sleeve, I heard one of the world's most humiliating noises: the sound of a zipper parting. My dress had divided itself into halves.

My husband, intent on peering into the darkness of the beer before him, took no notice. Lynne noticed at once. "Oh, dear," she said. "Turn your back to me. I'll try to get it back together." I did and she did and it wouldn't go back together. "Here," she said, "put your coat on." I did and, not soon enough for me, we left. At home my husband, in no mood to be sympathetic, said, "Well, you got what you wanted. Happy now?" As the clock struck twelve, someone set off firecrackers in the street outside. Inside, my husband snored.

And that was the last time, 1966 verging on 1967, I ventured out to celebrate the coming of the new year. Over time the possibilities of getting kissed at midnight lessened and then disappeared altogether. Over time, armed with the foreknowledge of what I was up against, I have maintained and even increased my capacity to mount a pout of epic proportions, lasting most of the holiday season—my only defense against the relentlessness of the cruelest night of all. Is it any wonder, then, that I remain kissless when the new year brings new life and lots of fucking to those who do not wander beyond the confines of respectability.

Of course, were I in New York, I could count on a few kisses from . . . whom? Is Sidney still alive? Graham isn't, at least not for me. Never mind, New York is alive, always, unlike me, who has suffered an emotional stroke, leaving behind only one feeling, the great big one: self-pity. What the hell. I'm going to New York. Again.

So what if my cottage gets sold in the meantime? My landlady and her family are moving far away. Not much I can do about that. Somebody new will buy the property, and maybe they'll let me stay and maybe they won't. I can't do anything about that either. I am not good at waiting. The years I have accumulated have not brought with them patience; I am, however, a champion hand-wringer and occasional sniveler. So while I wait for other people to make or unmake my life, there's nothing wrong with kissing an entire bottle of champagne by myself and then calling the airlines—*that* I can do. They're always open, even on New Year's Eve, and if I punch zero a lot of times and wait long enough, a real person will talk to me. Happy New Year, he'll say. How can I help you? Get me to New York, I'll say. And he will.

at the plaza

It is a truth universally acknowledged that a woman alone in a bar must be in want of a date.

—with apologies to JANE AUSTEN

he ride from JFK to midtown Manhattan takes about thirty minutes, except it never does, it's always longer. Which is fine with me. Coming across the Triborough Bridge into New York, through Queens and Harlem and Central Park, is thrilling. So, usually, is the cab ride.

It is very, very cold in New York in January, though not as cold as the holidays I just endured not at all gracefully. Outside the cab windows the dirty snow is banked along the highway, the sky is gray, overcast; at five P.M. darkness is almost upon us. I am in high spirits. My cabdriver is not.

"Sonofabitchin' traffic." The accents of New York are forever interesting to me; I can't make out exactly where this one comes from. The Bronx, I think, with black overlay or underlay; I like it. I will keep him talking if I can.

We pass Shea Stadium. "So," I say, "did your team win the Series?"

"No." Can you bite off a no and spit it out? Yes, he just did.

A dark green SUV eases its way onto the roadway.

"Sonofabitch!" My driver is bellowing. "Hey!" He opens his

window, puts his arm out, and gives the international sign for ag-grievedness. The icy wind renders me speechless. The driver of the SUV rolls down his window, does the same back. My driver leans his head out the window and yells, "Get your truck outta my way!" The SUV continues to glide slowly, confidently, into our lane. "Fuck you!" yells my driver. The SUV glides closer to our cab, whose driver has not seen fit to slow so that those vehicles from entrances can merge with the flow of traffic. "Fuck you!" yells the SUV driver, a young white man with a mouth as big as my driver's, and he moves the SUV into the lane ahead of us.

My driver is as livid as any American male can be. "Fuck you!" he yells, and in a burst of creativity, "Fuck yo mama!" The SUV driver leans his head out his window and yells, "Fuck you!" Equally creative, they are, but I will not argue, I will not beg for the window to be rolled up. I will simply endure.

My driver, no doubt sensing my cowardice, yells once again, "Fuck you!" and then, "Fuck yo mama!". In the absence of any re-sponse the cabdriver leans out his window and yells, "I got yo mama right here." He gestures out the window, his thumb point-ing to the backseat of his cab, to me. "Right here in my cab, you sonofabitch! You wanna talk fuckin', hey! Take a look!"

Surely not. There's too much traffic; he couldn't just stop. He couldn't even get off the highway, clogged as it is with slow-moving traffic, and even if he did, it's still daylight, people live all around in these neighborhoods, not to worry. Am I going to be a hostage? Nah, it's too cold.

The SUV, without benefit of turn signal, moves easily, rather grandly, into the right-hand lane. Smoothly the driver exits the highway, giving us the finger as he goes. No noise from my driver. Time passes. We have gone a mile in silence and with the window rolled up. "Feel better?" I ask.

"Yeah," he says. "Good to get all that out. Where you from?" Suddenly he pulls off the highway and onto streets I've never heard of or seen in all of my taxi rides from JFK to midtown Manhattan.

"I'm taking you some shortcuts. You got yourself the best driver going. Have you there in no time." The cab shoots up the street. I am at his mercy. He says, "People so grateful for me knowing all these shortcuts, they usually tip me big."

"I'm a teacher," I say. I don't say I'm a writer. When I do, people ask what it is I write, and then I have to go through this long song and dance about placing an ad in the personals and meeting men, and most of the time the other person turns speechless. If I lied and said that I write about economics or cooking or just plain sex, the other person would still be speechless; there's something about coming face-to-face with a writer that renders most people mute. Because I find this cabdriver interesting, I want him to talk to me, and so, "I'm a teacher." People are never speechless around teachers. Except you have to be careful not to say you're an English teacher, because the response to that is "Uh-oh, gotta watch my grammar" or "English was my worst subject" or "How come you people don't teach spelling anymore?"

A sigh of resignation from the front seat. What he doesn't know is that I am also a big tipper, probably bigger than people with lots of money, which they have, partly, because they aren't big tippers. I say, "Of course, whether or not you get a tip at all depends on how you're going to vote in the next election."

Another sigh, then a long silence. We are stopped at one of the many traffic lights this shortcut provides us. Finally, " I . . . I gotta go with Hillary. She's an all-right lady."

"Good," I say, "though we'll probably have to wait another four years for Hillary. Anyway, you've got a tip, an average to below average tip. How about the election coming up?"

Traffic light number twelve, another sigh, a long silence. "Whoever's runnin' against Bush," he says. "I gotta vote my conscience."

We are now friends. He tells me outlandish and fascinating stuff, better than what you can find in the supermarket tabloids: Robert Wagner murdered Natalie Wood out there on that boat. Whitney Houston is gay. "What? She is not!" Well, she is. My driver knows the neighborhood where she grew up. "Everybody know she's a dyke." Natalie Cole is clean finally, had a rough time. Bobby Brown is one bad dude, and "I never say nothing bad about babies, but that baby of his is ugly! Don't take him out in the light! The sun go down!"

As for himself he used to be a fireman, hurt his back, became an alcoholic, joined AA, sober seven years now. "I'm gonna show you something," he says, and reaches into his glove compartment. "Look at this." He hands me a piece of paper. "Barbra Streisand," it reads. "I drove her. This right here is her autograph." I return the paper quickly to his hand and murmur my appreciation. "Natalie Cole, she was in this cab, too, but she didn't give me no autograph. She's nice, though. She's clean, like I said."

We are making progress. The street sign says East 123. We are in Manhattan.

"So you're a teacher."

"Yes."

"Teachers don't get paid enough. They oughtta pay you more money." His voice rises. "Teachers do important things. Where would we be without teachers!" I expect him to roll down the window and yell "Fuck you," and he would, I'm sure, if either of us could identify the "they." I would help; I would yell, too, but outside this taxi people seem to be worse off than either of us inside.

Then he says, "I wanna ask you a question. You sure you're a teacher?"

"Mm-hmm."

"What's this word mean?"

"Yes?"

"'Conservative.' I hear people being that, being conservative. What does that mean?"

Now's my chance. I can proselytize, embroider, enlarge upon, propagandize, even tell the truth. "It means 'to conserve, to save, to pull in, to be tight, narrow.'"

He is silent, deep in thought. Then, "How about 'liberal'?"

"Ah, now there," I say. "Liberal is what you are. 'Liberal' means a person who is free, who thinks for himself, who grows, not shrinks. Wouldn't you say you're a liberal?"

"Yes, ma'am." He nods enthusiastically. The street sign out the window says ADAM CLAYTON POWELL.

He is not finished. We turn onto Central Park West, maybe my favorite street in all the world, and he says, "Which one is right?"

"You mean the political right?"

A nod.

"Conservatives are on the right."

He says, "Liberals are left, right?" and laughs.

"Yes, you are a left-leaning liberal."

He smiles at me in the mirror. "I am a liberal leaning to the left. A lotta *l*'s there."

"Indeed."

He pulls to the curb in front of the hotel. He hops out and walks back to open the trunk. He removes my bags, sets them on the sidewalk. "I want to thank you. This has been the best drive I had since Barbra Streisand."

"For me, too," I assure him. Once a teacher always a teacher, I must now reinforce the learning. "Hold out your right hand. Which is it—conservative or liberal?"

"Conservative."

"Now your left."

"Liberal. L equals liberal. That's me."

"Remember that in November."

"I surely will." He bends his head and looks straight into my eyes. "You know something?" he says. " I got educated." His smile is broad. "Now I can conversate with the best of 'em."

"Yes, you can." Give that man a big tip. So I do.

New York is just one big classroom where everybody learns from everybody else. No wonder I love it.

.   .   .

MY HOTEL IS down the street from the Plaza. You know, the big one with horses and carriages out front, and the fountain, where F. Scott Fitzgerald and Zelda danced their nights away, where Kay Thompson's Eloise lived, the one the new owners are ruining by turning most of it into condos for the very rich, who are, indeed, different from you and me. But all that is still to come. Now it is six P.M. and time for a drink, so why not at the Plaza? On an earlier visit I peeked into the famous bar, the Oak Room, and got scared off by its clubbiness; all that wood paneling did not invite a woman alone. My favorite bars are those in the lobbies of hotels, where in the midst of the hustle and bustle of people coming and going you can sit in the eye of the storm in a comfortable chair and sip wine or belt a beer or toss back a shot, and nobody notices, nobody cares. Lots of hotels have gotten prissy and prefer to hide their liquor and the people who drink it. Oh well, everybody has something to hide, why not hotels? Anyway, the bargain hotel in which I am staying does not have a bar in its lobby or anywhere else—it barely has a lobby—so I am forced out into the winter winds to make my way up to Fifth Avenue and the corner bar at the Plaza; the One is what it's called.

The One is not especially inviting at first glance. Well-lit and small, it sits at one side of a large expensive-looking dining room. But it must have something, because the people sitting at its bar (once it was Gore Vidal) and at the high tables along the wall are enjoying themselves, talking to each other, nobody sitting alone and sulky in a corner, maybe because there are no corners in this bar, it's too round.

At one of the tables a woman sits alone, though showing no signs of sulkiness, and since all the other tables are fully occupied, I ask her if she would mind sharing hers. "That's fine," she says, and continues her reading of the wine list. She orders a California white; so do I, and it seems ridiculous not to talk, at least a little bit. Clearly she is alone, as am I; we are approximately the same age, although, as is most of the rest of the world, she is some few years younger. She is dressed entirely in black, which means she is in mourning or trying to look as if she belongs in New York. Neither, it turns out. She is hoping to disguise the thickness of her waistline. So far we have a lot in common.

"I used to have a very thin body," she says, catching me eyeing her middle passage, then pulling at the waist of her black top the way women who don't like their bodies do in order to hide them.

"You look very nice," I tell her. "Are you visiting New York?"

She tells me all. And tells me. About the tradition she and her friend continue, even after the deaths of their husbands, of coming to New York for a week to see the shows and shop, and how her friend is at *Phantom* this very night and she didn't want to see that show again, though if it were *Cats* she would have, so she came here because she came here the last time she was in New York, and my, hasn't the cost of a glass of wine gone up! Goodness!

She is driving me nuts. I do not believe people are boring; it's just that sometimes their conversation—if that's what this is—is tedious. Greta—for that's her name, after Greta Garbo—seems certain and secure in the belief that everything she says, as long as it's about herself, will be of consummate interest to the listener. I envy her; it must be nice not to stammer in your head, turning over phrases and ideas, fearful that your every utterance will be misconstrued, derided, passed over. I doubt that Greta ever wondered why so early in every party she found herself standing alone. Here, in this bar, all the seats save ours are occupied by people who look absolutely fascinated, who bend across the tables and gaze into the eyes of those who seem to be truly engaged by the speaker's intelligence and wit, who speak, then listen, and speak again. Alas, I am not among them.

"I keep telling my daughter-in-law about ripening a cantaloupe before, not after, you put it in the fridge, but she can't handle it, she gets so upset right away, so I try my darndest to keep quiet, keep my mouth shut."

Oh, Greta, Greta, do it now.

"So why are you in New York?" she asks, her second glass of wine in hand.

Should I tell her I'm a teacher? And keep her talking? No. I tell her the facts. "I'm a writer and I'm here doing some publicity." This should shut her up.

"Oh, really, what's it about?"

So I tell her the title, the subject, and lo and behold, when she hears *A Round-Heeled Woman,* she laughs. She gets it right off. And then she goes to town. Married for thirty-four years, "I was not orgasmic, just never. Well, I was twenty-two when we got married, he was twenty-four; he didn't know what he was doing and neither did I, and things never got better. I did other things: the garden, children—we lost one—and then my husband died."

Greta lived for all those thirty-four years in what is now Napa Valley, "in a house we bought in the fifties for thirty-five thousand dollars. Well, gosh, here I was all alone with the children gone, and Hal dead, so I sold it. For $1.5 million! Imagine! Just a little three-bedroom house! I love New Mexico."

Bet you love California, too, Greta. Jesus H. Christ, $1.5 million. I stare in amazement and envy. This was a woman who had done it right: married a man who bought the two of them a house, which she kept clean and tidy for him and the children, who came soon thereafter. By following the rules—marriage, home, family— she has made out like a bandit. Think I'll let her buy me a drink.

"But gosh," she continues, "I was lonely. I was only fifty-six, you know, when Hal died. I went to a few bars, to singles gatherings in my community." And then one day at a hardware store she met Henry. "And I became a butterfly!" She puts her palms together and makes a V with her hands, and right before my very eyes the lines in her forehead smooth out, her mouth softens, her eyes shine; her cheeks grow rosy, she becomes a pretty woman. What a gift, this sexuality of ours.

Greta turns out to be multiorgasmic—"About time, wouldn't you say? I just blossomed and never quit!" She and Henry were together for ten years, and then "I got tired of paying for him, you know, when we traveled, or even when we went out for dinner. He was a painter and never sold anything, so—"

I protest: "But, Greta, he sounds like a gift worth paying for, as you say."

Greta knows her own mind. "He was fourteen years older than me, and frankly, he was running out of steam."

"Oh."

Now Greta and I look like the other patrons in the bar. I am bent across the table, riveted to Greta and her story. Her prettiness is, maybe, from the wine, but I don't think so. She is having a lovely time recalling her butterfly period, when she "just opened up."

"And since Henry?" I ask.

"No one," she says, "but I go on lots of Elderhostel trips, like the last one where we went to . . ."

Oh no you don't, Greta. The very tiptop item on my list of topics to be avoided is Elderhostel. Now, I know that Elderhostel is a wonderful organization, one of the few with no detractors, but I have heard more than enough about accommodations, good and bad, and bus drivers, ditto, from the ever-increasing number of retired persons I happen, by virtue of my age, to know. Alas, I am too late; she takes my silence for encouragement. "My main problem with Elderhostel, or any of the trips I've been on, is the single supplement, and should I pay it?"

Indeed this is a concern, and not a trivial one either, but seen perhaps from my own decadence, Greta is far less interesting and appealing when she talks about travel than when she turns into a butterfly. She goes on: "I hate it when we stay in college dorms. The bathrooms are down the hall, and sometimes they're unisex. I remember up in Oregon, where we went for the Shakespeare, I kept bumping into the bus driver in the bathroom, and then in Switzerland it happened once, too, though the bus driver wasn't the same one, naturally."

She is on a tear. "But this once, this one time I didn't pay the single supplement, I got put together with this really, really boring woman, you wouldn't believe . . ."

I tear a sheet out of the my little green writing book and write the title of my book on it. "Here," I say, "get this book. You'll like it." And I slip off my chair and out of the corner bar at the Plaza, into the wintry winds of West Fifty-eighth Street.

The following October I receive a letter from Greta, who did indeed like the book, as did her single women friends. Greta has just acquired a new home in a very large retirement community and invites me to visit her and "meet a wonderful group of women." A new house and with money left over, I'll bet.

The life expectancy of butterflies is short, and I wonder if Greta, like so many people, has gone to New Mexico to die. Probably not. Nabokov, in his lifelong fascination with butterflies, traveled many places to study and collect butterflies. In the Grand Canyon of Arizona he discovered and named a new species of butterfly: *Neonympha dorothea.* Maybe Greta is a new species, *Neonympha gretea. Nymph: One of the young of any insect that undergoes metamorphosis.* Wouldn't that be nice.

The next year Greta writes to give me an update on her sex life: neither she nor her women friends have one. They are all attractive and financially independent but cannot find a man who is not very, very old; they wish for men unlike those who come to mixers at the retirement center and, if they are ambulatory at all, shuffle. So how, Greta wonders, does one meet a man? Hang out in bars? Come tell us, she invites me. Me? Tell you how to do it? How to meet a man? What would I say? Don't give up, I'd say, Don't give up. Empty, hollow. Greta has not given up, nor have her friends; otherwise they would not ask the question I do not have the answer to.

This question—How does one meet a man?—will assail me wherever I go: to readings, to panels, to signings, to the speakers' dais. And I don't know what to say. I would certainly not recommend that everybody post an ad in the personals, though I would not recommend not doing it either. I do not like this position of authority my readers will carve out for me. I didn't write a how-to book; I did not write an advice book. I sure as hell would not recommend that anyone do what I did once the personal ad came out—traipse across the continent, heart in hand. I'm no expert! I'm no sexpert! Never mind. I am what my readers want me to be, and so as I move about the country giving readings, the question becomes a plea: "Tell us how to meet a man."

I fall back on my reading: In novels how do men and women meet? Elizabeth Bennet meets Darcy after Darcy's friend, Mr. Bingley, moves into the neighborhood and Elizabeth's father calls on him, thus paving the way to marriage, though not before the hurdles of pride and prejudice have been surmounted. Jane Eyre meets Mr. Rochester when she takes the position of governess to Mr. Rochester's daughter. What a mess that turns into! Well, in novels old and new there are dances and parties and church suppers and funerals and beaches and boardrooms where young women meet young men, and, if the writer takes kindly to them, they marry and, we are led to expect, live happily ever after. But, my women readers ask me, if I'm not young, if I'm widowed or divorced or just alone, how do I meet a man?

What am I supposed to say? The truth? That my outright boldness, my shamelessness, got me not just one man but five? And that they all live three thousand miles away? And that my all-time favorite dumped me for a younger woman? And that I can't get a date on the whole West Coast? Why are you asking me, for crissake? But I answer finally; we are all getting desperate here. I say something like, "This is the new millennium, ladies, go online."

Or we—okay, I—could write a personal ad and ship it off to Gotham, again. All this blubbering about getting a date and not getting a date, why not begin anew? Why not write an ad that says: "Wanted: A man to stay the course." The thing is, I don't know if that's what I want. I do know I haven't the courage to begin again. I do know that my heart has not mended; Lord knows what would happen if it got broken again. I am trying to hurt less, not more, and New York, where being alone is the norm, helps me heal. A little vacation from the slings and arrows of love is what I'm taking, though if that is so, what the hell am I doing in a bar? Alone?

My e-mail life, my whole life, is dreary because Graham is not in it. So in every Manhattan bar and restaurant I visit in this cold, cold month of January, I raise my glass and wish the newlyweds all happiness. And I hope that when Graham exercises his conjugal right, he thinks of me.

if there were world enough and time

Who breathes overhead in the rose-tinted light may be glad!
—SCHILLER

nlike Greta at the Plaza and despite my advice to the lovelorn—go online, don't give up—I do not feel like a butterfly. I feel like a collapsed lung. At home back in Berkeley, back in the real world, my new landlords are taking possession of their real estate. They are a happy-looking couple, she twenty-eight, he thirty-two. Where the hell did they get eight hundred thousand dollars? Never mind, they want to keep me; they need my rent money to pay the taxes. So they double my rent. I cannot pay double my rent. I will have to grovel. I do, I beg for a few months' grace period, promising to pay up once my book brings me a bit of money, sounding, I hope, more certain about that prospect than I feel. Now what will happen? What if they read the book and decide they don't want a notorious person living in their backyard? Or one they may find guilty of moral turpitude? And what's the use of lying awake at night worrying about all this? I can't do a thing about it, certainly don't have the money to go out and buy myself a place to live where I would be safe from the whims of the moneyed class. I'll do the only thing I can do: sit tight and hope.

At this point I can't even imagine an acceptable version of my future; I can imagine, however, a future that will keep me nervous and on edge from fear of eviction, of being dumped, rejected. Where is everybody, dammit? Graham is a happy, I suppose, husband. John is content to sit in his fully owned and paid-for domicile and complain about the weather in New England, Sidney is sometimes on the telephone, Matt is too off-and-on, and c'mon, these men didn't sign on to steady my life, to make me secure. They did what I asked: gave me good sex and fine conversation. It's just that sometimes I could use a little help, a little accompaniment in a world so uncertain, so uncaring, so random in its meting out of punishments and rewards, a world remarkable for, in Thomas Hardy's words, "the persistence of the unforeseen." With all that in mind, maybe I ought to look for another rental:

Bdrms: 2   Baths: 1   Furnished: no
Rental period: month to month
Unit has: stove, refrig, coin-op washer/dryer, carpet
Landlord pays: water, garbage, heat
Units/bldg: 20   What floor: 2   # Stairs: 10
Available parking: w/extra fee
Wheelchair access: no (too many steps)

Not yet, not yet.

Add to everything this fact: I am getting no sex. I am back at square one, and square one is looking pretty bleak. Here where I live, women my age don't go to bars alone. Women my age go to the movies alone—that's okay, nobody sees you, anyway—and to concerts alone and museums alone. I didn't used to go to all these things alone; until recently I went with my great good friend, Jo, a funny, irreverent, and marvelously intelligent woman, who at seventy-five got carried off by the cancer that had plagued her for the last twenty years of her life. During our friendship, when we weren't in a concert hall or a museum, we were sitting together at her house, talking about the books we had just read, about the ideas and people in them, about the times those people lived in, about everything in that world and this. Jo is the woman I would have been if I had had good sense and a good figure, a very good brain, and great hair. She looked after herself in all ways, and she did it without a man. Though she enjoyed the company of men, she was more or less content to go home—she bought it with money she earned herself—alone.

When she died, the lights went out for a while; for a while all the tickets we had ordered grew dusty in my drawer. Occasionally I would take a ticket out and show up at the performance hall, only to turn around and go home, my heart too heavy to bear it alone. Why are all the good ones dying? In my head I keep a list of people whose departure from this earth would make the world a better place. But so far the earth is poorer for the absence of my good friend Jo, who lived a rich life without a man to guide her or support her or buy her a house. She loved one man her whole life, who married everybody but her. She left a house that is perfect for me. We'll see.

Time does not heal all wounds, but now I do go to movies and concerts and museums—never bars, my butterfly wings having been clipped by the absence of Jo and by United Airlines en route from JFK to SFO. In the mirror of the plane's restroom, once we are "free to move about the cabin," my scalp shows pink. Jesus, I always had a lot of hair, What the hell happened to it? How long can I carry this off, this sensuality of mine; how long before I will have to fake it? Or not?

And even in New York in those months long past, after Graham and I made love and I turned to him when it ended, I knew that my face was folding in on itself. I saw myself in his eyes, with all my creases and lines, the looseness of my face and breasts and belly, and I pulled the pillow over my nakedness and wondered how he could make such amazing love to me. I never asked and he never told. And now he's gone, and nothing, absolutely nothing, can fill the enormous emptiness that is my center.

So how do we live alone at the center of our shrinking selves? Thank God for Freud, who in his depressed and pessimistic, yet wise and articulate, way convinced me long ago in *Civilization and Its Discontents* that art—music and painting and literature—could sustain us in the face of life's brutality. It does, indeed.

The concerts I go to, my favorites—Jo's, too—occur in St. John's Presbyterian Church three blocks from my house. The concerts are called Chamber Music Sundaes because they happen on Sunday afternoons and because they are sweet and, like dessert, well earned by those who have eaten all their vegetables for years and years and are now allowed to partake of the last and the richest part of the meal. We are all regulars here, and, except for the musicians, I am the youngest person in attendance, a fact I used to point out to Jo, who was a few years older than I. Across the aisle a woman colored brown and wrinkled by years of sunshine dangles her hand over the armrest of the end of the pew. She wears gorgeous turquoise rings, many of them, sometimes two on one finger, the turquoise set in heavy silver. They are beautiful, and I bet she can't get them off, for the knuckles of her fingers are knotted, swollen large and shiny, arthritis having come to call and deciding to stay. She will die with her rings on, for sure.

A woman down front, dressed in red, turns to the audience in search of her friend. She has had a face-lift and is a living example of why not to. Her skin, a sunburn-red, is stretched—God, it looks painful—across her cheeks, her mouth pulled to the sides of her face. Why is this woman smiling? Or is she?

In the pew in front of me a woman says to her friend, "We saw that cute little movie, the one with Diane . . . Diane . . ."

"Keaton," says the friend. "The one with Jack Nicholson: *Something's Gotta Give.* Fred and I haven't seen it. Did you like it?"

"It was cute. Not great, but cute."

The friend speaks, "We saw *Calendar Girls* last week. Now, that was cute."

"Is that the British movie where the older women pose nude for a calendar?"

"Yes. Helen Mirren was in it."

"Are you a Helen Mirren fan?"

"Oh yes, we saw her in a Chekhov play once."

"I'm not a Chekhov fan." Oh boy, she'd better watch out; those are fighting words in Berkeley. "Shhh." The music is about to begin.

Jesus! Why don't they talk about sex and romance and "older" women? Yeah, Keaton at fifty-something sure is long in the tooth, and when, midpicture, she discards her turtleneck and shows up in a black minidress, why, she doesn't look old at all! So then, meta-morphosis complete, Jack gets her, although he has to wait till prac-tically the end of the movie when, finally, she doffs the shroud of age and dons the spaghetti straps of youth. Isn't *Something's Gotta Give* supposed to be about "older" women and their aging bodies, and doesn't it show that young men—Keanu Reeves, for god's sake—can find "older" women attractive? What about all those "older" women, those Calendar Girls, over there in England get-ting naked, Helen Mirren included? Bet that sold some tickets. And what do the elderly women in front of me—they are not "older," they are "old"—think about this? Absurd? Embarrassing? No, they thought it was *cute*.

Occasionally my rational voice breaks in to save me from drown-ing in my own impatience; this time it says, "Not everybody has to be profound, you know. Not everybody has to think all the time." "But hell," my impatient self answers, "everybody's a critic, and a bad critic at that, rushing to judgment, leaving discussion in the dust, getting to the end as fast as they can before reason be-comes necessary. When they say 'cute,' the tone is dismissive."

Why don't they talk about the British film *The Mother*? It's playing right around the corner, and it puts the Jack Nicholson and Diane Keaton film to shame: Anne Reid, the actress who plays the mother, is a real woman, age sixty-five and beyond, and she *looks* sixty-five and beyond. She has a belly, she is broad in the hips, her chin has descended all the way down her neck. On the other hand her hair remains brown and luxuriant; I wonder why the filmmaker didn't decide to show it gray. She propositions the young man; she takes the initiative. They have wild sex of several sorts. We see her naked, at least her top half, and it's really her (or someone her age). In the end no one in her family—not her son or her daughter—not the young man either (who does have gray in his beard, because gray hair on a man is sexy), is good enough for her: They are shallow and callow, and she goes off alone to make herself a life. She's like Nora in Ibsen's *A Doll's House,* who leaves her family for god knows what, though anything must be better than what she leaves behind. Question: Why did the filmmakers of *The Mother* have to make the young lover snort coke and pop pills? Answer: Because were he drug-free, he would never take an old woman to bed. Question: Why do the moviemakers give him an autistic son he loves? Why do they make him married? Answer: To keep him home, to keep him from running off to France with an old woman and being happy. Breaking one taboo—an older woman and a younger man enjoying sex with each other—is enough for one movie. Giving the couple a happy ending would be way out of line. Audiences wouldn't stand for it. Question: Why do I have to keep talking to myself? Answer: Because my friend Jo has left me behind.

Completely unaware that the person behind them—me—is having this fascinating and intelligent dialogue with herself that they are missing out on, the women babble on. Finally I think, What the hell, I'm being unreasonably hard on these perfectly nice women. Who am I to condemn them? Maybe the ability to be dismissive, to relegate rational conversation to its appropriate venue—the living room, say—is what the women in the forward pew have gotten good at over the years, because the people in this church come to hear music, seem to be happy people. Their husbands and wives, many of them, are still alive, their children are grown and presumably self-supporting; they themselves are ambulatory and not festooned with breathing tubes, and clearly they are not poor. Their makeup's bad, though, the pasty cosmetic gunked into the lines of their faces, too much of it, greasepaint for old women trying to put on a good face for an audience that isn't much interested. Why did these women get their hair done this way: tight curls all over? Ah yes, to hide the pink of their scalps, the part where greasepaint won't go.

The man sitting to my left looks great, of course; the lines in his face make him handsome. His eyes glitter over the half-glasses he bought at the drugstore, and a lot of his hair is still there. He looks a little like Jack Nicholson will when he's really old, if he's lucky.

I ask too much. I want these very nice women, women who have lived long lives full of sorrow and joy and loss and love, to take up the cross for me, to plead our case to the world at large, to explain in words I can understand and then repeat—something about the vibrancy that remains in old age, the usefulness of us, the love in us, and yes, desire. Shhh, the music.

Unless your ears are especially evolved, you have to be old to like chamber music. We here today have heard enough bombast to last us a lifetime (which it has). This afternoon we get to hear Schubert's Quintet in C Major. When the violin sings the familiar melody to us from the first movement, some of us fall asleep or, at any rate, close our eyes, for the sweetness of this music needn't be seen, only heard. In chamber music there is no conductor whose flamboyance might keep our eyes open, whose sexy backside—think Michael Tilson Thomas, Riccardo Muti—might provoke fantasy. No, we are in the presence of a musical democracy whose members have talked things over, who have agreed on where to get louder or faster or slower. They understand each other and have set individual differences aside in favor of the common good:

Schubert. Don't snore, I beg silently of the man across the aisle, who is clearly asleep and whose wife is afraid to nudge him for fear his waking snort might shatter the concentration of musicians and audience alike.

In our younger years we preferred fast movements: allegro, allegretto—the best being presto: really, really fast. We skipped, or tuned out, the adagio, the slow stuff. Not now. This second movement is so familiar to us we are a bit nervous, for the high notes must be hit just right, and there are a lot of them. And if the violin doesn't hit them right on, eek, it's awful. You can feel it, a graphic wince, fingernails on a chalkboard, sliding down a banister that turns into a razor blade. Well, maybe not that bad, but pretty bad. The musicians here today come from the San Francisco Symphony, so for the moment we're as safe as we can be. Still, we have our memories of musicians less adept.

The music gets pretty heated up in the last movement. The musicians are going to town, which is a good thing, because everybody in the audience wakes up. Schubert is not shy about endings, and we are on our feet, most of us, at the last flourish of the musicians' bows. We applaud our thanks, smile our appreciation, as they leave the stage and hurry up the aisle to the long lives they have ahead of them. We're slower. But here we go, some on canes or walkers, others pulling oxygen cannisters behind, steadied by and steadying those near us, flushed from another Sundae with music. We have no doubt that our bodies are crumbling, that friends and family have betrayed and abandoned us or we them, that the society in which we have lived for so long has refused to grant our deepest desires. But as we leave this church made all of redwood, the late afternoon sun streaming in through the stained-glass windows, the sounds of Schubert, who lived such a very short life, fill our minds and hearts, and we know full well that life is good. Every so often it comes clear to us that, like chamber music, the last act of our lives is the cherry on top.

But the solace of music is not available to all. On my walk

home I encounter another sort of old person, this one clearly homeless. Maybe sixty-five, but she looks older; she has become a regular in our neighborhood. The grocery-store cart she pushes brims with clothes, newspapers, bits and pieces of glass and cardboard gathered from the waste bins of the town. Her legs are swollen, her back is bowed, she shuffles, she is going to die right here in front of us. She stares at the sidewalk, except, yes, now she looks right at me, although she does not see me. She sees, behind me, her car parked at the curb—an old BMW (a warning to fancy car owners everywhere: This could happen to you)—crammed to bursting with collected sacks, scraps of material, frames of bicycles, wheels from supermarket baskets, and plastic bottles of every size. In my neighborhood, in her car, is where she lives, so she is not, I suppose, certifiably homeless, though perhaps she will be when she is crowded out by the junk she has collected. For the time being she has a home and drags her feet over the sidewalk to it. Behind the wheel she starts the engine, and the car lurches forward. She drives as I have seen her walk: unseeing, unaware of other cars or people, weaving across yellow lines, slow, very slow. She stops traffic. She will be back.

Farther up the street, outside the post office, Leonard—a homeless man without music, without a car, without teeth—stands, his cardboard hand-lettered sign informing passersby that he is a veteran and in need of work. Unlike the lady in her BMW, Leonard is very aware of everything, as beggars must be if they are to survive. At our first meeting I dropped a dollar into his paper cup, and Leonard said, "Thank you, thank you. God loves you." I answered, "What if I don't believe in god?" and Leonard said, "That's all right, he still loves you." I put something in Leonard's cup every time I see him, and every time I do, he says, "Thank you. God loves you." That's faith for you. Leonard is fifty-six years old and has spent more than his share of time in the hospital: In the year we have known each other he has suffered a broken arm and shoulder from falling off a bicycle he had rescued from the recycling bin, and he has been diagnosed with diabetes. The other day I missed Leonard, didn't see him there behind the newspaper racks. I rounded the corner and heard a loud "Hey!" He called as he ran toward me, "I gotta have a operation. I'm going to see about a job. There's one down on Milvia, a warehouse, shoving things around. I'm going to see about getting it." I wished him good luck, handed him some money, and smiled as he said, "Thank you. God loves you."

I have Freud; Leonard has god. Let's hope one of them can get Leonard his operation.

This morning, no job. "They tell me I gotta have transportation and I don't have none, and the bus don't run that far out. So here I am back on duty." He grins his toothless grin, and I say, "You know, you don't look fifty-six; you look much younger." This is not true, but my cheering-up skills have diminished since Jo died, and this is the best I can do. Leonard looks at me bemusedly, and suddenly I understand how irrelevant appearance is, how foolish we are to be caught up in the futile efforts of looking younger, dredged in the fear of looking our age or, worse, older. I stand before Leonard, speechless for once, and recall T. S. Eliot's "Words strain, / Crack and sometimes break . . ." Tomorrow I'll just give him some money and keep my mouth shut. Will that help?

This evening my three hundred fifty square feet, my rental, my home for the nonce, looks even more welcoming than usual. Before I go in, I check my car, just to make sure nobody's moved in.

be careful what you wish for

Any love, be it happy or unhappy,
is an absolute disaster when you
wholly surrender yourself to it.

—TURGENEV

eonard and I, each of us better off for knowing the other, soldier on. So do most people, though mostly in straits less dire than Leonard's. Those of us untethered by marriage, like Greta at the Plaza and the women I encounter at readings everywhere, aren't content to just be, but continue to be propelled into adventure by the desire for human touch. I am considered by some an expert; I do not feel like one. But I find myself, every so often and against my better judgment, making pronouncements. In fact, I've gotten interested in how people live their lives, especially women who are older and therefore marginalized, women for whom rules to live by no longer exist. So what do we do? We make up new ones. Because today, while debutantes continue to debut and churches—however changed from those of yore—still offer social gatherings, the machinery of matchmaking for most of us, even for young women, is less sturdy, less dependable, than it once was. And for older women it does not exist.

Tanya, age sixty-two and as droopy as a rabbit in the rain, sits across the table from me at my corner café. We have not met before; I am here at the behest of Tanya's friend, whom I know slightly and who assures me that reading my book has changed Tanya's life. "Please," the friend urges, "talk to her."

Tanya looks as if her life needs to be changed. She is pinched all over, like a raisin, like a little worm that shrinks at the sign of danger. She looks over her bifocals at me and tells me her life: She is long divorced; her two daughters are grown and far away; she works as a teacher's aide in an inner-city middle school; she is lonely and, as we talk, desperate for the company of a man who might lessen the misery of her life. "I have not been with a man in many years," she says shamefacedly. "When I read your book, I thought, 'That's me.'" Then she looks at me full on and asks, "Do you have any suggestions?"

Allow me to pause right here and say once again that in my new life as a public person I have resisted giving advice, even though at every reading, every dinner party, every little speech I give, I am asked that question or a variation of it. I answer, "I don't give advice, though I will say that doing what I did—placing such an ad—is probably not in the best interests of the whole family." People laugh then, some with disappointment. So I perk everybody up by adding, "But if you do—do what I did—don't send your best picture; send your third-best photograph. That way your potential suitor won't look at you and turn away in dismay." Well, good, now everybody has something to do, and we Americans are always needing something to do. I have provided a service, and we can all go home. But I leave always feeling oppressed by an unmet obligation. What have I written, in all innocence, that makes people think I have answers? To anything?

Still, here sits Tanya, her shoulders rounded, both hands warming themselves on her coffee mug, her blue eyes alight with hope. That's it: My book seems to have given many people hope, and with so little of it in the world these days, I am happy that hope flies out of my book and into the lives of people who want it.

Tanya, however, is not about to be satisfied with hope; she wants details, some rules; she wants explanations, a plan for the future. Driven to speech by her intensity, I lean across the table and say, "Lighten up." I've done it now, no going back. "It seems to me we jump to the end too quickly; we tell ourselves we want a mate for life, a man who will be a companion and lover and who will stay with us, never abandon us, until death do us part." Tanya nods, downcast. "That's asking a lot," I say. "If I were a man sitting here, I'd get up and run." She's still nodding. Enchanted by the sound of my own voice, I race on: "We forget to have fun. We're so intent on ending up not alone that we miss out on what can come before the end, and sometimes in our desperation we drown the possibilities of life." I am aghast at myself; I have delivered a sermon. Tanya rises and says, "Maybe" and "Thanks." I wish her good luck, which really I mean, and in my eagerness to help I offer a plan of action, however futile, to counteract the sententiousness of my sermon. "Go online," I say. In the weeks hence she will e-mail me to tell me that, well, she is online and might be about to have some fun. But she's not sure.

Way off in Thailand, where Betsey from Iowa went to teach English, online is serving Betsey well: She and Howard in New Jersey have been corresponding regularly for almost a year and will meet for the first time face-to-face in July, when Betsey comes home to visit. Betsey is sixty-five, Howard *"a few years your senior,"* he writes in an e-mail. Watch out, Betsey: This purposeful vagueness could mean that Howard is anywhere from seventy to a hundred. I'll bet that if he were "a few years younger," he'd specify, he'd shout it out and then make a big deal about being "the younger man." Don't ask me how I know this; I just do.

In August, Genevieve in Chicago flew to meet George, USAF Col. (Ret.), in Seattle. Genevieve, at sixty-three, decided to give up her married lover, who was in his own way wonderful, but never ever available on holidays. Genevieve had had it. She wanted a life that resembled other lives, and while she knew there is no such thing as a normal life, she wanted to wake up on New Year's Day with a man beside her. Cyberspace to the rescue, perhaps, for Col. George (Ret.) was out there, too, waiting for her, she hoped. Off she went, only to discover, via a phone call to her hotel room, that Col. George had wrenched his back while renovating his condo, and wouldn't be able to keep their date. Hmm. Well, nothing ventured, nothing gained. Or, in this case, everything ventured, nothing gained. Col. George is a bum, whaddya bet?

Online dating, though I have never done it because you have to send a photograph right away, seems safe enough, certainly safer than sitting in a bar, even as nice a bar as the Plaza's, where likely the most interesting person you'll meet is another woman. Online dating certainly worked for Ilse; it worked for my neighbor, who actually married the guy. And even if it doesn't bring you a lifetime of happiness, you can sit at your computer in your old clothes, no makeup, a little light-headed from the glass of wine at your side, and you can create a self you like, not terribly far from the real you but just a little better, a little more appealing. You could have a relationship in practically no time at all. And you don't even have to change your underwear.

Online seems safe; everybody's doing it, so it must be safe. The Internet offers something for everyone: JDate for Jews, LDS Singles for Mormons, even Arab2love and the Muslim-specific Zawaj.com. If you don't fit in any of those categories, perhaps HOTorNOT .com is for you. The question is, Why are millions of people across the world on the Net? Okay, so it's fast; okay, so it's safe, a way to connect, if only by way of ether. It offers hope where there was none. What else?

Andrea Orr, in her fascinating book *Meeting, Mating, (. . . and Cheating),* offers the example of one of her office mates, "a typical single white male," as one explanation: "His ad was nuanced, funny and self-deprecating . . . that little 400-word piece of prose was witty and intelligent." If, as she says, his profile was not strictly literary, it came close. As writers everywhere do, this young man created himself in his own image, only better. Where else do we go to reinvent ourselves? What are our chances of becoming the person we admire? On the Net our chances are pretty good; after all, we never have to actually meet. In the meantime we can make a new life, our own, in the privacy of our computer. This time around we'll have control. We can be the boss of us. And if someone answers back, if we should fall in love, then we get to add a new dimension to ourselves; we'll see ourselves through the eyes, albeit cybered, of another, and it will be good.

Amy writes to me from Nebraska that she has read *A Round-Heeled Woman*. *"When I wasn't crying, I was smiling,"* she says. She goes on to say that a wonder of online relationships is that *"someone sees and responds to every word 'uttered.' What could be more seductive than to be heard?"* And so Amy embarked on *"a love affair of words only. No face-to-face contact, no bodies entwined, just words."* She became, for this man ten years her junior, everything desirable in a woman, a woman adored by someone unlike her real-life husband, someone who was *"a young, funny, talkative, energetic, silly man with blue-green eyes."* Monday became the best day of the week, weekends being exempt from contact. When she woke on Mondays, her first thoughts were of him, *"the warmth and excitement of him"* slipping over her *"like a shield,"* protecting her from disappointments to come her way in the course of the day. They *"loved each other . . . through our fingers,"* when suddenly, out of nowhere, he wrote, *"I can't do this anymore."* At this, Amy turned herself into someone she had never known—a woman full of self-hatred, a woman unable to let go. She sought the help of a therapist, who prescribed pain medication. She lied to her family, told them her depression came from the death of her sister, and all the while she continued to look for him on her screen, to send off witty, light-hearted notes, some even *"playfully sexual,"* until at last he wrote her about *"One of those things that just seemed to happen."* He had found another. Three years later Amy cries. She looks in the mirror, sees *"a well-tended body attached to an ugly woman with baggy eyes—pathetic, the proverbial spurned lover . . . a woman . . . who would rather die than continue to experience this . . . daily self-inflicted torment of abandonment, rejection, and invisibility."*

Holy cow, this is as bad as real life, worse even. Amy in her desire to be *"a standout,"* as she says, *"a shining star,"* got dumped, but all the while, parallel to her secret life on the Net, she cooked and cleaned and took care of her husband and went to her book club and her volunteer job at the hospital and her exercise class, and tried not to let her secret life spill into her real life; and all the while her online life was more real, more desirable—even in the anguish that resulted.

Here was high drama in which Amy played many roles: the ingenue, the older woman, the heroine whose injury at the hands of one less worthy made her life as large as tragedy itself. She wrote herself a life and writ it large. She is a woman out of Ibsen, a Hedda Gabler. But, Amy, don't do what Hedda did; she shot herself. Take a break from misery; go buy some shoes, get a manicure, take lots of walks. Fitzgerald wrote about American life, "There are no second acts." He was wrong, wasn't he? We do it all the time, for fiction and for real—first, second, all the way to the fifth act, with epilogues when called for. So, Amy, you made a life. Do it again. It's what America is all about.

I, of course, never went online. I thought about it, I even booted up a matchmaking site. I thought, Well, hell, I'll pay some money. But I got to the part where it said "photograph required" and quit. The photograph, the one I had sent via snail mail to Robert the Rat, had been my downfall. One look at me in real life, and he said, "I didn't recognize you." Things went from bad to worse, and it was then that I swore that if I ever sent another photograph of myself I would send the third-best. That way the other person would be relieved instead of disappointed.

Now, Ilse, of course, beloved of Robert, whapped her best photograph up there on Match.com—the one of her standing in a field of flowers, skirt lapping her thighs, wind ruffling her tresses—and got immediate success, had tons of dates. The thing was, she really looked like her picture. Most of us don't, though; most of us look like our third-best.

So that's my online experience, hardly any at all. And even though I recommend online dating services to women I hardly know, I do not take my advice. I'm not ready to face the unknown all over again, to risk life and limb, to know in advance that while joy and happiness might be just around the corner, so might rejection and sadness, and I've cried quite enough, thank you, at least for now. Besides, why doesn't somebody come and find *me*? Why do *I* have to do all the work? Well, I'm sitting out a few innings, cleaning the infield out of my cleats, hoping for a brief shower to cool things off.

However, down the block from me my neighbor has hit a home run. She just married a man she met online. He lives in Germany and she lives here, and he is coming here when the papers get done, and in the meantime she went there to get married to him. Isn't that nice? Xenia is a very adventurous lady and a computer whiz. She's also very cute. And she has a bunch of money. So, one might ask, if she wanted to get married, why couldn't she find someone here? Xenia has had it with American men, she says. She has had it with American life, the kind of life that she claims is particular to this country, where every social event has to have a purpose: a book club, a birthday party, a wedding. These kinds of events eventually find the men in one room and the women in another. "Hasn't this changed?" I ask her. Xenia is fifty-six, almost a generation younger than I. "No," she says, "and another thing that hasn't changed is that if you're single, a single woman that is, you don't get invitations from couples for dinner or the theatre, where you'll be number three or five or seven." I sigh: All of that has been true of my own American life, and apparently remains so.

"In Europe," Xenia tells me, "men and women come together in cafés or each other's homes, and they talk. And they talk about important stuff." She puts a finger on her pretty lips and says,

"Hmm . . . I think it's that they smoke. Everyone lights up. They're equal right there, and they relax behind their little streams of smoke, and they just talk."

"Here, in this country" I say, eager to be a part of Xenia's wisdom and good fortune, "we have to get drunk. Not necessarily drunk, but we have to have enough wine or beer or booze to disinhibit us, and then we don't listen very well, do we?"

"No, and pretty soon the men go off to the backyard and the women stay in the kitchen, and where's the fun in that?"

Xenia is hooked up intercontinentally by her computer. She has this neat gizmo for her Apple, this Ichat AV program that connects her to the world. She has this little microphone she clips on to her computer, and as she talks, real-time pictures of the other person appear on her screen! It's amazing! Her new husband—I got to talk to him today—looks and sounds like a nice man, and Xenia is so happy with the beginning of her new life that I think, Hmm, maybe I ought to try that. You have to have OS X, or something like that, and it costs over a hundred dollars. Besides, with a real-time picture I wouldn't be able to send the third-best.

Before Karl, Xenia had had tons of dates by way of the computer. After her entirely amicable divorce and after two of her three kids went off to college, she wandered around in her sizable house, shopped, and did good works. But then, why not? Why not try this online dating thing? James broke her heart: A professor with a messy divorce-to-be was wonderful in bed, where they went not long into their online exchange. They traveled well together, they talked well together, but then . . . The divorce stayed messy and never turned into an actual divorce—surprise, surprise. It took Xenia some time to understand that she was not going to be a bride, and at fifty-six Xenia wanted to marry again, to be with someone forever. Her forever, unlike mine, being quite a long time.

I hope Xenia is right in her judgments of this country. Well, no, not right, but convinced enough to keep her happy. I did wonder, "Why is Karl moving here if European social behavior is so superior?" Xenia explains that she needs to see her last son into college; then she and Karl will move to Germany, and when this happens, this country will have lost a bright spirit and a warm heart.

I hear that a lot these days: Susan, my friend, and her husband moved to Paris; Georgeanne left California for Ireland. Georgeanne suffered the dot-com bust in Silicon Valley and, as a single woman in charge of making a living for the rest of her life, believed chances for a career were better in Ireland, along with a more reasonable cost of living. As for Susan, she spent every summer of her long teaching life in Paris and loved it so that each year on her return home she went into a deep depression, emerging from her house only to exchange one French video for the next. So on retirement she and her husband moved to Paris, where she is happy, although, for the first few months of her emigration she stayed inside their flat for fear her misuse of the French language would make her a figure of fun. When she came out, it didn't, and now only the Parisians can tell that Susan's first language is American English. Canada, of course, is full of Americans fed up with this country's political misbehavior. I hear that Toronto has become what Paris was in the twenties when Fitzgerald and Hemingway expatriated themselves in order to live on the cheap and write. Mexico harbors some of our young and not-so-young émigrés. But most of us stay here, our romantic enthusiasms dulled by the descent of the dollar. We remind ourselves that there are worse places to be, that while we threatened to move to Canada after the last presidential election, we didn't, did we?

One day there in the post office is Tanya, who seemed so defeated by her life, who thought perhaps she might try to have a bit of fun by way of Match.com. She looks terrific. Her blue eyes sparkle, her smile is wide, she is slim and cute in Levi's and a sweater. "I did it," she says. "I went online and I met someone." Her smile is wider. "We got together and had a fairly decent sex life, and well . . . You know what?" She doesn't wait for me to answer. "He wants me to retire from my job and travel with him, and I've decided I like my job and my friends, and actually, I've decided I like my life better the way it was before I met him." She takes a breath. "So I told him no."

I am impressed. Not many women would dump a man who could give her a fairly decent sex life *and* trips to faraway places. But Tanya, well, she had a choice, and she chose the life she wanted, and here she is happy and as bouncy as a june bug. Ah, that Online works in mysterious ways.

the snows of yesteryear

Seek not, . . . endlessly to know
where now they are, why time has passed.

—François Villon, "Ballad of the Ladies of Old"

ow do I know this stuff? How is it that I can tell you about the lives and loves of all these people from all over everywhere? It's because they tell me. Here in Berkeley I am recognized by people wherever I go, and then pretty much ignored, as the good people of Berkeley are sophisticated enough to do. I don't mind being recognized; people are nice to me and, for the most part, pleased with my success. One day as I walked down the sidewalk in front of my landlord's house, a pleasant-looking woman came toward me, in her hand a book, my book. She came closer, looked hard at me, and threw her hand over her mouth: "Omigod," she said, "it's you! I'm reading your book! I like it, I even bought it, I didn't even get it at the library." Words tumble from her: "Did you know there's a long waiting list for it at the library?" That was nice; she was nice; I felt good.

On another day, as I was leaving the post office, a woman strode purposefully toward me. Now, I knew this woman, or rather I knew of her; she lived in a big house a few blocks away; she intimidated the hell out of me. She knew just about everything there was to know about any subject anyone might bring up—politics, gardening, the Seine, the Grand Canyon, not to mention Chopin and George Sand—and the way I knew this was that I had been trapped in an airport van with her and her husband, an understandably taciturn fellow, who spoke not a word during this very long van ride, though neither did I, there being no need or opportunity. Forceful, that's what she was, and now here she came right at me. "You wrote that book, didn't you," she accused. "I read it." Uh-oh, here it comes. She stood before me, eyes blazing, and shook her index finger in my face. "Don't ever," she said, "don't ever leave the neighborhood. We need you."

Did my landlord and my landlady hear that? Things are a little dicey right now because the media have come to call and have brought cameras and lights and microphones, and my landlords like their privacy, understandable of course, and No! I call to the photographer from *Oprah* who is at this minute photographing my landlord's house. "Stop!" and I motion for them to tiptoe— hah—up the drive, push gently on the gate; then they can set up, then they can stay forever if that's what they wish, just don't bother my new landlords.

Another woman, whose name I will probably never know, passed by in her car one morning as I wandered along the sidewalk on my way to my café for my morning low-fat latte. Suddenly she stopped, didn't matter that it was in the middle of the street, in a crosswalk. She got out of the car, called my name, and gave an energetic thumbs-up. "Loved it!" Traffic at a standstill, honking its loudest, she returned to her car. Even now, whenever she sees me from her car, she calls, "Great book!" or "Loved it." Though lately she has ceased stopping traffic. Every time something like this happens, I am surprised and pleased all over again that women have found the book useful or comforting or encouraging or simply a good read.

And it still goes on. Today, in fact, a woman walking her dog passed by me, looked closely, and said, "You wrote that book." She put her hand over her mouth. "It has meant so much to so many women." I thanked her, we walked on, and suddenly she turned as if she had just thought of something. "You know," she said, "it's probably the influence of your book, but tomorrow I leave for four weeks in Europe—alone—and my husband doesn't even enter into my consideration."

Encounters like these make up for the rare though always frightening "You're a fucking whore!" They balance out the letters that urge me to find god, that express dismay over the downturn of my life. So reading e-mails and letters and answering the phone keeps me busy, but not busy enough to stifle the truth—some days I curse my former analyst for making me dredge up the truth and then pay attention to it—that there is no man nearby who will touch me, who will wrap me up and like doing it, who will buy me a house of my very own, who will be, in Katharine Hepburn's words, the perfect lover: "Lives nearby; visits often." Oh, there are men who offer; I am not without opportunity.

My phone number, although I pay to get it unlisted, is apparently available to all, either from old phone books, which pursuers find in the library, or from Google, god bless its great big engine that could and does. "Hey," says Larry from somewhere in Alabama, "I am sixty-two and self-unemployed and I enjoyed your book." I thank him and give him my e-mail address, not wanting to spend more time on the phone. Next day he calls again to tell me about his last relationship. (Lots of men want to tell me about their last relationships.) Larry wishes to impress me with his generosity. "For her birthday I gave her one Chippendale," he says, his Alabama accent a fascination in itself. How nice, I think, to give what was surely a very expensive piece of furniture. Larry continues: "For her next birthday I gave her two Chippendales." Wow. "And for her next birthday I gave her three!" I imagine a dining room table surrounded by those graceful chairs, with perhaps a sideboard against the wall. Then I hear, "And if you think I felt left out, no way, José, cuz I got to watch." Hmm. Something's askew here. I thank him for his call and hang up, bemused.

offices were not far away. The waitresses were topless and their breasts enviable. I know because I went there, too, with a male acquaintance who was curious, who wanted to have a little harmless fun. These were real breasts, breasts before silicone had become de rigueur for nude dancers, when Carol Doda, a tiny dancer at the Condor, grew her breasts by way of silicone implants to a 44DD, and then the silicone hardened and she had to have surgery to get it out of there, but then she went and did it again, so much did her career depend on her breasts. Most dancers avoided implants if they could because the surgery was expensive and not at all guaranteed. So in the heyday of the topless clubs the breasts were all sizes and shapes. What they had in common was that none of them drooped; they jiggled ever so slightly as if they were having a good time, loosed from the constraints of brassieres. Perhaps at dinner some of the customers, a few drinks in them, felt compelled to touch. Maybe at night in a back room lap dancing went on. Maybe in booths somewhere out of sight all-nude girls performed behind glass for men who watched and took their pleasure alone. Those activities go on today and probably did forty years ago. But there was in the sixties and seventies an innocent enjoyment of bodies, too, that is no longer part of the seamy clubs of North Beach in San Francisco or the blatantly aggressive sex shops of London.

I have my own nostalgia, my own naïveté to sort through, but when I do, it seems that the cover of night is no longer so mysterious and inviting as it was; with the advent of AIDS in the eighties, night came to cover the day and tarnish us all with the reality of sex as death, of sex as business, where performers unionize, where hookers are called sex workers. It's the economy, stupid, that renders the most delicious fantasies banal and turns sex into a commodity. Of course, sex always was a commodity, something to be bought and sold; but the scrim of let's pretend has been rent by the need of performers for money and the greed of owners who don't want to give it. Chaucer reminds us, in his *Canterbury Tales,* that *"Radix malorum est Cupiditas":* It is greed, not money, that is the root of all evil.

dwelled on the rosiness of the—at least at lunch—unattainable. On top (so to speak) of it all, I relished the freedom these girls seemed to feel about their bodies; they looked to me as if they were having fun. I wanted them to be having fun, because I wanted that kind of fun, not the fun of serving sandwiches naked but the fun of liking my body, maybe even being proud of it. Never happened.

Forty years later, with a body to match, I have become a sex symbol, though one fully clothed to all but a chosen few. So Walter calls. Walter is seventy-two and for the last several years has lived with his sister Anna. Last month Anna died. "Could we meet for a cup of coffee?" he wants to know. "I am so very lonely." How do I forgive myself for turning him down? What harm could a cup of coffee do? Oh, I was too busy, too busy, and of course Walter understood that I was so very, very busy. But I wasn't too busy; I was just selfish. I didn't want to comfort the lonely, heal the sick, or soothe the needy. Perhaps it was the headiness of the attention I received that crowded out compassion, when a few European editors and journalists, thinking that I represented the new senior sexuality in America, took me to lunch and photographed me posing beneath a willow tree or the Golden Gate Bridge. Perhaps it was the memory of my men in New York, against whom any man I could imagine paled in comparison. Whatever it was, I am not proud of my response to Walter. A cup of coffee. No big deal.

I chose not to have a cup of coffee with Barry either, who lived in San Francisco and was ready to hop on over to Berkeley at the drop of a hat and who, as an added enticement, sent me a sex toy. A pocket rocket, I learned this little flashlight-looking thing was, a vibrator, I guess, for inside and out. Bet you want to know what I did with it.

When I showed up to do readings, someone who worked at the bookstore would meet me with what we decided to call mash-faxes in hand: fan mail, I suppose you could call it, faxed to the bookstore in advance of my appearance there. "Hello, my name is Romeo, I am twenty-six and very hairy." From Simon: "I envision a déjeuner sur l'herbe, pistachios and foie gras, sparkling cider (I don't drink) and melba rounds and then, if we are so inclined we will incline ourselves to my apartment."

And always there were the Men at the End of the Line. It got so that while I was doing the reading I could tell which of the men in the audience would stay around afterward, would install themselves at the end of the line formed by people waiting for me to sign their books, would suggest future meetings, just the two of us.

One night there he was. Couldn't mistake him, sitting alone (these men were always alone) in the back, slouched against the wall, pale face, skinny, blue jogging suit, white stripe down the pant legs. Sure enough, here he came, all six-feet-plus of him, all one hundred fifty pounds of him. He looked down at me, tugged the jacket out of his pants, and began to roll down the waistband of his jogging suit. There was his bare skin, very very pale, like his face, with blue lines just beneath the surface—his veins, for god's sake, which got bluer every time he stretched his arm up over his head, which he did several times, no doubt to impress me with his muscle tone and his execution of the perfect stretch-your-arm-over-your-head form. Everybody was gone; the bookstore people were folding up chairs, noisily, and stacking them in the back room. Don't go, don't go, I pleaded silently. The man leaned down from his great height, looked into my face, and spoke, his waistband now just below his navel: "I run," he said. "I lift weights, I work out." He tugged at something hanging from his waist. "Here," he said, pulling out a little clock-thing, "I want you to see how many miles I ran to get here, just to hear you." Clearly I had no idea of how to read this pedometer, so he said, "Seventeen. Seventeen miles. Just to get to your reading." I was supposed to say something; it was my turn. What in hell . . . "Thank you," I said. He straightened up and stood there looking down at me, disappointed at my failure to announce that I adored at first sight men who worked out, especially men who went to great effort to meet me, to suggest we run off together that very night to put our mutual good health to work for what would surely result in our mutual pleasure.

In the silence one of the bookstore employees returned from the back room, saw this odd scene out of a silent movie, and said to the man, "Jane has to go now." I want that employee's name; I want to send her a million dollars, or at least a copy of this very book you are reading now, in which she is a hero or heroine. (I miss feminine endings.)

And of course, I made mistakes. One man at the end of the line (this line being at yet another bookstore), again tall but this time nice-looking and sort of normal, whatever that is, handed me his book to sign and said, "I drove a hundred miles to get here. I read about you in *The New York Times* and thought, Well heck, I need a little excitement in my life. So I found out where you were going to read, and here I am." I smiled and said, "Thank you." He continued: "I liked how you read, and I liked the question-and-answer thing you did afterward." I thanked him, and he said, "Well, that's about all the excitement I can handle right now, so I guess I'll go home. Good night." And he left.

My mistake was not jumping out of my chair where I sat to sign books and running after him. My mistake was not pursuing this normal-looking, undoubtedly kind, and rather shy man who, a hundred miles from here, probably led a normal, plain, and maybe even sometimes boring life. This was a safe man, a nice man, and what was wrong with me, anyway, that I didn't offer my phone number or my e-mail address or just follow him to his car and get a lift to a life less dizzy, less complicated, a life of peace and quiet. But I think what he told me was true—that that night had been enough for him and he was ready to go home—without me. I am dangerous, I guess. I have upset all the applecarts for everyone to see, and one evening is as close as any nice, sensible man wants to get to cleaning up the debris. Alas.

We shall skip lightly over two ugly men who stayed late in order to regale me, and anyone else within shouting distance, with their exploits of women, how easy they found it to get women, especially older women, to do whatever they wanted, how especially in Berkeley women were desperate for male attention and how they—these two fat, hairy blowhards—got laid whenever they felt like driving over the bridge. "You give men a bad name," I said, and walked away.

And on one foggy night in San Francisco, in a tiny bookstore filled to the brim with people come to hear me read, I glanced out over the crowd—Who would be at the end of the line this time?—and saw in the back of the room, leaning against the wall, arms folded over his chest, a half smile on his face, an absolutely wonderful-looking man. I undressed him then, and found big shoulders, strong arms, broad chest, and an ass to last the night. Watch out, I cautioned myself; I felt my face grow hot, and so I returned quickly to business, reading and signing books. The next time I looked up—the end of the line was near—he was gone. Maybe he undressed me, too, and found me wanting.

So there you have it, my opportunities that came via e-mail, telephone, letter, and in person big as life. Did I find The One? Everybody asks that, and I answer, I'm not looking for The One. I say that so often I must believe it. I keep quiet about Graham and his marriage, for I do not want to let myself believe that he was The One. How ridiculous, everyone would say. How could you let yourself get swallowed up by your passion for a man half your age? And now you hurt. Serves you right.

So there lies my innocence, dormant in the snows of yesteryear; and here comes wisdom. It reminds me that night awaits, that lunchtime was over a long time ago.

"Tell us how your life has changed." I am asked that again and again. My answer is always the same. "I still live in three hundred fifty square feet and go to the laundromat every week." There is to be a change, however, not long from now; my landlady is pregnant.

And another change: an e-mail from Graham. *"Dare I phone you?"*

CHAPTER 12

identity theft

How suddenly the moonbeams turn to worms.

—NORMA SHEARER to CLARK GABLE in *A Free Soul*

n the three seconds it takes for me to answer yes to Graham, in those three seconds that change me from sad to happy, from mean and grumpy to loving and generous, I toss all the caution I have accumulated over these months to the wind. Common sense? Who needs it? A nice age-appropriate man? Nah. Wisdom that comes with all my years of experience? What wisdom? With one e-mail I come fully alive to the possibilities of life, and once again they are all mine. In my newfound enthusiasm for just about everything, I say yes to Hannah, an acquaintance who begs me to hear her story, which came about after she read my book. She gave me her permission to tell it. So here it is.

One night Hannah's husband of twenty-six years went out for a pack of smokes and came back a crack addict. It happens that way, sometimes, one hit and your life is no longer your own. That's what the man in the next cubicle told her when she went to work the following day. Not long after, her teenage daughter ran off with her soccer coach, and her son, away at college, sent home letters of despair promising to end it all before Thanksgiving. Hannah had not gotten over, and never would get over, the death of her firstborn, drowned at age three. Life was beating her up. She could curl up until the referee rang the bell, or she could pick herself up and do what she could to even the odds.

Hannah left her husband, drove long miles to console her son, and sent her daughter a money order for bus fare home, should there come a time to use it. She wiped away the tears of lives gone awry. She went to work every day. She saved part of her salary. She went to the movies alone and with friends. She took long walks. She told her husband he could not come back even though he swore, falsely, that he was rehabilitated. She got a lawyer, then a divorce. She sold their house. She rented an apartment. A year and a half later Hannah was, in her words, "ready to be with someone with hair on his forearm, ready for a man to touch my wrist."

At fifty-six Hannah is small and trim, her face unlined except for crow's-feet, her expression open and cheerful, the look of a midwesterner, which she is. She sits on the couch of her small apartment, her legs crossed Indian-fashion, and tells me what it was like to fall truly, madly, deeply in love—for the first time—in middle age. "It's not that I didn't love my husband," she assures me. "I did in the beginning, and for all those years we were more or less comfortable with each other. Oh, there were problems with his depression, I guess it was, but all marriages have problems, and I never once thought about ending it or being untrue to him. And then all hell broke loose." She smiles. "I know, there's nothing funny about such upheaval, but it's that my old life ended and another began. And this time I was in control." Her smile turns ironic. "Or so I thought."

Once she settled into her apartment, she dived into Match.com and the profiles of men who wanted to meet women. She felt deliciously risky and wild and sexy—"I hadn't felt deliciously anything for years"—as she pored over the responses to her online profile. She felt powerful as she discarded men interested in bowling and NASCAR, and anyone unable to spell "cuddle." And she fell in love with the language of Wayne's profile, which rendered him witty, self-deprecating, confident, intelligent, whimsical, sensitive, curious. *"Grounded, independent, and not stuffy . . . Interests: black raspberries and fresh green peas, prairies, hepatica when it first blossoms in the spring . . . Goals: to massage the foot of my read-aloud partner, make macaroni and cheese 52 different ways, play second base, build a rowing shell . . . Ideal Match: one who can banter, who knows how to flirt. Smiles, good teeth, youthful brain . . ."* He ends his profile with *"If you've ever stolen a guy's long-sleeved, soft white cotton, button-down collar shirt and worn it without accessories, please write."*

Who wouldn't write! Hannah did, Wayne answered, and for weeks they wrote up a storm; they spoke on the telephone, and then they met. They made love. And Hannah grew beautiful, for she loved and was loved in return.

> *These violent delights have violent ends*
> *And in their triumph die, like fire and powder,*
> *Which, as they kiss, consume.*

So warns Friar Laurence when confronted by Romeo's declaration of his love for Juliet. The friar, well-meaning dunce that he is, is at this moment wise, for have we not known such passion first-hand from the time of our first love? Should these violent delights arrive so unexpected in middle age, should they gallop into our later years, they will trample common sense and the wisdom that long life was to have provided us, in exchange for the combustability of passion. When love hits, we turn sixteen.

In person and online Hannah and Wayne communicated in romantic prose and poetry. Erotic and dreamy. Together they made up a fantasy woman named Nora. In e-mail they played with Nora, a shy loner begging to escape her dull, conservative life; Nora: the single, isolated secretary. It was fun, Hannah thought, harmless enough and clearly an exciting way to connect with her lover.

But then one day Hannah received a real e-mail from Lily, Wayne's old friend and lover. Lily was married, taught in the humanities at Georgetown, was a *"hard-core introvert,"* and yearned to correspond with Hannah. Lily enclosed a photograph of herself—blond, blue-eyed, great teeth in a wide smile—that Wayne had taken a few years before. Lily is wearing a man's white cotton shirt, long-sleeved. She and Hannah shared a birthday, and the two of them, according to Lily, were "in love with the same guy." Hesitantly Hannah wrote back to her, not yet aware of the truth: Lily and Wayne *were* the same guy.

It was the weekends that made the bumps in the course of true love. Wayne was busy with conferences, out-of-town visitors, trips to "hide out" from a busy weekday life. Hannah felt abandoned, herself a working woman for whom weekends were golden. And there was a secrecy about those weekends; Wayne's explanations were less and less convincing—how many conferences, how many out-of-town guests could one person manage, and just where was this girlfriend Wayne claimed was entirely in his past. Angry with what she felt was his cumulative dishonesty and refusal to account for his behavior, she broke it off, and she broke it off again and again, and always he was gone on Friday and back on Sunday. His evening e-mail just right, so loving, so sweet, so provocative, so powerfully erotic, she went back again and again, only to stop herself finally. She wrote Wayne that she was returning to Match.com to look for a full-disclosure relationship that included weekends.

Oddly, though she found several new matches, contacts seemed to evaporate before her very eyes. She wrote to a man with whom she eventually had a date, a great date, she thought. But then he never called. Through e-mail Hannah wondered why. He answered, *"Because you wrote to me and said you were no longer interested."* He attached the note. It took Hannah's breath away. She hadn't written it, but there was her name, there was her e-mail address. She had been hacked.

Match.com employs an abuse person, a bit of information that might come in handy for many of us. Together Hannah and the abuse lady figured it out. Wayne had created an e-mail address close to Hannah's, with just the slightest change—an added dash. Thus he was able to place himself in the middle of Hannah's correspondence, write to her suitors, and, in her name, turn them away. At fifty-six Wayne's life was full: There was his own male self, the self who wrote to and wooed Hannah; there was Nora, the fantasy girl he and Hannah created together; there was the fabricated Lily, so blond and blue-eyed, so eager to correspond with Hannah; and there was Wayne as Hannah, who rejected all would-be suitors.

If e-mail relationships allow us to remake ourselves into someone we would like to be, we might conclude that Wayne made himself into a woman. How remarkable to find both male and female in oneself—for both are present—and bring our androgyny safely to life. Hannah's husband went out one night and came back a crack addict, Wayne went out one night and came back a woman. For a while, anyway.

It was long enough, though, to end the real-life love affair between him and Hannah. She felt betrayed, invaded, confused, and frightened. Who was this man with whom she had experienced such loving intensity? Whoever he was, she decided, there was no question: She needed to rid herself of him. And that's what she did.

Phone book in hand open to the Yellow Pages and the letter p for "psychiatrists," Hannah walked into Wayne's office. "I'm not leaving," she said, "until you pick up the phone and make an appointment." He nodded. She closed her eyes, circled her index finger above the page, and let it drop to a name. "Call this number." He nodded. "I do not, of course, trust you to keep the appointment," she said, "so I have taken your colleague, in the office next door, into my confidence." She had seen her son cornered by his fear of self; she was seeing it again, and worried that Wayne, his back to the wall, would hurt himself, and so she was resolute. "If you fail to keep the appointment, your colleague will alert the head of your company. Do it, Wayne," she said, and held out the phone. He dialed, and finally, "Thursday at four," he said. "Goodbye, Wayne," said Hannah, and walked into another new life.

She and Brent, the date who had been denied by the combo of Wayne, Lily, and Nora, are content, she with his great good sense, he with her sweet sensuality. But, "I can't stand how much I want him," she said. The "him" is Wayne. Or is it "her"? "He was the best girlfriend I ever had."

At fifty-four Brent is not only stable, he is useful. He cleaned junk off Hannah's computer and, lord above, found a spy program. Wayne had not only stolen her e-mail address, he had planted a spy program so he could read her every keystroke. She shivered for weeks at the creepiness of the man she had loved so passionately. But she went to work every day, paid her bills, and cooked Thanksgiving dinner for her daughter, whom she collected at the bus station, and her son, eager to return to school. Brent carved.

Hannah has no plans to return to Match.com, suspecting as she does that Lily and Nora and Wayne live there quite happily.

How many hours did Hannah and I spend together, me at one end of the couch, my mouth agape in amazement, Hannah's at the other end going a mile a minute? What struck me, amidst her unraveling of the truly bizarre events in her life, was her great good humor and her determination to make life do, for a little time at least, what she thought it was supposed to. Never for a minute did she blame anyone, seek a shoulder to cry on, give up on her responsibilities for making things work or for being a good mother and a good friend. Listening to her, I made myself a silent promise to quit whining about my rent and my sexless life. Though with Graham's begging a hearing on my e-mail, perhaps my unwanted celibacy would come to an end—Wait a minute, Graham is married now. So just cool it, Jane. Have you no shame?

And, with Hannah's experience indelibly fixed in my mind, I will stop tossing out so carelessly the advice to go online. With apologies to William Shakespeare, There are more things on the Net, Horatio, than are dreamt of in your philosophy.

CHAPTER 13

the body electric

O pumpkin plump! O pumped-up corpulence . . .
O fatty dishes of love!
—from "Ruben's Women," Wisława Szymborska

n her pregnancy my landlady is getting more beautiful every day, and oh, how I wish I could admire her unrestrained by my fears, which come with change. Just when I am beginning to manage my increased rent, there looms a new threat to my stability: a blessed event. So I'm a little paranoid, but I can easily—too easily—imagine her house becoming crowded when the baby arrives, and so they sell and move away, leaving me once again at the mercy of strangers. Or they stay: I look at the tiny—and getting tinier—backyard that separates her house from my cottage. Where will this child play? On my patio. At night, in my dreams, I see rocking horses and miniature fire trucks outside my door and hear the scraping of plastic shovels and buckets and the thumping and falling against my French doors when he begins to walk. And then, in no time at all, he will have playdates: There will be a passel of toddlers flooding the banks of my privacy, little fists hammering at my door, cries of "Juice!" ringing in my ears. My life will become a natural disaster. Maybe I wish they would move. Maybe I wish I would stop having nightmares. Maybe I wish I had some control over any of this. But I have no choice save one: If I wish to avoid an ever-darkening cloud of depression, I must try to enjoy these months of gestation along with this gorgeous mother-to-be.

She parades her pregnancy around the neighborhood for everyone to see. Like her belly, her breasts are plumping up, her skin is radiant, and I wonder where her maternity clothes are, those clothes I wore only forty years ago, smocks that billowed out like umbrellas meant to hide the somewhat embarrassing matter of a baby growing inside, a baby the result of—shhh—sexual intercourse. Forty years ago, my income from teaching the sole support of my husband and me, I begged my obstetrician to lie about my due date. Forty years ago my school district did not allow a woman to teach past six weeks of pregnancy—purposes of insurance, I was told, though I suspect it had more to do with purposes of propriety. I pretended for as long as I could that simple weight gain accounted for the tightness of my blouses and my skirts and my trousers; the kids, of course, knew all along that pregnancy was upon me, and behaved rather better than when I was not pregnant. The district office, usually dumber than the kids by quite a bit, remained oblivious, and I managed to extract three more months of pay before the smock took over.

The intervening decades have brought some improvements. It is no longer necessary to hide one's pregnancy; indeed, flaunting it is the style now, and I do believe a healthy one; women are allowed to work as far into their pregnancy as they see fit. My landlady does not have a job, but if she did, she would undoubtedly share her pregnancy with the workplace as she has with the neighborhood. She is a lovely creature to watch. I do wonder, however, what will become of the diamond in her navel. Will it pop out? Will it, at some point, shoot across a room or straight out back where I live? I would catch it and take good care of it, for I would like a jewel. I don't have one. I did have a ring—a star sapphire—from my aunt, given her by her husband. I never wore it. It was too big, someone might actually see it, think I was showing off. So it's stored in my underpants drawer, where no thief will think to look, or if he does, he won't see it because I have hidden it still further in a wadded-up sock. Boy, am I clever.

I love my aunt for having willed me her star sapphire, but what I would like now is for a man to give me a jewel. I know, I am not being modern, I am being a cliché and an old-fashioned one at that. Okay, I could buy myself a jewel, even a diamond, but it wouldn't be the same as if a man went to some trouble, thought enough of me, to buy me a diamond. I would like him to think I was pretty enough to wear a jewel. A diamond is my first choice, thank you very much. However, I would be willing to start with an emerald and go from there.

I had a wedding ring, one I paid for myself since my affianced was not working and I was. Six years later, when the divorce was final, I took it off and put it in the jewelry box my mother had given me for my graduation from high school and which, fifty-two years later, still holds my National Honor Society pin, my Delta Gamma anchor pin, my high school ring, and the Add-a-Pearl necklace with one pearl, a gift from my grandmother, which never got added to because she died. My wedding ring, a circlet of little diamonds, got stolen by the neighbor kid, who was a thief and a junkie and meaner than sin. He knew what was hockable, left behind the pins and the necklace, helped himself to the ring and a bottle of scotch, and skedaddled to the Nevada desert, where it was too much trouble for anyone to go after him. I don't miss my wedding ring any more than I miss my marriage. But it was pretty, and as it was deemed appropriate for a married woman, it was the one and only time I would wear diamonds.

In the forties and fifties, when I was growing into girldom, modesty was all the rage, which is to say that our bodies were to be kept under cover. We wore pearls made of paste on our unpierced ears and around our necks, where the necklaces descended onto the cashmere (if our dads could afford it, orlon if they couldn't) of our sweater sets, cut loosely enough to suggest the presence of breasts but never ever to celebrate them. Pearls for purity, I suppose; diamonds were a girl's best friend only if the girl was a slut or engaged. We good girls stuck to pearls and, as we launched ourselves into adolescence, added the circle pin, often made of pearls or the more humble silver alloy unadorned with jewels. We wore our circle pins sometimes at the neck just below our Peter Pan collar, sometimes on our lapel if we had one, most often on our sweaters and blouses, in the soft space below the shoulder and above the breast. Everyone had a circle pin, me too, a little halo announcing the angelic goodness of its wearer. There we were, an endless stream of virgins all in a row, ready for plucking. Mind you, one did not wear both a circle pin *and* pearls; that would have been too much, too bold. Gilding the lily was frowned on and not just in the Bible.

The most coveted jewel of any sorority girl's first twenty-one years, outside of the engagement ring, was the fraternity pin, the precursor of the (diamond) engagement ring and its promise of marriage, and it came with the right and responsibility to let the boy unhook your bra on a warm spring night in the arboretum. "She got pinned!" rang through the sorority house, a celebratory call of triumph. Before pinning, dating couples were relegated to a nook beneath the stairs of the house, called the beau parlor, where our housemother saw to it that the door remained open at least three inches and the feet of the boy and girl in it On the Floor at All Times. The road to pinning rarely ran smoothly, so when the fraternity boys came to serenade the sorority girl just pinned by one of their brothers, their music, an acknowledgment of what eventually would become betrothal, was sweet in the ears of the girl who had, so far as anyone knew, lived her life according to the rules. She had earned the right to display his pin on her left breast alongside her own pin of sisterhood. Two pins, she was the envy of every girl she knew. Her future was secure.

Not so incidentally, girls who hadn't pledged, who hadn't made it through rush to the very last party, who still lived in the dorms, "unaffiliated," rarely got pinned, because fraternity boys looked for sorority girls, not independents. This was the reason my all-knowing mother wanted me to rush, to make it through to the acceptance, signaled by an invitation from one or more of the top five sororities to final desserts, where, seduced by candlelight and cream puffs, not to mention the sweet sound of sorority girls all gussied up and singing "If You Wanna Be a DG" or "Not Thy Key, O Kappa" or "Pi Phi Arrow Forever," I would be asked to pledge my loyalty, my purity (though the word was never used) to an organization whose chief purpose was the exclusion of others. Keeping people out was my sorority's blood sport. I hated it and thrilled to it, spoke against it and never missed a hash session, where we determined whether this girl or that girl was pretty enough, smart enough, connected enough—Was she a legacy?—and, of course, virginal enough to become one of us.

All that earning our own pin and then the pin of a boy kept us busy. The Korean War came and went, noticed by us only because it decimated our football team. While we watched *Mr. Peepers* in the television room (separate from the beau parlor) and hoped for a panty raid, Julius and Ethel Rosenberg were put to death. We smoked Pall Malls and wore our camel hair coats open to the winter winds. We wore our Wigwam socks and white Keds through the slush of spring while Senator McCarthy, whoever he was, marched across the country, purging our nation of the Red Scare, those Commie pinkos. And we went to the movies, *On the Waterfront* being as close to blue collar as we wanted to get, but oh boy, though we'd never have admitted it, we wouldn't have minded being Eva Marie Saint (What a name!) in that slip.

Our real jewel, that jewel beyond compare, was our virginity, and our duty was to keep it safe until our wedding night, when our husbands could do whatever they wanted to our bodies and then we would have babies, our true purpose in life. Today we wonder, my friends of the fifties and I, where our heads were, how to account for our true ignorance of national events, our lack of interest in anything beyond our cashmered selves and the boys we hoped would claim us. We were indeed the Silent Generation, the generation that came after the Second World War, whose end returned women from factories and fields to the home, where my mother, a proud nurse's aide during the war, counseled me on how to mix a highball, how to make a tossed salad, how to miter the corners of the sheets, how to play bridge, and, by example, how to defer to a man. All of these practices, so long as I got in to the right sorority, would make me pinnable, thus certifying my fitness for marriage to the right kind of boy, and the assurance of a diamond on the third finger of the left hand.

Thanks to my mother, who had been a Delta Gamma in her day, thereby making me a legacy, I got into the right sorority, but then things went downhill, for I never got pinned, never got engaged, never even brought a boy home for inspection. After college I put my lonely sorority pin into my jewelry box and, as a working girl in San Francisco, looked longingly into the windows of jewelry stores where diamonds winked back invitingly.

Now, at age seventy-one, I still want a jewel to wear. I want a jewel to do for me what it seems to do for so many women—Elizabeth Taylor, for one, who is my age and sparkles with diamonds so brilliant that no one thinks to look below them to where her waist used to be. Then, of course, there is the queen. In 1976, Queen Elizabeth came to the Olympics to honor the athletes of England and Canada. I was there, too, a guest of one of my college friends who never got pinned either but who nonetheless married a man of some importance. Through him I was invited to the reception given by the queen. Now, we all know about the queen's notorious dowdiness, how her hats made her look older when she wasn't yet, how her skirts midcalf hid any possibility of femininity, her jackets tailored to create a sort of upholstered bosom. So the anticipation of seeing the queen in real life, while an event, since after all she was the queen, carried with it no glamour. However, on this night, the night during which she would shake the hands of athletes old and young, the Queen Got Dressed Up. Here she came through the doors at the end of the hall, white shimmering gown as décolleté as ever a queen would wear, long white gloves, even a train. And around her neck, ropes of diamonds, and in her hair—a diamond tiara. Omigod, she was beautiful, she was awe-inspiring, she shone, she was alight with diamonds, and in the presence of her radiance we bowed our heads and gave her our hearts. Next day she was back to her sturdy no-nonsense self, but for that one night in my life she was an unforgettable splendor.

Today women, in their independence, buy their own diamonds with their own money if they don't want to wait for a Hearts on Fire 2 carat surprise from a man suckered into purchasing it by the relentless advertising campaign. I, as a woman of today with enough money to buy maybe not a two-carat but a real diamond nonetheless, could walk down the street, where two blocks away the windows of two jewelry stores wink and blink and glimmer with diamonds aplenty. But I don't want to buy myself a diamond. I want a man to give it to me.

So let's say somebody gave me a jewel, like a diamond. Where would I put it? Jewels, I think, are to be set off by the background, by a woman's skin. What skin would I offer? Not the neck. Why would I want to call attention to my wattle, to the looseness of skin that started in my forehead and every day continues its descent to my neck, my bosom, and so on. So, where? If my jewel goes on my finger, which one? On my left hand I have bitten the nail of the index finger, and since I try to keep it hidden, a jewel would give me away. My right hand is pulsing with the enlarged veins of age because they've got too narrow to keep up with my heart. Do I want to call attention to my hands? Where else? My hair? Diamonds would get lost, my hair being the same color. My belly button is out of the question, couldn't even find it. So why do I want a jewel, anyway?

There is always the hope that beautiful jewels will draw atten-

tion away from the ravages of time, will in themselves be so
breathtaking that the woman wearing them becomes beautiful,
too, as happened with Queen Elizabeth, though jewels or no jewels, she is undeniably queenly. As a member of the bourgeoisie and
so not eligible for a royal position, I would like one part of my
body to be a proper setting for a precious stone. And there isn't
one, not one part I don't keep as covered as I possibly can, though
my nose isn't bad, come to think of it. And of course my ears are
okay, and what the hell, my lower lip is still full and—bereft of
adornment. When young women began all this body piercing, I
was horrified, but maybe I should be less scornful. After all, their
bodies and faces and ears and tongues can accommodate many
jewels; there may be a method to what I took to be their madness.
And those beautiful Indian women: little diamonds in the soft
part of the nose between the nostril and the bone. I could do that.
If I did, I would glitter when I snored, and the man lying beside
me, who had given me the diamond, would think me beautiful
and well worth the enormous amount of money that one perfect
diamond had cost him. Yes, I could accommodate a fine jewel.

In Santa Rosa, California, still jewel-less, I have come to do a
reading from the book I wrote about being naked with men.
Waiting for people to find seats, I hear a woman in the audience
whisper to her friend, "She seems so comfortable with her own
body, so at ease." The friend answers, "You would, too, if you were
getting all that sex." They are talking about me. Well, with my
clothes on, I'm pretty comfortable, and, truth be told, the attentions of men, their ministrations to my body, have loosened me
up. So the women in the audience are partly right. Yet, at another
reading, during the question-and-answer period, I am asked the
age range of the men I got naked with. "Eighty-four to thirty-
two," I answer, and there is a gasp. Then, from a woman who looks
directly at my torso, "What would a thirty-two-year-old want
with you?" Again and again, wherever I go to read, to sign books,
the question or a variation of it arises: "How do you get undressed

in front of those men?" My answer, which always brings laughter, is, "Fast." But it's true. Faster than a speeding bullet I have covered myself from top to toe in, if I'm lucky, 400-thread-count linens while he was still wrestling with the top button of his shirt. More powerful than a locomotive, I have dived beneath bedclothes while he's still pulling at his socks. "Where did you go?" he asks, and, half-hoping he won't find me, I whisper from the depths of sheets and blankets and pillows, "Here I am."

> . . . *the expression of a well-made man appears not only in his face;*
> *It is in his limbs and joints also, it is curiously in the joints of his hips*
>   *and wrists;*
> *It is in his walk, the carriage of his neck, the flex of his waist and knees—*

Walt Whitman knew what he was talking about; maybe only a homosexual male can truly appreciate the male body. If that is so, I run a close second as a fan of male nudity. I have never ever seen a naked man who was not comfortable in his skin, who did not walk naked from here to there with no thought of clutching at a robe or a bath towel or a curtain, who did not turn this way and that without self-consciousness. I have seen more than one man strut his stuff while I, swaddled in sheets, lay on my side and offered up my heartfelt praise and admiration and (silent) envy. My memory conjures up Graham in all his beautiful nakedness, and I see him striding about, smoothing his hands over his very flat belly, prideful and happy that I share his delight in the splendor that is his body.

Age entirely aside, how is it that men are like this while women, like me, prefer the dark to the light? Why do most men prefer to make love with the lights on? Maybe it's that boys see each other naked at younger ages than girls do. Maybe it's that girls' bodies change more dramatically than boys'; maybe it's that girls learn shame while boys learn pride. Girls' bodies every month become a bloody mess; we are unclean in some cultures, men will have nothing to do with us. No matter how antiseptic the pads and tampons, no matter how floral the scent of vaginal douches, there is no escaping the sight and smell of blood that comes from us every month for thirty or forty years of our lives. I am hopeful that all this is changing. Surely girls—excuse me, young women—today take pride in their bodies; surely they prefer to make love with the lights on; surely, like my landlady, who glories in her pregnancy, they, too, stride about naked, comfortable in their own skin. I am not convinced. If what I wish were in fact true, advertising would have found a new tune to sing; instead, the relentlessness of the ads that drive us to oils and creams and rinses and gels and powder and paint and foundation and blush convinces old and young alike, if we are not careful, of our bodies' imperfections. Shame on advertising.

Maybe nothing at all has changed, for here comes Eve Ensler once again, who, having shown us where our vaginas are, has raised her sights to the belly. In her one-woman show, *The Good Body,* she exhorts us to love ourselves, even the ugliest part of our bodies, our bellies. "I think that when we truly end the internalized self-violence, when women actually live in their bodies, actually love their bodies as they are, feel safe and empowered in them, then the world will change." Well, who could argue with that? So there she is up there on stage, pulling up her spaghetti-strapped top to reveal to the audience this loathsome thing, this hideous part, this post-forty belly that, in the next hour and a half, will become lovable. The problem, at least from where I'm sitting, is that she doesn't have a belly, or much of one. What is she talking about here? Wait another twenty years, I want to tell her, then I'll listen to you. Ms. Ensler, still in her youth as far as I'm concerned, has only a slight idea of the power of self-hatred that has lurked throughout most of our lives and threatens to explode unless we strike first: Smash all full-length mirrors, enter only those dressing rooms where the light is muted, insist on lights-off for love, stop reading women's magazines and buying all that junk.

Ensler's audience, mostly women in their thirties and beyond, gives her a standing ovation. I leave depressed. The wheels of progress grind exceedingly slowly.

In *The Last Gift of Time: Living Beyond Sixty,* Carolyn Heilbron wrote, "Seventy does terrible things to a woman's face." It does, and not just to her face. Carolyn Heilbron, at seventy-six, killed herself, and, since she left no note, we can only guess at her reasons. I cannot believe it was vanity, that the damage to her face wrought by age would drive her to her death. But suicide is so cruel to those left behind that one wonders how anyone of sound mind could do it. How I wish Heilbron had left us something in writing about how she knew it was time to end her life. She wrote us about living after sixty. Couldn't she have stayed the course and told us how to live with a face badly treated by time? Well, she doesn't owe any of us, I guess. It's just that she left a lot of readers unfinished; we had hoped she would help us all the way to the end.

At a reading in Arizona a young man at the end of the line, apparently unfazed by my seventy-one-year-old face, stays to tell me that I am "tantric kundalini," whatever that is. Because he is too stoned to explain, he weaves off into the night, leaving me face-to-face with a woman who sat riveted during the reading, who hands me her book to be signed, and who whispers, though we are the only ones in the room, "I am seventy-three and want so much to have a man in my life. But my belly has dropped and rubbed all my pubic hair off. I'm so afraid that any man would run away in disgust. I know about plastic surgery and tummy tucks and all that, but I just don't have that kind of money." She drops into a chair and sighs, "What should I do?" I could say "Undress fast." But I don't; neither do I say "Go online." I say what perhaps is true, "I think men see different things."

Back home I call John, my New England cabin-in-the-woods John, my great good friend with whom I have enjoyed long hours of sex—lights off, my choice. I ask, "Do you think men don't see the imperfections of women's bodies when they make love?" John answers, "Oh, no! I'm a real lookist, most men are. I like to see everything." I am surprised. Given my imperfections and John's enjoyment of the visual—apparently he can see in the dark—how is it that he takes such pleasure from me? He says, "Men are not nearly as hard on women as women are on themselves."

True. Feasting as we do on a steady diet provided by women's magazines, it is no wonder we doubt ourselves. So we paint, shave, and spray, and hope to god we smell like gardens, at least until after he goes home. If he stays the night, my friend Julie programs herself to wake up very, very early, so that while he is still asleep she can apply makeup anew. Julie's latest beau, with whom she has been intimate for over a year, has never seen her without her face on. She is twenty-seven. She plans to stay forever young, and when the powder and the paint are not enough, she will look to surgery to lend a helping hand, or a face or a breast or a belly. Given that most of us do not have Julie's discipline, that we do not take full advantage of the wonders of cosmetics, that we lack the money and the urge to reconstruct our bodies, it's amazing we get laid at all. John must be right: Men are much easier on us than we are.

When I think about the bodies of the men I have come to know, when I recall the enjoyment I took from a body that was seventy-five years old, a body that was thirty-two, and a few in between, I remind myself that much of the pleasure came because I liked, even loved, the person who inhabited that body. I remember unhappy encounters with men whose bodies became repellent to me, not because they were ugly or old, but because the men who wore them were selfish or greedy or ill-tempered.

> *i like my body when it is with your*
> *body. It is so quite new a thing.*
> —E. E. CUMMINGS, from Sonnet XXIV

Better cummings than *Vogue,* better Whitman than *Harper's Bazaar,* better John than our mirrors.

And best of all, Graham, my favorite person in my favorite body, phones. He is repentant, not about marrying but about not telling me in person, such as the last time we had lunch in New York, when he knew he would be getting married and said nothing. "I wanted to tell you," he says, "but I just couldn't find the words." I am so happy to hear his voice, to hope that he will enrich my life again, that I do not scold, upbraid, or otherwise chide him for his lapse, and soon we ease into talking once again about everything, about Thucydides—he knows more than I—about George Eliot—I know more than he. Our conversation runs in and out and in between and fills the gaps of my loneliness. For a time we are together, and I am soothed and at the same time exhilarated. I love what he does to my mind. He forces it awake; he keeps it running, though not always smoothly. At times my missing of him becomes palpable and I stumble, lose my train of thought, and then he says, "I miss you," and I say it back, and for that small moment everything is right.

This love affair between a man of thirty-six and a woman of seventy-one is odd but no less real for being so. "I worry about you sometimes," he says, referring I suppose to my dui's, those impassioned e-mails I fire off in the dead of night. I am surprised, and say so: "Why would you worry about me?" And he says, "Because you are the woman I would have married." I am moved to tears with longing and love for this man, with despair and regret for what cannot be, but I know the right answer, and so I stop my tears and say, clearly and with certainty, "Yes." And we fall silent.

friend Zoreh, who ought to know, whose experience is firsthand.
Zoreh grew up in Iran. As we come to know and like each other,
Zoreh and her Persian friends and family will dispossess me of my
self-absorption and replace it with a fascination for her and the
world from which she comes. I welcome the change, the chance to
turn off the burners, front and back, where love and loneliness and
desire threaten to boil over or, worse, curdle into something foul. I
am incensed: Graham is going to Italy without me. Of course
without me. He is taking his wife. They will have a good time in
Italy without me. I want to go to Italy. With Graham. But I am
not for public consumption. It's fine with Graham when we sit
across from each other in a restaurant and he looks at me all
moony-eyed until I say, "Stop looking at me like that; people will
see." His green eyes are practically melting into his salad. "Like
what?" he asks, pretending innocence. "You know, that love stuff."
He smiles, leans across the table, takes my hand, and says, "In the
entire world there is no one like you." Now who's melting? But stay
in your seat, Jane, don't travel abroad, lie low; I am pissed. Obvi-
ously my sense of the other needs stoking. Zoreh no doubt knows
many men and, while the image I have of Iranian men is not to
their credit, in the pictures I have seen of them they are very handsome. I can look but not touch. A valuable lesson in self-control.

At our first meeting at a bookstore in San Francisco, Zoreh, elegant in Western dress, stood out in the crowd of people come to
hear me read. I was briefly uncomfortable. Her dark eyes were un-
wavering, and they seemed never to leave my face. What could she
want of me? She waited in line for me to sign her book, said a
heartfelt thank you, thank you, and a week later at another reading was there again. Again she bought a book, asked me to sign it,
said, "Thank you so much" in a voice as rich and dark as the Turkish coffee she would serve me in a few weeks' time. She wrote me
notes inviting me to her home for tea, offering anything I might
need anytime at all. And finally I accepted her invitation to morning coffee. "Turkish," Zoreh will tell me, "best in world."

I was reluctant to accept. There was an intensity in Zoreh that I found unsettling. I wondered about her persistence in befriending me; what could she want? Still, she was fascinating and beautiful and held worlds of secrets I wanted to learn. Surely the world from which she came was nothing like mine, nor could the two of us be in any way alike.

It is eleven o'clock in the morning, and the ad for Zoreh's house, were it for sale, would read something like, *Grand Lake area, 5+bdrms/3baths, formal dining room, 2 fireplaces, sweeping Bay views, $2.2 million.* This ad would not include *washer/dryer* or *washer/dryer hookups.* No, that would be tacky, for in this house it's a given that someone *else,* not the owner, will trouble herself with laundry. For a moment I don't even want this house; it's too grand. But in the next instant I know that if someone gave it to me and promised I could stay forever, I would manage. I would even grow to feel at home here.

I roam from room to room, all of them smelling faintly of incense, which Zoreh tells me is jasmine. "And you can get it to put on your body, too." Outside the windows of the enormous kitchen it is raining, and the overflow from the hot tub into the blue, blue waters of the swimming pool makes a lovely waterfall. Zoreh tells me, "This Turkish coffee you can sip, not like espresso, which is bad-tasting. And then I will give you a wonderful lunch." Oh boy, I am stuck here in this great big house for a while.

Zoreh is wearing her hair loose today. It undulates in deep dark waves halfway down her back, and frames her face, which is free of makeup and has high cheekbones. Her dark eyes are shaped like the almonds in the dish she has placed before me. It is easy to imagine that face framed in a black scarf, as it was when she lived in Iran. Here she wears jeans and a turtleneck that fit her slim body well. It is not so easy to imagine her shapeless in a robe intended to disguise her femaleness, a robe she wore for many years.

She turns from the sink, where she has been washing lettuce leaves for our salad, and says to me, "You are so free! Iranian women think they are free. And they are, compared to women in

Afghanistan, but they are not really. American women are much freer, and you . . . you are freer even than that!" I decide not to confide in her the abiding self-consciousness I feel about my body, though there is something in Zoreh that makes me think my doing so would not change her opinion. Zoreh has made up her mind: I am freer than anybody, and that's that.

"I tell my daughters, both of them, stay away from Iranian men, and look—both of them, who do they marry? Iranian men." She laughs the rueful laugh of parents everywhere. "But my younger daughter, her husband, this boy, has lived in America for many years; he is the most gentle young man. My daughter is fortunate." She stirs the couscous she has made for our lunch. "All Iranian women are good cooks," she says. "In my culture women learn early on from their mothers about herbs and spices, about basmati rice, how not to let it get sticky, must be fluffy. I cook for many people even when there are only a few." She places a bowl of dried fruit and nuts on the counter and says something she will repeat in one way or another every time we meet: "In my country people get together all the time—young people and old people and rich and poor—we are always getting together to talk and to laugh and do much dancing." Zoreh's energy electrifies me into silence, and I imagine her dancing, whirling around a room, a beautiful and exotic creature. "In Iran we have wonderful times inside our houses; you can do whatever you like inside your home."

Where is Zoreh's husband? Surely she does not live in this great big house all alone. As if she has read my mind, she says, "My daughter and her wonderful husband live with me. They go to college." So where is Zoreh's husband, the father of this fine daughter married to this wonderful young man, so enlightened and kind, so not like Iranian men? I don't know how hard to press or whether to press at all. I am a guest so, at least for the moment, I will act like one. Besides, Zoreh needs no encouragement to talk. "Take more," she says, "chicken, couscous, you eat too little." I take more, and she hands me a platter of beets. Lonely for the sound of my own voice, I say, "I love beets. I can never get enough beets. The other day I bought one beet, boiled it, and ate it just like an apple." I marvel silently at my talent for small talk—and my first language is English. "Now tea," she says, and rises from her chair.

"My daughters' father lives in Iran. I am divorced three years. He is a kind man, a gentle man, wealthy, good father, everyone likes him, but . . . two of us, we fight from very beginning, never stop. My daughters get grown before divorce. Never would I get divorced in Iran. In Iran man gets the children, just automatically; he gets the house. Single woman in Iran no one will rent her a place to live—'Where is the husband?' they want to know. I come here to get divorced. Here are rights. But I wait long time for my green card. Now I am a single woman." She tosses a strand of hair back over her shoulder. "I love parties. I love people coming to my house, to cook for them, to dance. My husband very, very jealous all the time, he thinks I'm flirting, thinks I have eyes for other men. No, no, I do not, I just am happy to be with people, but he never believes me. So fighting goes on and on. My husband did not want me to come here. 'If you go there,' he tells me, 'I will lose you. I don't want to lose you.' I tell him, 'It is too late. You have already lost me.'" She piles more couscous onto my plate. "You eat." I obey.

Outside the window the autumn rains pelt her herb garden and her fig trees and her vegetable garden, all of them thriving through her own efforts. "In Iran there are four seasons, each one different. In Iran it snows in winter. Winter very cold, snow on the mountains. Very beautiful." She catches herself from her wistfulness and says, "March twenty-six is our new year. It is our tradition to start over, to throw out the old, begin the new—new food, new clothes, new thoughts. I will have party here. I will invite you. Singing and dancing and much food. I will cook."

"Thank you," I say, and rise to leave.

"Can you wait one minute?" she asks. "I want to ask you something. What is it with Americans?" Ah, that's it; she thinks I know something about Americans. And then she says, "When I moved here eight years ago, I give party. I go up and down the street inviting all the neighbors. At the party one man who lives next to me here"—she points to her left—"says to another man who lives next to me there"—she points to her right—"'You look familiar, don't I know you from somewhere?'" Zoreh is scandalized. "They are neighbors for twenty years and they don't know each other!" She looks at me expectantly and says, "Why is that?"

Hell, I don't know. I mumble something about Americans and work, how people here work hard all day and are just too tired. Zoreh interrupts me: "American women are lazy." Oh boy, here we go; I'm going to have to defend American women. Can I? Will I want to? I needn't worry, for Zoreh is on a tear. "Let me tell you, you listen. Iranian man married to Iranian woman: end of day, both work, man brings home four people, surprise, for dinner, not a problem. Not so for America. Iranian man married to American woman says, 'I don't dare do such a thing! My wife will be angry!' American women spoiled."

I nod, yes, American women are spoiled. Of course, being one, I don't think we are, or at least I'm not. Though here I sit while Zoreh serves me this wonderful food she has cooked in this lovely room overlooking her gardens. It comes to me then that Zoreh doesn't want answers from me. She wants to talk to someone who will listen to her. She wants to cook for someone who will eat with her. I rise to go, and she says, "If you need a place to come, to write, to stay anytime, as long as you want, you can come here." She wants to live with someone. She wants to spend her generosity, to share her warmth and her talents and her love, if not with a man—never a Persian man—then with me. She would be happy to spoil me. She is remarkable.

I waddle down the driveway, chewing on my Iranian pistachio candy, and turn to wave good-bye to Zoreh. She is not there. But a minute later here she comes, running down the driveway, waving something in her hand. "Wait! Wait!" she calls. I stop the car, and

Zoreh thrusts a jar through the open window. "Beets," she says. "From my garden. For you."

I have spent the morning with a woman who thinks of others, who cooks for others, gardens for others, who does not dwell on the misfortunes of her life, past or present, who ought to provide a model for me to follow. I will consign Graham to oblivion while I practice extending my frame of reference beyond the two of us. With this in mind and the hope that it rains for forty days and forty nights in Italy, I accept at once Zoreh's invitation to dinner.

I DID NOT expect a crowd, but there is one. Four couples, Zoreh, and me make ten; that's a crowd. Here, at last, I will meet Iranian men.

His is the dominant voice in the gathering. Slim, sleek, and beautifully dressed in Ralph Lauren, salt-and-pepper hair cropped close, pale of cheek, he looks as upscale as any American man of means. His eyes give him away, for they are almond-shaped and large; they are beautiful. He is Iranian. "Do you like our governor Mr. Schwarzenegger?" he asks me, and before I can answer, he says, "I believe he is doing a fine job. I like his budget."

Though it is clear that his answer is the one he wants to hear, I say, "We'll have to wait and see." I do not want to get into a political discussion with this man in this place. I am a dinner guest and do not want to offend my hostess. Besides, from long experience I can tell an actual exchange of ideas is not something this man is familiar with, particularly if one of the discussants is a woman. Zoreh, who proclaims that as a devout Muslim she can nonetheless enjoy wine, pours another glass for me, then for herself.

Ralph Lauren persists. "Did you like the previous governor, that fool Davis?"

"No," I say, and decide to shut up about the way Arnold Schwarzenegger was elected, the nasty business of ousting a legally elected governor before his term was up, the frightening power of money in the hands of idiots.

Next to me sits an adorable woman. Her name is Missa. She, too, is Iranian, has been in this country for twenty-two years. She is plump, her skin like satin. Her accent is strong. "I sell real estate," she tells me. "Zoreh tells me you write book. What did you write about?"

On the other side of the room the women are quiet, listening to Ralph continue his monologue on politics both here and in the Middle East. He is joined by another man who, with his wife, has come late. So we are twelve. Enough already.

Missa is here without her husband, who will come later—thirteen! I answer her question. "Sex." Missa and I are sitting on high chairs, perched on them at the bar that separates the kitchen from the family room. Missa almost topples, catches herself, and, her beautiful eyes large and a-sparkle, says, "Yes? Really?"

"Yes, really," I say.

"I will get that book. Where will I get that book?"

"Zoreh will tell you," I say.

"I will get that book and put it on the table where my husband puts his papers, and he will read it."

I advise her to read it first herself.

"I never read one book," she tells me, "in my whole life. I am busy with my children, my work. My husband, now our children are gone from home, he never talks to me about that, we never would ever talk about sex. That part of our life is over."

The word "sex" has penetrated the room, and Ralph Lauren's audience becomes mine. Everyone is silent. I whisper to Zoreh, "What have you got me into?"

Zoreh smiles; she is having fun. I suspect she is breaking some taboo.

"What is this book?" Ralph wants to know.

So I tell them. I repeat the ad as I have so many times before, though perhaps in this venue a bit faster. I explain that the book is about what happened after the ad appeared.

Silence. Rapt silence? Shocked? Angry? It lasts forever. Then Ralph speaks: "After childbearing women lose interest in that sort of thing. Many men, too."

And oh, lucky us, he offers the joke about the ninety-five-year-old man who marries the twenty-three-year-old woman, then is warned by his doctor about the dangers of a long honeymoon. The man says, "Well, if she dies, she dies." Everyone laughs as if to say, How ridiculous, an old man having sex.

Ralph says, "Sex between old men and old women is . . . degrading. A good thing not much is going around."

And I laugh and say, "You are so funny!"

Everyone, all the women, too, laugh, and Zoreh says, above the laughter, "He is not funny; he is Persian!"

Indeed he is, but he and his derision go far beyond Persia. Tonight it will include men, and some women, from everywhere in the world. I say, "In my experience there is great interest in sex among men and women long past childbearing. From what I have seen and known, there is much activity."

"A search for intimacy perhaps," says Ralph, "but the rest, the rest is . . ." He can't find the word. I do it for him. "Disgusting."

"Yes, disgusting. Can you tell me that old women can even do it?" Ralph takes another sip of wine. "Can they get wet, aroused, you know, what has to happen?"

Ralph's wife sits to my left. She, like the other women here, is impeccably groomed: She wears a dark suit perfectly fitted to her slim body; she has pulled her hair back into a large bun; it has not gone willingly, the waves and crinkles of what must be a wild unruliness when free are visible under the light, along with glints of red. She is silent, stone-faced, and I'm not sure if this is her reaction to her husband's outrageousness or if in the presence of her husband she is like this all the time.

I mention something about physiology and testosterone in women, and nobody hears me, nobody is interested any longer in what I have to say, only in what Ralph will tell us next about sex.

Ralph says, "The only reason for older people to have sex is from deep love of each other, from long lives of loving each other."

"That would be nice," I say.

Now Ralph gets himself into trouble. He says, "I can understand how someone could do that maybe to get published or in the newspaper—"

I cut him off. "Are you suggesting I placed an ad in order to write the book?"

"No, no . . ."

"I had no intention of writing a book when I began my adventures." I am surprised at my curtness.

Ralph is silent. For a while.

Zoreh has once again made wonderful food: chicken and saffron rice and cheese and prunes, and all the while the wine flows. She has seated me at the head of the table; Ralph has seated himself on my right. The women, all five, sit together on one side of the table; the four men line up on Ralph's side. Not one of the men will utter a word, leaving me to assume that Ralph speaks for them or that conversation with a woman—me—is, for a man, unseemly. Fine with me; it turns out that Persian *women* hold my interest. I want them to talk. I ask, "In Iran are there standards of beauty?" Not well asked. "I mean, what determines, in your culture, if a woman is beautiful or not?"

Zoreh speaks: "It is inner beauty, we are not concerned with outside. In Iran we say, Don't be proud of your beauty; it can be destroyed in one fever."

"But," I press, "you are all beautiful; you are very pleasing to the eye." I do not say "and you are very skillfully made up and gorgeously dressed," though they are. They are also silent. "I read somewhere that *Baywatch* is a very popular TV program in Iran. Is that true?"

Ralph is helpful here. He smiles and says, "Yes, it is true." In a voice of certainty acquired through a lifelong confidence, he continues, "I like my women blond and long-legged."

Finally his wife speaks. "It is the eyes."

"And the eyebrows," says another woman.

I am so stupid. These women have grown up beneath burkas and head scarves. Of course, it would be only the eyes and the eyebrows that were visible. Zoreh, however, is not to be deterred: "We all have same eyes! Black, black, same difference. It is inner beauty that matters."

We move away from the table and into the living room, where Zoreh serves a special tea, the elixir of heaven. If I go out and kill infidels, I want my reward to be this tea, forget the virgins. Ralph's wife, who has apparently determined me to be a source of lascivious information, leans toward me and asks, "Do you think Michael Jackson did what they said?"

"I think he is a sad young man. He has tried to re-create himself so many times."

"Yes, he is trying to escape from being black," she says. "Do you think he did what they said?"

"I think he probably did, but I also think that he doesn't believe he is guilty."

And so the talk turns to television. "I cut off Cinemax," says Zoreh, "too much women with women. Who wants to see that?" Nods all around.

"And men with men. That *Queer Eye* program is disgusting."

Ralph says, "Homosexual marriages should be banned, homosexuality should be banned. It is wrong."

"Is a fad, don't you think?" a woman asks of me.

"No matter," says Ralph, "should be stopped."

"What would you do with homosexuals?" I ask.

"I would send them away. They can come back when they know proper behavior."

Ralph, who has waved away the offer of tea, continues to drink red wine, and, echoing Zoreh's earlier declaration, announces, for my benefit I suppose, "I am a good Muslim, I pray, and I drink wine, too." I excuse myself; it is late, my drive is long. Ralph rises from his chair, everybody rises, and I shake hands with everyone, and Ralph claps his arm around my shoulder and walks with me to the front door, giving me a little squeeze before I go.

I have done a very un-Muslim thing, two very un-Muslim things: I have shaken hands with four men, and I looked them straight in the eye. And they looked back, though only briefly, and returned my handshake, though not at all firmly. The Islamic Republic would not approve of their behavior or of mine. In the Republic, men who are good Muslims keep their hands behind their backs and their eyes averted; they never touch women not their wives or daughters; they never look directly at them. Men who do are frowned upon; some are forced into exile—like Ralph, like the men at this gathering who have remained silent, letting Ralph speak for them. How, I wonder, do they like their exile, self-imposed though it seems to be? I want to ask them, What of *your* behavior would you need to change in order to go home? What parts of your own true selves would you be willing to hide?

At the car Zoreh says, "Next time we will have tea with women, only women."

"I would like that."

"You see what I mean?" she says. "Persian men. Bah."

MY OWN EXPERIENCE with Persian men came in the early eighties. It was entirely unhappy. One year, when the term began at the school in Concord, California, where I taught, our student body changed. Into it came boys, clearly foreign, very handsome, their skin like ivory satin, their dark eyes pools of disdain. These newcomers—on the verge of manhood—dripped in gold: gold chains, gold bracelets, gold rings, all that Persia could provide them, and they opened their shirts, rolled up their sleeves, so that we could see that they glittered when they walked. Their English was limited if present at all. For this reason, because my school's English as a Second Language program did not yet exist, these boys were assigned to my class—to my 1C class, the 1 indicating grade level nine, and the *C* indicating failure in English up to this time. Until then my students had all been native English speakers who, for one reason or another, had bottomed out of their middle-school English classes, whose test scores urged immediate remediation. Assigned to bring these students up to grade level or as close to it as they were capable of getting, at first I had no idea what to do. But I made stuff up, and in the few years preceding the influx of Iranian immigrants it seemed to me I was learning how to teach. Then came Persia. At least the Persia that fled Iran after the deposing of the shah.

Their insolence was astounding. By 1981 I had been teaching for almost twenty years. Although I knew that every new year would bring with it problems of discipline—kids who didn't want to be in school, who hated school, who didn't know how to go to school—I was unprepared for the Persian boys. As I walked down the aisle of the classroom, their feet would shoot into my path; sometimes I would stumble. Their feet remained, unyielding in their obstinacy, in their insistence on showing me my position as a woman, my unacceptability as their teacher. They slouched in their seats, daring me to "teach" them; they laughed at me openly, not bothering to cover their mouths. Tired of that, from behind their gold-ringed hands and always in Farsi, they "talked behind me," a phrase I would learn from my Iranian women friends almost twenty-five years later, the phrase that describes the running commentary of ridicule with which they filled the classroom. In my long life I had been disrespected as a teacher, abused as a woman. But this was different: I had never been publicly humiliated, discounted, disappeared, if you will—my unworthiness revealed to the world at large, by boys to whom I was a flea. They were princes, sons of princes, princes who would have assumed their rightful roles had circumstances allowed; they were royalty dumped without ceremony into a corral of the common herd. They were not happy. Neither was I. I hated them, these boys so arrogant, so rude, so comfortable in their superiority. And then suddenly, midyear, they were gone. No one knew where; we knew only that we were happy they were gone. We never saw them again. When we regained our senses, we realized that in those few months of our persecution we never saw a Persian girl. But I had learned how it felt to be one.

"Persian men, bah!" I get it, Zoreh, I do.

This time, at morning coffee, we are all women. I look for Ralph Lauren's wife, but she is absent. The sun is warm and Zoreh is happy to have a reason to bring people together. Once again she says, "Back home we do everything together, even after revolution, not outside but in our houses."

By now they have read my book; they are fully aware of my outrageous behavior. They look at me curiously, suspiciously, admiringly, awe mixed with disbelief. I am no longer the mystery guest, and so I allow myself a bit of boldness. "How did you meet your husbands? Did you marry for love?"

Nima answers, "Before the revolution in '79, marry for love. After, is common for younger woman marry older man who can give her things, take care of her." The women laugh and repeat their mothers' advice: Marry a doctor, an engineer. Hmm, I think, sounds familiar.

Zoreh, who will perhaps remain angry with Persian men, maybe all men, forever, bursts out with, "We grow up with this cloud of 'No, no, no.' We must never enjoy sex, must remain pure, even when right in the act, we must remember husband is first. If we leave, if we divorce, if we do a bad thing or not, men will lie, talk behind us, tell whole neighborhood we are sluts. And we cannot talk anymore to our families because they say we shame them. Even if we not do anything, men can make stories about us. Everybody believe them. Bah!"

The other women nod. "Is true. But you"—they turn to Nima—"did marry a doctor." Nima smiles. "At first," she says, "he didn't get my eyes," then explains to me, "He was not handsome enough for me to notice." She tosses her blond hair over her shoulders. "But then everywhere I went there he was, and finally my friend said to me, 'He's interested in you. Talk to him.'" Nima, fair-skinned, strawberry-blond, and buxom, looks very un-Iranian, if one is to judge by the other women present, who are small, dark-eyed, and dark-haired, dressed in well-cut suits in somber colors. Nima wears a beige linen top, sleeveless, over matching pants. The top is V-necked, pointing to cleavage that surely would get her jailed back home. Nima turns to Zoreh, who says, "Even now since I am divorced, the cloud put by my mother remains."

Nima nods and says, "That cloud came with me, too. I was the youngest of ten, the youngest girl, and my mother warned me every day, told my brothers to watch me, to keep me on leash, I would disgrace family one day. She would not let me wear a bathing suit, so when I was a teenager, I sew my own suit with my own hands and walk around inside the house in my bathing suit. My mother is horrified. 'I want to learn to swim,' I said. 'Take that off,' my mother said, 'no swimming, you are too wild.' To this day I cannot swim. But my husband, he trust me and love me."

"Not like other Persian men," says Zoreh.

"I never ask him can I do something. I tell him I wish to go here or there, and whatever I want or need to do is fine with him." Nima's voice softens, her eyes grow moist.

Nima does not wear a ring. Nor do any of the other women. They are all divorced. Sami, before the revolution, worked in the American consulate in Tehran. Her husband was a journalist. Came the revolution, he was jailed for six months. When he was released, he was confined to his house. Then Sami lost her job. At home together, unhappy, they began to argue. They divorced. Her husband went to England, where he could write. Sami came here. Her husband remarried; Sami did not.

Nima's husband remarried, too; Nima did not. Nima explains: "When king deposed, new religious government kill anyone they like, rich people just because they are rich. We had to leave because all houses we know will be searched, and in our house are some photographs of me and the king and others, and this would be very bad for our friends. So I take papers and go, with my children, who are then two and a half and six months, but without my husband, because under new regime is forbidden for doctors to leave Iran. He says he will get visa and follow us to America. And then six years go by, and he can't leave unless he has somehow got academic appointment. So I find him one in Los Angeles, and he calls to say he is in Switzerland. 'Tell the children I am on my way,' he says. I answer, 'I will tell the children when you call me from New York.' Good thing, because my husband, he goes in line at the consulate to get visa, and when is his turn, the window closes, last visa given to old couple who want to visit their children in America. People at consulate say try again. No luck. He returns to Iran, tells me to come home. I say yes, when I get my green card, which is my visa, because without a green card I could go to Iran but I would not be able to get out again. Our children are now six and eight years old, and finally he says we should divorce. And now he is remarried. When my son turned fifteen, I took him for five weeks to Iran. To meet this stranger, his father. Is very sad."

"Is very sad," says Zoreh, and we all nod. I wonder how often Nima has told her story, this one about loving and losing a husband. From the brightness of her eyes, tears unshed, I gather that although she has often explained the reasons for her exile, she has chosen not to include her regrets, her sadness, the enormity of her loss. To do so would threaten the recovery that has been her life for the past twenty years.

Nima decides to alter the mood. She tells us about a gathering of Iranian women, her tea circle, all over fifty. She asked them, "How old were you when you first came to know your body?" Silence.

"Don't you masturbate yourselves?" A woman said, "What is that?" Nima answered, "It is touching yourself, here." "Oh my god!" a woman exclaimed; another woman grew faint. Nima announced that orgasm is a good thing. Not one of the women was familiar with the term, not in English and certainly not in Farsi.

We are astounded by her audacity. Zoreh says to me, "Nima is scandal just like you!" We laugh together, and I wonder silently if my own outrageous behavior is the reason for their interest in me.

Zoreh breaks in, "Yes, I hear some Iranian men say about their wives, 'She is cold.' Well, I tell them they have to warm them up!"

Nima laughs. "Yes, they think one look at them and women go hot." She goes back to the story of her tea circle. "I told them, you can touch yourself all alone, even when you are driving. Everybody horrified, gasping, everything. I said, You have to be careful, though, SUV does not come along higher than you and look in your window."

Oh, my stars! Even I am surprised! Zoreh says to Nima, "You are hot. You like boys."

Nima nods. "Old men can't do much; old men too set in their ways, old men just more of how they were when they were young. I like sweetness in men; old men are sour, young are not." I wonder if Nima is fantasizing or if, in fact, she has managed to collect a few young men. I suspect the latter, for this is a woman who seems to be at home in her own body.

"If a man can't do it," says Zoreh, and she looks over our heads out to her garden, "if he's too old or a little bit sick, I don't mind. It's not the sex. I just want to rest near him. His arms around me." She comes back to us: "Just not Persian."

The longing in this room is palpable. The yearning for a sweet man, a kind man, fills us and the air around us, and we grow quiet. In their eyes I have found what they want and what, with the possible exception of Nima, they believe they have no possibility of finding. Their world of exile is small yet influenced by the rules under which, as Iranian women, they were born. They are free of the burka and the scarf, free from the fear of imprisonment, but not free of desire. They are women alone with high spirits and great beauty but little hope. I leave our gathering sad and ashamed of my whimpering over Graham. What these women have lost is incalculable. What they have gained remains under cover of clouds.

Intentionally or not, with Ralph Lauren's help my new friends have set me against Persian men, although I am sensible enough to know that Persian men are everywhere and are not always Persian. They can be American or English or Japanese or Finnish or Brazilian. What makes them all Persian, at least the way Zoreh describes it, is their supremacy, actual or imagined, their belief that women are to be enjoyed, that as men *they* make life possible, women make life pleasurable. I grew up with Persian men: my father, my brother, my teachers, my bosses, all of them dead now. I am happy that era is over, and fortunate to have outlasted it. I am confident that obeisance to men is behind me, that now I can look them straight in the eye without blinking or flinching or even flirting. I am grown up and so is America.

So how in heaven do I end up in Berkeley, California, with a gastroenterologist who is Persian?

Like all sensible women of seventy-one, I am having a colonoscopy, and Dr. Bahri is going to give it to me. Wait till Zoreh hears about this!

Dr. Bahri wears gorgeous clothes, probably more expensive than Ralph Lauren's. I think I am looking at Armani. When he questions me in our pre-procedure interview and I tell him about some discomfort in my nether region, I am immediately suspicious when he looks at me very sympathetically—a ruse, I am certain, intended to befriend me and make his life easier than it would be with a patient genuinely hostile to his invasive plans. Zoreh and Ralph have prepared me well. I go on the offensive: "Do you read Persian poetry?" I ask. If he answers yes, then the seduction will be complete and I will obey his every command. "Not as much as I wish," he says. "I have a beautiful book of *The Rubaiyat* in four different languages, which someday I will spend much time with; for now, however, . . ." Okay, he's got me. I ask him if stress could play a role in my discomfort. "Absolutely," he says. He looks closely at me and says, "I see much stress in you." He places his hand on my shoulder: "It is okay to cry, you know." I do. I feel better. He has cast a spell.

At the endoscopy center the man who prepares me, who takes my history, who administers the wonderful stuff that will knock me out, I hope, is named Ardalan Parsi. He is Iranian. "Like your doctor," he says. He sits close to my gurney and asks me about drugs, allergies, familial inheritances. "Do you drink alcohol?" he asks. "Yes," I answer. "What kind?" "White wine." His eyes light up. "What kind of white wine?" "Macon Uchizy," I answer, "from the Loire Valley, and it's under ten dollars a bottle." He takes a pad of paper from his shirt pocket. "Tell me again. I am on the lookout always for good wine. Where did you find this?"

Wait a minute, is this another ruse? I say to him, "You are very good at questioning. I feel so secure I could tell you anything. Even if I were a spy."

He puts his hand on my shoulder—I am swaddled in hospital gowns—looks deep into my eyes, and commands, "Tell me everything."

"I will tell you everything. Where shall I start?"

"Start from the beginning."

"And if I don't?"

"Then"—he shakes his finger at me—"we will send you to that corner over there for a time-out."

I like this man. I tell him about my Iranian friend Zoreh, who cautions her daughters and everyone else to stay away from Persian men. Ardalan grows serious and says, "She is probably right. I came to this country when I was fourteen, your Dr. Bahri when he was twelve. If we had stayed in our country, we would have been as your friend says. It is impossible to escape. It is all around you, this all things for the man, women here to serve." His beard and sideburns are sprinkled with gray. "My friend," I tell him, "would like a man in her life. Are you married?" He smiles and says, "I am." Happily? I wonder but don't ask, because, after all, this is our first meeting. However, the look on his face, the ease with which he touches my shoulder, my foot—covered up—suggests a good marriage, a good profession, a good man.

In the endoscopy room, just before I slip under the valium, I say to the RN, "Ah, these Persian men, aren't they handsome?" She answers, "And they are so very nice." Outside this room I see Ardalan striding down the hall. From the back, his robes flowing, he looks like a sheik in the desert. He turns and gives me a thumbs-up, and I disappear into semiconsciousness. Dr. Bahri is at my side. Here I am in their tent, drugged up, half-clothed, and vulnerable to their every command. Who would have thought a colonoscopy could be so wonderful.

AND WHAT OF Persian women? I ask them, "Do you think the younger generation of men is an improvement over the men of your generation?" They are thoughtful, then nod in definite agreement. The good things of marriage and husbands have passed them by, they tell me. They believe themselves too old for the good young men of today and too young for the traditions into which they were born. They are so admirable, these women. With courage, intelligence, and determination, in a new world where the rules, if not entirely absent, were close to invisible, where guidance came, if at all, from an uncle, a sister, or a brother, or from each other, they built new lives for themselves and their children. Unaccompanied women now, they—and I—are desirous of the company of men. "I just want to rest near him. His arms around me."

Here with a little Bread beneath the Bough
A flask of Wine, a Book of Verse—and Thou
Beside me singing in the Wilderness—
O Wilderness were Paradise enow!
—from *The Rubaiyat of Omar Khayyam**

As for me, I am captured and captivated by both Persian men and Persian women. Both sexes have a force that is visceral, in the presence of which I feel bound to do their will. Always when I leave these women, I feel guilty, as if I have failed to do what they wished me to do. Zoreh, the most outspoken, tells me outright she would like to find a man; implied is her hope that I might find her one. The other women are silent, but I sense that Zoreh speaks for them, too. I have failed them. However, I am a good listener and I am a writer. And they know it. It is very possible they want me to hear their stories and write them down and send them out to the larger world. I am happy to oblige.

*Translated from the Farsi by Edward Fitzgerald, 1859

oh, dear, what can the matter be?

He promised to buy me a pretty blue ribbon
To tie up my bonny brown hair.

—a song

My Iranian women friends are lonely for the attentions of men. I'm not doing all that well either. I continue to maintain, during the question-and-answer sessions that accompany my readings and signings, that it is possible to love more than one man at a time, that I do in fact love more than one man, that I would never turn monogamous because I would have to give up too much, like Graham. Nods all around. I don't go into details, like Graham got married but he loves me anyway, though probably we will never make love again in a bed, only over the telephone. I do admit to my audience that I am having a hell of a time loving more than one man at a time when the men I love live so far away! So well, yes, of course, I am open to meeting someone here, someone within reach of me and me of him, but no matter the letters and phone calls that arrive almost daily from men "only an hour's drive from you" or "a few blocks away" (scary), I just don't find anyone interesting enough to change out of my sweatshirt for, except that man at my reading with the great ass who didn't even get in line, who took one look and took off, oh well. I look with greater and greater interest at the pocket rocket that came in the mail—"to keep you company until we can meet." It's hidden in my drawer, for heaven's sake. On the other hand, it's not in the wastebasket. A pocket rocket in the hand is worth how many you-know-whats in the bush. However, all is not lost. Just in the nick of time, London calls. I am wanted there to do publicity for the book. Do I think it over? Do I weigh the pros and cons of such a trip? No. I ask one question: Who's paying? And since it's my publisher, off I go. Romance and adventure are right around the corner. Because, as it happens, Barrett will be in London at the very same time.

We have met once—in New York—a natural next step after exchanging many, many letters. His first letter came in answer to my ad in *The New York Review.* I did not answer it. His next arrived on the heels of Alex Witchel's article on me in *The New York Times.* His letter began, *"I'm one of those who answered your delicious ad, so I can't resist asking a most personal question: Why didn't I make the cut?"* The punctuation of that sentence alone—capitals and commas completely correct, assured, comfortable in their places as accompaniments to and clarifiers of thought, never overriding content—blew out my brains and replaced them, once again, with curiosity. And hell, I couldn't resist him. However, judgment—a small piece—remained intact, and when I wrote him—of course I wrote him—I told him why I had not answered his very first letter. *"You were married."* And he wrote back, *"I'm not anymore."* And so we began.

Barrett is, despite his glamorous international life, seriously East Coast. Born and bred in Connecticut, he will make all kinds of slams at the West Coast, particularly at California, which, *"while beautiful to look at, soaks up every bit of intellectual energy before extended thought can attach itself to a human person residing out there wherever it is you live."* He writes me this before we have met and is careful to append, *"None of this applies to you, my dear, for of course, your wonderful book is a demonstration of a remarkable mind and glorious spirit."* Omigoodness, what a wonderful thing to say!

It helped, of course, that when he wasn't in Paris or Rome or Vienna, he lived in New York. Everything about him and his life—he dabbled in finance "subsidized by a fair-sized family trust"—and everything he wrote made him so goddam glamorous. I didn't have the clothes for that or for him. I didn't even know where, if I had the money, I would go to buy clothes for having even lunch, let alone dinner! As surely you know, if you are a woman of a certain age, most clothing stores do not offer departments for Women with Breasts or Ladies with Bellies, and the designer Eileen Simpson, bless her heart, can do only so much. It would be best, I decided, if Barrett and I never met. And then he wrote me something about my photograph in *The New York Times,* the one in which I am wearing that now oft-remarked-upon red jacket. Punctuation as perfect as ever—you could tell he was born with a sense of it—he wrote about the photograph: *"The* Times *has displayed you in a most refreshing manner. Red is your colour."* He spelled "color" the British way! Is that cool? Am I seducible?

I had never known a rich man, one who was also so finely educated (Harvard and the London School of Economics), so well traveled (see above), and so, apparently, fond of me, at least from a distance. We wrote each other every day—fountain pen and ink on real stationery, his monogrammed for real. I knew because my grandmother had showed me how to tell if the paper was monogrammed or just printed, and this was the former—he had his own plate!

He started out with flattery: *"Your book handles earthquake events in your life with a lovely delicacy and a fine self-deprecating humor."* Wouldn't you write back?

His letters went on to discussions of the Greeks: *"Creon and our president are one and the same: 'Antigone did wrong and you're either with me or against me.' Dangerous for everyone when the leader thinks thusly."*

I rarely disagreed with him, except for the fun of disagreeing with him, so I wrote, *"Creon is responsible for law and order, for keep-*

ing rebellious pieties from infecting his kingdom; how else, then, could he deal with Antigone?"

And he wrote, *"He could have let her be rescued by his son and sent them both to live in the hills with the shepherds. That, as you no doubt know, is another version of the story."*

No, I didn't know. But I did now. This man was a treat, just a treat. And so I decided we should meet. I wrote him I was going to New York. I decided to wear my red jacket.

Why am I doing this? Haven't I had enough? Am I just so god-dam vulnerable to flattery from an articulate man that I will walk, even run, up the garden path? In one of Barrett's letters, he asks where the men in my California are. *"Aren't they coming out of the woodwork? Surely, your book has been read there by men who want to meet you; yet, from your letters, you seem not to have found companionship."*

He's right, I have not found companionship of any sort from any man within driving distance of my cottage. It's not that I am still stunned by all the life in and around New York, though I suppose I ought to be. On the contrary, I am fully aware of the cost, financial and emotional, of carrying on romances with men three thousand miles away. How long can I sit around and recall Graham's passion and Sidney's gentle affection and John's prowess? Although they are still part of my life, they are so very far away, and despite letters and e-mail and phone calls, I can't *feel* them. I am as desirous of touch as when I wrote the infamous ad, and oh lord, I have turned seventy! Cast your eyes around the room, Jane. Empty.

There is, of course, the possibility that I don't want a man in the room, or even next door, that I prefer long distance to up close and personal, that I prefer a life uncluttered by a man on my doorstep. Maybe I was just out to prove something, that I could be attractive to men or that I could love 'em and leave 'em or . . . Well, okay, what I hoped for was that I could be like a man or like the men I had read about: people who had sex without consequences, who had no intention of being faithful to one woman, who could have a fine time making love and not worry about it in the morning, who had multiple partners at their beck and call. If that is so, I am working on failure: I worry like hell the morning after about did he like me, will he do it again? I attach myself deeply to every man I sleep with. For me there is no such thing as casual sex, though, if you want my honest opinion, I don't think sex is casual for anyone, though they may wish it to be. I think "casual sex" is a term made up by someone who had bad sex and didn't want to think about it, who just wanted to dismiss it from memory.

Casual or not, in my sex life over the past several years—currently suffering an unwelcome hiatus—I came close to becoming this fictive cool dude only in that I had not been faithful to one man. And by god, I had no intention now of becoming so. Actually, come to think of it, to whom would I be faithful? Sidney has become a friend, not a lover, John is searching hard for a woman who lives within driving distance of his cabin, and Graham, my beloved Graham, is about to turn thirty-six in the company of his child-bride, age thirty-three. Let's face it: My lovers are getting on with their lives, and not one of them has asked me to move to New York, no one has gotten down on bended knee to beg me to share his life, and truth be told, if anyone had asked, even Robert, I would have said no. I did not want to move three thousand miles from my son and his fear of flying and from my newly born granddaughter. Still, I don't want my adventures to end, not just yet; I don't want to settle for the friendship of only three intriguing and wonderful men. So, given the apparent absence of such men in the entirety that is California, I think, What the hell, it's only lunch.

But it isn't. It's lunch all right, but never such a lunch have I had in such a place as Barrett took me. It's lunch at his club.

I am a club virgin. In my growing-up days my parents belonged to the country club so they could play golf, and sometimes they hauled me along, not to play golf, for heaven's sake, but to . . . I don't know. I suspect they wanted me to hang out by the pool where similarly clubbed kids gathered, but I never did, because I was ashamed of how I looked. I never wanted those kids to see me in a bathing suit, mine being the only one with a skirt designed to hide my beefy thighs, and abnormally wide shoulder straps to hold up my way-too-early breasts. So mostly I sat in the car with a book or drank a lot of Cokes in the 19th Hole until my parents came to drink their own drinks. So that doesn't really count. My life after that never called for club-joining, since I never learned to play golf at all or tennis very well, and since I had no idea what else went on at clubs and no interest in finding out. In college I belonged to that sorority, which, if you want to get picky, could be called a club. At the end of my junior year, after the political science department at Michigan finished turning me into a socialist, I decided my sorority was something to be ashamed of, and I spent my senior year, not moving out, as I would have done had my principles been genuine, but staying on in my sorority house and making fun of it. Shame on me. And about to be deflowered at last, I had no idea what I was in for.

I scarcely notice the small man pacing the floor of the vast and marbled lobby. I should have worn a dress. But then there he is, here he comes, smiling warmly and, dare I say, wetly. "We meet at last," he says, and I smile a smile that will occupy my entire face for the rest of the afternoon. Smiling is better than ogling this incredible building, this incredible dining room. Smiling is better than talking, which I seem to have forgotten how to do. No matter. Barrett talks. And I watch. He must be of Scottish ancestry. That would account for the redness of his face and hair, which, probably, there used to be a lot of. He talks and talks some more. I am a champion listener; I can appear to be listening when I'm not, and I'm not—in this incredible dining room that opens onto a library with books up and down the walls and comfortable chairs to read them in. MEMBERS ONLY, reads a small brass plate bolted onto one of the columns. Do they take women? I am assured they do. This is a totally classy place.

Barrett points out a few illustrious people who have come to lunch. And then my cell phone rings. It never rings, so I never think to turn it off, just leave it there at the bottom of my purse, which it seems I cannot get to, for the phone continues to ring. The headwaiter appears quickly, and before he can cut off my hand, I rise and follow him into the marble foyer, mumbling my apologies as I go. He consoles me politely in French.

Back at the table I order a cheeseburger with mayonnaise, take a look at Barrett's face, and switch to crab cakes avec un sauvignon blanc, s'il vous plaît. "You're wearing your red jacket," Barrett says. He is enamored of me because of my book. He has read it and fancies himself in love. Watch out. Apparently he skipped the part where I warned readers against falling in love with writers, where I argued that it is unfair to hold the person to the standards of her writing, that writers can revise themselves as people cannot, that the real person is sure to disappoint. However, from the look on his face he is not disappointed, not yet anyway. He says, "Have you noticed what I'm wearing?"

No, I had not, but I am touched when he explains. "I'm wearing all Brooks Brothers because you say in your book you like that kind of men's clothing." Indeed, he's spanking new in a blue blazer with gold buttons, a rep tie and button-down shirt, gray trousers below. In his enthusiasm he is winning me over. Barrett is like the bright little boy eager to please the teacher, the kid whose hand is always up and who usually has the right answer, who can be an example to the class, a help to the teacher, and an utter distraction to everyone. By the end of the crab cakes, Barrett is endearing and exhausting. And I am flattered that such a fascinating man wishes me for a friend. On the street, Barrett puts me into the taxi and says, "I adore you." Safe and alone in the backseat, I breathe a sigh of relief. Wonder of wonders, while I am close to cherishing his friendship, I do not want to sleep with this quite charming man. I am not a slut, after all. Instead, I am happy, because this very night I am going to cook for Graham.

And I do. I have borrowed a friend's apartment, she having escaped to the country for the weekend. Barrett has taken up more time than I had expected, so I have not had a chance to grocery shop, or even to find a grocery store. In California greengrocers thrive on every corner, organic foods line the shelves of groceries large and small; farmers' markets clog the streets; Whole Foods is everywhere, grains and fruits and berries spill from baskets, fresh fish and aged cheese and olives of every size, shape, and taste are to be had for the asking and a sizable amount of cash. Where the hell do New Yorkers buy their food? They don't. Well, they do, but they buy it at the deli. Or they go out. Graham and I are going to stay in if I have anything to say about it. So . . .

I figure that at thirty-six Graham does not worry about (1) cholesterol, (2) hypertension, (3) arteriosclerosis, (4) gastric occlusions. So I buy meat and potatoes at the deli, likewise a salad, and—I should be ashamed—a little apple pie. Now, I happen to make the most sensational pies of anyone in this day and age still making pies. My crust is to die for, my filling to live for. My pies are auctioned off at charity affairs. Rich ladies pay me to bake pies and smuggle them into their kitchens during their dinner parties, where they will pass them off as their own. Unaware of my expertise, New York is not supporting my artistry: My friend's kitchen is too small for a pastry board; neither does it hold a rolling pin, and the grocery stores must all be in Queens. So Graham will have to forgive me for going native. He does, even raving over the pie, though only out of ignorance of what a pie made by a true artist tastes like. Poor fellow.

We have a vertical evening, Graham and I. By the end of it I am close to screaming. Jesus, there he sits over there on the couch— How come the living room is so large?—*not* patting the cushion next to him but smiling over at me sitting stiffly in the chair. He is more wonderful than ever to look at—his eyelashes are longer, his nose slimmer, his lips plum-perfect—and to listen to: He is full of complaints about John Milton's poetry; he brims with admiration for London's Exposition of 1849; he is reverential toward Proust, nastily critical of Kafka, scornful of Hemingway, affectionate toward Turgenev. I feast on my young man. But I never get to dessert. Without ever mentioning his wife, he has made it clear that infidelity, at least on this night, is not on his menu. At the door he kisses me and says, "This evening was good for us; it proves we can transcend the carnal." WHY? I want to scream.

Graham takes his leave, and I take a cold shower. It is time to get sensible, to stop this churning inside whenever I think of him. It is time to give up hope that this wonderful man and I will ever again share the horizontal. It is time for me to transcend the carnal. But I don't: Alone in my lonely single bed I imagine that the next time will be different, I tell myself that he was tired after a long day's work; I am utterly unconvincing. An evening with him and at the same time without him has taken its toll, and my tears drench my friend's pillow and dampen the blanket United Airlines lends me on my return flight.

Barrett, not one to avoid the carnal, remains smitten and, after I return to Berkeley, writes an e-mail that, written by hand, would have set the stationery on fire. It makes me blush, his description of a position he learned in Nepal, in which I'm supposed to kneel with my legs parallel to his chest and then he can fondle—Well, I'm not doing that. First of all, I have glass knees, so the kneeling part is out because even on a soft mattress I can hear them crunch. Second, there I'd be fully frontally naked, no pillow, no nightie. Well, maybe if it were dark. Barrett assures me that I could then control when and how deeply he would enter me. He intends his description to arouse me, I suppose—at least to interest me. But it doesn't. I don't want to do it.

I write him my truth: *"I live three thousand miles away and will not . . . cannot begin another long-distance relationship. I am emotionally stretched to the limit and now am stuck with loving three men who are far, far away. None of them is you, and I will not risk another sadness. I like writing to you; I like reading what you write to me, but I must not add the*

other dimension which seems to be so important to you. I understand if you
choose not to continue this correspondence."

He chooses to continue. And on and on we go. His e-mails are
frequent and ardent, full of advice about writing and publishing
(sound), descriptions of his house in Paris (yum), compliments to
me (I blush). He signs them "A kiss in the night . . ." and *"Abrazos
y bezos . . ."* and *"Âme soeur."* Jesus.

I don't know why I don't just tell him the truth, that I do not
want to sleep with him. I should want to, I suppose. He's certainly
willing and appears able. Maybe it's just chemistry. Maybe, just
maybe, I've had enough sex. Maybe, after all this time, I'm calm-
ing down. Celibacy could be kind of restful if I could keep the
memory of Graham at bay. In any case I sit atop the horns of a
dilemma (a fun place to be sometimes): I do not want to make love
with this man, but I do not want to lose his friendship. And here
comes an e-mail inviting himself to California, to Big Sur, to a
long, slow drive down the coast. This is not good.

Fortunately my book has created something of a stir in London,
and my publisher flies me to the city that will give New York a
run for its money in my affections. Barrett is in Paris. Shall I tell
him my travel plans? If trouble does not find me, I tend to go
looking for it. I fancy myself in control. I truly believe I can have
exactly what I want: friendship sans sex. I am fooling myself, because Barrett plus me in London equals trouble; how else to read
his e-mails but as invitations, increasingly impassioned, to make
love. And well, okay, I am flattered. It's nice that a rich and successful man seems to adore me. I like it. I don't want it to end. I
write to him the times and the places of my travel. *"I shall be with
you soon,"* he breathes into my e-mail.

We have a wonderful time in London. The museums, the theatre—Barrett knows tons about everything, and as long as it's
daylight, I am as happy as I've ever been. We dine at his club, even
grander than his club in New York! While Barrett goes into an
antechamber where he will put on a tie beneath his jacket, I stroll

to the small bar at the far end of the oak-paneled room—big, big room; very, very quiet. The man in a stiff white jacket behind the bar bows stiffly and says, "Good evening." I nod and say, "Good evening." Interrupting the silence that ensues, I say, "May I have a sauvignon blanc, please?" And he says, "Are you a member, madame?" and I say, "No, but I'm with a member who will be here shortly." And he says, "Then we'll just have to wait, won't we."

The food is good. We read all the newspapers in the world in the book-lined room, in chairs with footstools and little tables on which white-coated waiters set a little port or perhaps a flute of champagne. Nobody is smoking. How about that? And this is London, too, where Californians go to smoke. Barrett and I, having years before transcended the need for tobacco, are off to the theatre. It is Stoppard, his *Jumpers*. On our walk to the theatre, across Waterloo Bridge (my second favorite movie—though I recommend the 1931 original with Mae Clarke), I can see how Vivien Leigh (in the 1940 remake) would have been able to jump from it had not Robert Taylor stopped her. The lights from all the other bridges brighten the sky and my mood, and Barrett says, "I want to give you a present. I adore you." Now look, I want to tell him, I am seventy years old and far from adorable. But I don't because he is indeed smitten, and I must admit that his mind is so quick and so filled with information and learning and wit that I lose about ten years and talk right back at him. "You can buy me a house," I say. My goodness, what hemming and hawing, and finally, "It's a bit beyond my capacity at the moment," he says. Drat.

At intermission I tell him, "I love Stoppard but not *Jumpers*."

"How can you not love a play about logical positivism?" he asks.

"Logical positivism does not a play make. He should've just written a book."

"It's a play about something," he says, "which is more than you can say about most contemporary theatre."

I agree. "However, would you agree that *Jumpers* is not Stoppard's best."

"It's an early play, 1972."

"So we agree."

"Of course we do; I want to make love to you. I want to give you a night you'll never forget."

"No," I say, "you want to give yourself a night you'll never forget."

"That, too."

If I didn't want to sleep with him, why did I agree to stay with him at his club? Well, one good reason is that I am off my publisher's grid. That is, my publicity duties are over and done with, and I am my own financial advisor and, as such, I tell myself I can't afford London hotel prices, which is true. So what is a fully adult woman to do? Go home. Had I been then—or ever—fully adult, that's what I would have done. Instead I accepted Barrett's offer, and now it's time for him to collect. The play is over, nobody in it ends up happy, and there is only one thing left for me to do: get drunk.

For the first time in my life the word "nightcap" does not sound dated, like something out of Noël Coward; for the first time it is useful, as in when I say, "Shall we stop somewhere for a nightcap?" We do, and now that I'm used to the word, I say, as we draw nearer his club, "How about a little nightcap?" There we are at his club, the stiff-coated man still behind the bar and, "Why not a nightcap?" And another. With each succeeding nightcap, I get soberer. Instead of the interior dullness I'd hoped for, instead of unconsciousness, I am alert, steady on my feet. Hell, I could drive. And up we go to Barrett's room.

Inside the room, Barrett in silk dressing gown, me still fully clothed, I think, Why not? Sleeping with me can't be that big a deal. Why am I fussing as if it is? I do my lightning-flash disrobing, slide beneath the covers, and here he comes on top of me. Jesus, I hate this, and after a decent interval I claim orgasm, and soon after, thank god, so does he. "My favorite time to make love," he murmurs into my hair, "is in the morning." Jesus Christ, he's going to want to do it again.

In the morning I moan and groan over the hangover I do not have. Barrett isn't feeling tip-top himself so I am spared. He says, "You like my body, I like your body, so we'll do this again."

At last my dilemma is over. No, we will not do this. I feel like shit. We say good-bye; Barrett goes back to Paris and I go home to California. Barrett writes and I don't write back. Soon all is silence.

I stayed too long at the fair, didn't I.

FROM THE SAFETY of my desk I write to my friend Lisle: *"Did you ever sleep with someone you didn't want to sleep with?"* She answers immediately, *"Yes, my husband. For ten years. Any cock in a storm."*

Men are probably different, so I write to Graham the same question. He replies, *"Yes, once. She wanted it so badly."*

I ask John. His reply: *"I never didn't want to."*

I tell all this to my friend Jenny, who has just turned forty and so must be smarter than I in matters of this sort. I explain that I felt I had to. She answers quickly: "No, you didn't. You did not have to do that." It is not a reprimand, she does not explain, but I feel she is right. Yet I am a part of my history, part of the books I have read, books in which women marry out of the need for economic survival, and submit to the desires of their husbands in payment for social acceptance and financial security. A woman alone lived in great danger. Jane Austen's Elizabeth and Darcy, two fine and beautiful people united in love at last, are fantasy; more real is Charlotte, Elizabeth's best friend, "who accepted [the ridiculous Mr. Collins] solely from the pure and disinterested desire of an establishment . . ." And even Elizabeth's mother is more real, addled as who wouldn't be, giving birth to five daughters, one after another, in short order, by way of a husband who ridicules her for the silly woman she has become?

Edith Wharton, in her novels of New York, showed us what happens to women who do not have the sense to marry and stay married, who are foolish and independent and prideful: They die as does Henry James's Daisy Miller, Tolstoy's Anna Karenina, and Flaubert's Emma Bovary. Of all these writers only Mrs. Wharton uses the word "money," and frequently, too. Behind Tolstoy's Anna and her icy-cold count of a husband, behind Eliot's Dorothea and the dreadful Casaubon in *Middlemarch,* and behind the beauteous Gwendolen and the sadistic and ironically named Grandcourt in *Daniel Deronda* is the matter of money. By the turn of the century, when Wharton, clear-eyed and imperious, writes about American society, she puts money where it really is: up front. Young women of social position are for sale and so are bought by men unworthy of them, men who by virtue of marriage exercise conjugal rights regardless of the feelings of their wives.

But then comes Ibsen, who, with the exception of Hedda Gabler, keeps his women alive. His heroine Nora leaves her husband and family, casts aside the safety net of her marriage, gathers up her pride and honor and goes . . . where? Ibsen doesn't tell us, but wherever it is, Nora is not going to have it easy. Look at the benighted Mrs. Linde, an old friend of Nora's: Husbandless, bedraggled, and poor, she serves as a warning to women everywhere.

Yet come on, Jane, you cannot blame history—growing up in the forties and fifties. Well, maybe a little. We weren't called the Silent Generation for nothing. And you can't blame your lifelong absorption in nineteenth-century literature. Well, maybe a little. Look at what literature did to Emma Bovary. And you can't blame your mother, who did her best to bring you up a lady, who wanted you to marry someone who would give you the life she had led you to expect. "What if I married a Negro?" I asked my mother one day when she was showing me how to miter the corners of sheets.

"Marriage is difficult enough without the added problems a marriage of that sort would bring with it." Made sense to me.

But the fact is that Barrett, unlike nineteenth-century fictional men, in his desire to bed me did not offer security of any kind. The fact is that I was not looking for social correctness by way of a man. The fact is that I was financially independent, past childbearing, and unencumbered by those things nineteenth-century women had to do. It was myself I was not free of. I was determined in this day and age of equality between men and women to prove to myself that I could be as I assumed men were: free of sexual guilt, free of the need for fidelity, free of jealousy and envy, free of the need for love. I wanted to have sex with a man I liked. Here he was. I liked him. He was nice to me. He would help me prove that I had risen beyond—transcended, if you will—the pettiness of female neediness. I wanted to be like John, who said, "I never didn't want to." Never not wanting to would free me from wanting to love and be loved, from wanting someone who stayed, maybe even forever, to help me bear the cruelty of life. Besides, I had been taught to be a nice girl, to be grateful to men who were nice to me, and now, in the twenty-first century, offering this man whatever pleasure he might receive from sleeping with me seemed the liberated thing to do. At seventy, I didn't have all that much time to get liberated. This was no time to get fussy.

Back home once again, I go round the corner to my neighborhood movie palace to see *Gloomy Sunday.* In it the beautiful heroine agrees to have sex with the Nazi officer, who in return promises to save her lover from Auschwitz. After the officer finishes with her, she rises from the bed, her loathing of him and of what she has been a party to so palpable as to reach into the far corners of the movie house. But it is clear that she has lost none of her integrity, nothing of herself, in the ugly encounter, not even when she discovers the officer's betrayal of her and her lover. I cannot get the movie out of my mind, and of course I see that in the light of her sacrifice my experience pales in significance; worse, I had no such excuse. I had no good reason to pretend to Barrett an enthusiasm I did not feel, to let him do with my privacy what he wished, to remind myself again and again that this was, after all, just casual sex. I didn't have casual sex, I had bad sex. I had sex I didn't want to have. There is nothing as scuzzy as lying back and letting a man go about his business, unless it's letting him go about his business and pretending you like it. Somewhere along the way I lost the control I thought I had and gave it all to Barrett, forfeiting a friendship and my own integrity as I did. What the hell, I thought, sleeping with me can't be that big a deal. But it was. So don't give yourself away. Keep some for yourself. That's not bad advice. I plan to take it.

"Misunderstanding and separation are the natural conditions of man," writes Katherine Ann Porter. Here we are, our whole lives, searching for understanding and connection, which in turn results in misunderstanding and separation. Round and round we go. What a struggle, and how brave—and foolish—we are to keep at it.

the 92nd street y:
something for everyone

And learn upon these narrow beds
To sleep in spite of sea

—from ARCHIBALD MACLEISH'S "Seafarer"

ohn phones from his woodsy hideout. "I've taken your lesson to heart," he says. "I've placed an ad in *The New York Review.*" I race to the library to scour the ads: Which one is John's? He is a very, very good writer, so I cannot identify any of the ads as his because clearly he does not want me to. Several of them specify the Boston area, which is John's bailiwick, sort of; they are well written; any one of them could be his. The next time he calls, he says, "Good lord, I don't know if I can handle this. I've already got more than fifty letters. You would be amazed at how many women have convinced themselves that Cleveland and Saint Louis and Chicago are in the "Boston area," and are willing to travel huge distances to get to it." No, I wouldn't be amazed. I am the last person who would be amazed at a woman's eagerness to take extreme measures to have sex with a man she might like. And, knowing John, he would be worth the trip.

Of course, I am minutely jealous. At seventy-two John shows

no signs of a slowdown: He is perfectly happy to make love with the lights off; on is fine, too; clothed or not; summer, winter, or fall; springtime, too. During one of my visits to his lair—unclothed, springtime, lights off—I ask him why he had answered my ad. Another nice thing about John is that after the deed is done he does not roll over and go to sleep. So he plumps the pillows up under our heads and answers my question with alacrity. "Three reasons," he says. "First, I thought the sex would be good. Second, there were no strings attached. Third, the pillow talk promised to be terrific." He got all the right answers! So why aren't I enough? "You are plenty," he explains, "just not close enough. You're not going to move here and I'm not going to move there, so . . ." Just like me. He wants the same thing I want: a life made richer by another person or persons more easily accessible, though as yet undiscovered. He wants to have a lot of sex with a woman he likes who does not live on the opposite side of the country. While I understand completely, I fear for the future of my sex life: Given John's charms in and out of the bedroom, he will have no trouble finding the woman he wants—some intelligent, attractive, cultured, independent female who asks of him only one thing: fidelity. Hello, Ms. X; good-bye, Jane.

The geography of my love life seems to be shrinking. But the interest in my love life is expanding: People all over the country want to know how to do it, how to inspire one's life with the juices of desire. Even the 92nd Street Y in New York City wonders. They call me up and invite me over. Would it be possible for me to come to New York? You betcha. Finally I am going to play the Palace.

The 92nd Street Y is a fabled New York institution. Founded in 1874 for the purposes of bringing young Hebrew men together, it has grown. Now, in one way or another, it addresses everything missing from your life. Physically unfit? Sign up for Pumping the Prime or Flamenco. Sexually deprived? Sign up for Moving from Serial Dating to Lasting Love or How to Make Anyone Fall Madly in Love with You! Politically ignorant? Go listen to David Brooks or Maureen Dowd or Bill Moyers. Culturally starved? There's Dick Hyman on piano, Yo-Yo Ma on cello; there's drawing at the Met, collage on the East Side, Kabbalah on the West Side, gallery tours all round the town.

For me it is the writers who have read their work at the 92nd Street Y that make it magical: Dylan Thomas, T. S. Eliot, W. H. Auden, Langston Hughes, and now Joyce Carol Oates, and . . . Yes, I could go on. At the 92nd Street Y, I will sit on the shoulders of giants. Or crouch in their shadows, for I have not been asked to speak as a writer; I have been invited to share the stage with three other women over fifty who, so thinks the Y, have stored up enough liveliness to get them through old age. We are empaneled in the catalogue as Juicy Living after Fifty. The room is full.

The panelists are: a psychoanalyst who has written many books about the goddess in us and who will suggest to the audience of almost all women hovering over fifty and beyond that they create a circle of women and light a candle for those who cannot join them; a well-regarded journalist who, after detailing her long and wonderful marriage, will tell everybody to go on long walks and don't forget to vote; and, on my right, a onetime model, scorned by the beauty industry while still in her thirties, who will tell us do not despair, age will bring tolerance and an appreciation of things like her teenage son's hip-hop music. At this I can no longer remain silent. I say to her, "When you reach seventy, you don't have to listen to that junk." As for the rest of the advice, "Don't forget to vote" seems the most useful. I am loath to add to all this nonsense, but finally I do, more out of frustration than anything else: "Do something hard." Had I been in the audience, I would have asked for my money back.

Backstage I sit at a table and sign books. I am surprised when two lovely young women, in their late thirties perhaps, hand me books for signing. The woman with light hair says, "You're the one we came to hear. I'm recently divorced and my friend here is newly widowed." Oh, my. It is not the New York winter that has chased the color from their cheeks; it is grief. "We were wondering what to do with our lives."

I am stumped. If I were braver, I would get up and put my arms around them both; maybe our very own circle of women would help ease the despair that is sucking the life out of them. But I am not brave, and besides, I sense they are here not to be hugged but for some real-life advice. Banality to the rescue: "Have you thought of going online?" I ask, and hate myself as I do. How can I suggest this, knowing as I do the disappointments, even the dangers, that await the online naïf—the veteran, too? I think back to Hannah and Genevieve and Tanya and their trials and tribulations, though all three of them came out all right in the end; nobody got murdered, not that I know of. But what am I to say here and now? These lovely young women have left their houses on a search for something to *do.* My suggestion back in the hall—"Do something hard"—was enough to bring them backstage. Well, going online can be hard, that's for sure. I don't say any of this. They do not look eager for a lecture, however brief, on the complications of Internet dating.

"I am not the one who wanted the divorce," says the light-haired woman. "I'm not sure I'm up to that sort of thing. Actually," she bursts out, "I'm still in love with my husband." The brown-haired woman, circles so deep and dark beneath her eyes, says, "My children are eight and ten, so dating would be difficult, and dating strangers, well . . ." They look at me expectantly as I murmur something inept and useless about time and how the right time will come along, and of course they look disappointed, and I stammer out something having to do with saving one's own life, and dissolve into "Thank you for coming." They thank me for coming and wander into the night, their shoulders a-droop on their slim young bodies.

Sometimes just the right words come in the dead of night, when they are no longer of use to anyone, when the time and the people have passed you by and all that is left is "Darn, why didn't I think of that then?" But later that night no such words come to me, only the wish that I had been able to summon them, whatever they might have been. For surely it is language that soothes, that heals the wounds of experience. But I remained mute, I had run out of words. There I sat, in my red jacket, looking up at these sweet young women through my bifocals, silence gaining on, and finally vanquishing, me—the writer, the one who is supposed to have words for any occasion. What a failure. And yet, in the silence of the long night to come, as I imagine these women in their grief, they are surrounded by words from family, from friends, words of consolation, of sympathy, of advice. It is likely that by the time they got themselves to the 92nd Street Y, they were not in need of words; they had heard just about enough, thank you. Maybe what they needed was just to look at me, to verify for themselves that life is a renewable resource and will not desert them forever, just for a little while.

My front yard is her backyard, and on it, in my absence, there has appeared a serious contraption that looks like a teepee without its cover. One pole of the tripod is red, one is yellow, and one is purple, and on the yellow pole are little designs, like Navajo graffiti, painted in orange. From the apex of the teepee two really strong-looking rubber bands hang down, and hooked onto the ends of the bands are slings, which are red and will hold the legs of my landlady when the baby decides to come. When it comes time, she will push hard, and the baby will drop onto the grass, I guess. The baby is late. It was supposed to come last Tuesday and here it is Sunday, and my poor landlady is kind of fraught, now that even the midwife has gone home. My suspicion is that the baby peeked out, saw this contraption, and decided the hell with it, it was going to stay inside where it was safe. Or it could have gotten pissed off at the flute playing on the deck overlooking its backyard/my front yard. "Greensleeves" over and over accompanied by a lot of swaying of the flutist. She's gone now, too. That leaves the grandmother-to-be and a sister who does the dishes. The baby's father had to go back to work. Uh-oh, here comes a guitar. Now it's "Moon River."

So I say yes to the invitation from an instructor in women's psychology at a nearby community college. Anything to get out of my front yard, where I want to stand and yell up at the birthing room that for god's sake, the hospital is two blocks away, and go there!

The invitation from the college offers me the opportunity to teach the class for a day. Teach what? I have nothing whatsoever to say about the psychology of women, don't think much about it, mostly don't care. Long ago my mother instilled in me a disdain for women. All their talk about food and babies and lotions and laundry bored her; she preferred the company of men, where she could talk about what she truly loved: sports. Women were silly, always complaining about something: cramps, husbands, their weight, recipes gone awry. As I grew up, I preferred the company of my younger brother and his friends and ignored their sighs of resignation as I tagged along behind them when they went out into the night to commit their adolescent skulduggery. They were a pack of trouble.

My favorite trick of theirs involved cars and took place in the days before freeways, when the fear was manageable, not amplified and magnified beyond our control by Hollywood and its special effects. Still too young for drivers' licenses, the boys terrified those who weren't. Uninvited, I tagged along ignoring their protests, which, by the time we reached the road, would dwindle to nothing, for they knew I was a good sport, for a girl, and would not get in their way or rat on them. They divided themselves into two groups, one group on the right side of the road, one on the left. They stood one behind the other—I hid behind a tree—waiting for a car to shine its headlights on them. When it did, the boys shouted, "Pull!" and made as if they were pulling a rope tight across the road just at the level of the headlights. Cars screeched to a halt, drivers yelled or gasped; we ran away laughing at our—okay, their—boldness. At fifteen I was too old for this, but I preferred tagging after twelve-year-old terrorists to painting my toenails and wadding my hair up in pin curls.

Today, thanks to the words and deeds of Kate Millett, Betty Friedan, Germaine Greer, Gloria Steinem, Helen Gurley Brown, and others, I consider myself a feminist—although Catharine MacKinnon makes me nervous and Andrea Dworkin makes me mad, though I did not wish her dead, which she is. Still, I did indeed get liberated and am now a woman who believes that we should receive equal pay for equal work and respectful attention to our humanity. On one hand I remain suspicious of college courses and departments called "women's studies," fearing—needlessly, I hope—that male-bashing is part of the curriculum, that literature and life will be explored through too narrow a lens. On the other hand, today I admire women who cook, sympathize with women who have cramps, and paint my toenails whenever I feel like bending down there. Still, I don't know a damn thing about women's psychology.

Sensing my hesitation during our phone conversation, the instructor suggests I talk about the double standard and aging. I don't want to do that either. I am asked all the time to pontificate on sex after sixty—hell, I just got back from presenting myself as a juicy liver over fifty—and at a recent conference of women writers someone actually demanded, "Tell me something cosmic." I suppose I could make up something about almost anything, except maybe cosmic, but I would feel a charlatan, and besides, I don't find those topics very interesting. What I do find interesting is engaging people in conversation about topics not usually confronted in the open air of the classroom, topics like sex: like doing it, like talking about it, like arguing about it, like laughing about it. I maintained for most of my teaching career that the more incendiary the topic, the more certainly it belongs in the classroom, where the clean, clear wind of reason can cool it. And yet, do I really want to go way out there where these kids could very well ridicule me, if not worse?

The instructor tells me on the phone, "I've included your book in the Collateral Reading List. Our bookstore will be fully stocked." My gosh, she's selling my book for me. Okay, I'll go.

In the intervening weeks I receive maps and instructions on how to get there and where to park, the latter being a matter of such significance that ominous consequences will befall me should I do it wrong. And then, one week before I am to journey eastward, the instructor's e-mail announces that when she issued the invitation and placed the book on her reading list, she *had not read the book.* Now she had. *"I am apprehensive about our meeting next week,"* she writes. *"Please know that my students are diverse in ethnicity, religion, and culture."* And attention span, I bet. She ends with, *"Please try not to offend anyone."*

I fire off an offended e-mail offering not to show up at all, and reminding her that those students who had read the book would already be offended—or not—and that so far as I am concerned, offending people is one way of getting them to care about what's going on, and to think about whatever that may be (though the two things rarely happen at the same time). So, unless she is going to rescind my parking permit, I am going to be there.

The truth is that I want to escape the impending drama in my front yard, but there's another truth as well: I miss being with kids. I miss the tension of a good classroom, the storms that threaten, the excitement of it all. I miss the insouciance of kids, even their bad manners: the lack of attention, the rude outbursts. I want—just one more time—the challenge of grabbing their minds and making those minds work. So into the valley I ride, kids to the right of me, kids to the left of me. My mission: to offend them and to make them think. If *A Round-Heeled Woman* has done its job, my mission is halfway completed. Now, about the thinking.

"We've combined two classes," says the instructor, "and a few faculty will be joining us. Your reputation precedes you." Another packed house.

A classroom is a pile of kindling; the least little thing can start it up, and before you know it, you've got a three-alarm fire. My highfalutin pedagogy aside, it has been a long time since I have shared space with assorted young people, and I am nervous as hell, so I have written a lesson plan. I will not go in there unarmed. This lesson plan is so boring it will deflect any outrage from any person under thirty: I will tell them how the book came to be— the writing of it, the publishing of it, the changes in my life brought about by the book. The kids will be asleep in no time, and I can claim victory. I am a stealth fighter.

And then I get a look at them. They are diverse all right: All the colors of the world shine from their faces; they wear costumes from exotic lands, from their sisters' closets, from the mall. The boys' trousers threaten to fall, the girls' T-shirts to rise. They are all beautiful. They look at me expectantly, warily, politely, curiously. Can it be that they want to learn something? I throw out my lesson plan.

What the hell, I decide to begin by reading my ad aloud. I read it slowly, loudly enough for everyone to hear, and don't look up until the end. Nobody looks outraged or offended; a few faces register mild disgust, nothing that would send me into retreat. I decide to read some of the letters that came in response to the ad. "I put each letter into one of three piles—yes, no, and maybe; I'll read some of them, you tell me which pile they should go in." This is a goddam brilliant stratagem, student involvement right off the bat in a subject of (prurient) interest. I can't fail.

"Call me at the office between two and five on Thursdays." "Yes!" they call. Uh-oh, we're off to a bad start.

"A letter from you and I'll spend more time with warm glaciers and cuddly icebergs." "Bogus!" yell the boys. "Yes!" from the girls.

"Have Viagra, will travel!" A unanimous "Yes." They are getting all these wrong.

"I'm seventy-two and very horny." "Yes!" Oh, God.

"Much of what goes on in the world amuses me, and I tend toward the sardonic view while remaining appreciative of life's ironies and serendipities." The drop-in faculty are into this: "Yes!" they cry in unison. The kids are, "Maybe."

It's a good thing I'm not grading this. Every single answer is the opposite from my own when I first took these letters from their envelopes, but that's okay. Now we are all warmed up and can talk with ease and candor. I dig my little green notebook from my purse and say, "Is the word 'slut' still in use?" My pen is poised over the notebook. This is a fine bit of teaching: The teacher becomes the student and the students become the experts. In this case the turnabout is genuine, since I no longer know what's really going on in the valley of the kids. "'Slut,'" they tell me, "is still used and sometimes for guys as well as girls."

Argument breaks out. "No, guys can't be sluts."

"If you go with a lot of guys or girls, you can be a slut."

"I never heard a guy called that."

"Well, start listening."

I break in. "Do you talk openly with each other about sex?"

The girls do. The guys not so much. In the front row a terrific-looking young woman—she is quietly but unquestionably more experienced than a girl—says, "I think sex for a woman is different than for a man." The room grows quiet. This is a bold statement. I nod my encouragement, and she continues: "In sex a woman is being penetrated and she may feel assaulted. So she may be more reluctant than a guy."

Everybody in the room looks at me. What do I think? What I think is not important. What I think, if I make it public, will end the discussion, for the teacher will have spoken, end of argument. Rather than my opinion, I offer another view: "There are those who believe that when a woman is entered, the void is made full and the woman completed." The passive voice has its advantages.

I look at the clock, five minutes to go. I say, pointing to the young woman in their midst, "I think you are lucky to have in your class a most intelligent and articulate young woman." Three minutes to go; kids are performing their velcro symphony, opening and closing their backpacks, and in the noise I say—well I just can't help it, I have an opinion, and what the hell, they'll never see me again, so—"The quality of sex"—the symphony pauses—"depends on the people having it."

A boy shifts his backpack onto his back and calls out, "I just want to say that guys think about sex all the time."

From somewhere in the crowd a sweet, high voice answers, "So do girls."

I am exhausted. How did I do this sort of thing—five periods a day, five days a week—for thirty-three years? I am also elated. Nothing profound got decided. Nothing life-changing. At least I don't think so, though teachers can never be sure. What did happen is that all these minds—every single one was working, I could tell—filled this room with the electricity of thought. Mission accomplished. I am ready for a nap.

Not yet. The line of girls waiting to talk to me is out the door.

"Would you write an advice column for our newspaper?" "Will you give me your agent's name for my dad?" "Would you speak at our Christian youth group?" Near the end of the line stands a tall blond, blue-eyed girl, a California girl if there ever was one. Her turn come 'round at last, she looks at me shyly and says, in uptalk, as if she were asking a question, "I have this problem with my boyfriend?" My smile is her encouragement. "We've been going together for six months and three days, and we agreed right from the start that we would see other people, not just each other, but lately I don't want to see other people, I want to just see him and he doesn't feel that way, I don't think, and . . ." She takes a breath. "I'm jealous. I hate myself."

Sometimes you just have to give advice. Sometimes you just can't get out of drawing a conclusion, forming an opinion, saying it out loud. This lovely creature standing before me is in pain, so I say, still in my avoidance mode, "Have you talked about this with him?" She shakes her head. I tell her what to do, and it's not "Go online." "Give yourself three weeks," I say. "See what happens. After that, if the problem still exists, explain it to him." The sun breaks through. "Thank you so much," she says, and off she goes.

On the way home—a soldier home from the war, a sailor home from the sea—I congratulate myself on a successful campaign in which no limbs were torn, no lives lost, not one drop of blood spilled. I wallow happily in the possibility that the kids in that class will be more respectful of each other, will listen to each other, will think about sex and its rightful place in our lives. Peace, it's wonderful.

MY LANDLADY IS in the swing, her belly the size of a beach ball. Holy god, how did she get her feet through those stirrups? She smiles at me! and says, "We're hoping this will widen the birth canal and make it easier for the baby to pass through."

Oh. I certainly hope it works. I offer a reminiscence of my own labor pains, more than thirty years ago: "I'll always be grateful to the nurse who gave me that shot."

"I'm having natural childbirth," she says. "No drugs." She's still smiling!

Her husband joins her on my lawn and helps her out of the contraption and back into the house. That evening my landlady's moans fill the cool spring air. The neighbor on the left, herself a physician, paces nervously in her backyard. On the right the neighbor, who works at home, has given up working at home. He tosses his briefcase into his BMW, and roars off. Across the street the woman who gave birth to twins when she was forty-eight and has lived to tell about it wrings her hands. Natural childbirth is wonderful. But NIMBY. Or in my case, NIMFY.

Isn't anything private anymore? I know, I have just promoted an open discussion about sex to thirty-three young adults and their teachers. I write about sex, I talk about sex, but I do not urge a public display of sex: I don't go around saying, Do it on the sidewalk! Likewise I support all the talk in the world about birthing—upstairs, downstairs, in my lady's chamber—but dammit, do I have to watch?! I suppose I could move, couldn't I? Nobody's forcing me to stay here. Maybe I could hide out in my car till it's all over.

CHAPTER 18

just one of the boys

It's a boy. Nine pounds ten ounces. No wonder it took so long for him to come out. He is adorable and everyone flutters around him and his mother, cooing and oohing and blowing germs on him. Of course, I don't hate a baby; besides, this one is too cute to hate; however, he will need a yard, like next week. And there's just one yard. Hey, kid, this yard is not big enough for both of us; one of us will have to move. Already the house in which he was born looks smaller. Are his parents going to move? I don't know, but the anxiety of not knowing grows every day. On the other hand maybe I'm paranoid; maybe I have nothing to worry about. But yes, I do: My cottage is not mine, never will be. The winds of change blow hard without ceasing.

They have blown me into my seventy-first birthday, and where is everybody? No one is paying any attention to me. Where's my party? My son and daughter-in-law gave me a surprise party last year on my seventieth birthday, so they no doubt think they're off the hook for the rest of my life. And since it's Sunday, I'll have to wait until tomorrow to pry out all those cards, letters, and small gifts that undoubtedly crowd my post office box. Is anybody going to phone me? Take me out to dinner? Pour me a little champagne? Give me a present? Be my date?

Fifty years ago today, when I turned twenty-one, by god there was a party. It took place at the Pretzel Bell in Ann Arbor, Michi-

guys and a few girls who were serious drinkers. The Pi Phis, very neat girls, came in the dark of night to tap me for membership in their drinking club, the Blue Blazers, the initiation being to set on fire a shot glass of gin and drink it without burning your eyes, nose, hair, lips, tongue, or chin—or the floor when you got too scared, literally, to hold your liquor. At three o'clock in the morning, ten girls standing around my bed in (100 percent, Dad) camel hair coats, kneesocks in Keds, I did it, thank you very much. This was a great honor, for the Pi Phis had so far restricted membership to their own house, and here I was a Delta Gamma. What that meant was that my reputation had broken out beyond our sorority house on Hill Street and found its way to the Pi Phi house on Forest, and I could not be denied. What probably secured my reputation was my friendship with a couple of dissolute DKEs, Dekes, the fraternity of our nation's current president, the most disreputable fraternity on campus, always on probation for one thing or another, filled with rich boys intent on humiliating their fathers by behaving badly. The fathers, unimpressed, posted bail, paid their sons' fines, found abortionists, argued their sons back into school, and returned to making money. Not long after, the boys joined their dads in the firms and eventually turned into them.

Detroit was only forty miles from our university, and surely, there, some ghost of a person was smoking marijuana or even shooting up. But we never thought about Detroit or Cleveland or Pittsburgh or anywhere else; on the campus we knew, drugs were unknown except as stories in newspapers, which we rarely read, or in the books that I *did* read—not one of them on any college reading list—about "mary jane" and smack and the denizens of the underworld who made money from buying and selling them. Our drug was tobacco: No one knew of its addictiveness and its far-reaching consequences; it was simply something everybody did, even my roommate, the single Phi Beta Kappa in our sorority, who referred to cigarettes as "coffin nails" just before she lit up. Our clothes reeked of tobacco. Camel hair coats became sponges for the smoke from Pall Malls, and our hair was infused with the carcinogens of Chesterfields and Luckies. A very neat thing to do was to light a kitchen match on your teeth, spark your tube that way. I was the only girl who would do that and did. Made me one of the gang, kind of a guy-girl.

But while everybody—absolutely everybody—smoked, drinking—hard drinking—was something else, and not many girls won medals in that category. Nice girls, girls who would marry fraternity boys, watched their ways. Got tiddly, sure, silly enough to let their boyfriends undo their bras, but rarely if ever lost total control. Girls who did got reps overnight. I never lost control and hardly ever got tiddly, just remained a good ole virgin, never offended by the vilest joke and always capable of finding my way home alone. Every weekend offered the opportunity to get drunk, to pass out, to wake up with a hangover and swear never to do it again. If one were a guy, doing all that stuff was desirable and necessary for personal growth. In addition you had to get decent grades, not a 4.0, for god's sake, but nothing much below a 3.0. B's you could get on a hangover, A's required protracted periods of sobriety.

Since I tried to be as much like a guy as a girl could get, I got fairly steady B's with fairly little studying after my roommate took me in hand and impressed on me the importance of memorization. Once I learned to memorize huge chunks of text and reams of lecture notes, all of which I deposited into the blue book, even though I forgot every single item of information I had "learned" the minute the final exam was over, a 3.0 was mine. My parents were relieved and left the socialization of their eldest daughter up to the sorority, sensing, I suspect, that I was lagging behind my peers in that regard, but not knowing what to do about it. I didn't know what to do about it either, and I was terrified of doing what some of my sorority sisters were doing: climbing out of the window at night, kissing right under the porch light, getting pinned, staying out after hours, trying on the scents and shades of womanhood. So I did the only thing I knew how to do; I did what I had done when I was fifteen: I hung out with boys who would treat me, if not exactly as one of them, then like a buddy, not a date. I was happy to drink beer with Ted and Barry whenever they couldn't find a girl who would go all the way in the arboretum. And I was popular, sort of, though not exactly in the way my parents had imagined. I could hold my liquor and had a ringing laugh. I had friends who were boys but no boyfriend. The distinction made all the difference.

My four years of drinking at Michigan prepared me well for graduate school in 1959 at the University of California at Berkeley, where I lived in a one-room cottage in a courtyard. On the other side Frank and Bob and Bruce and Tom, PhD candidates in one science or another, lived and studied; at least, they must have studied, because they all got their degrees and went off to positions at ritzy universities. As graduate students in the sciences much of their studying and their TA-ing went on in the labs of the university, where there lived an apparently inexhaustible supply of grain alcohol. At Michigan we had injected oranges with vodka or gin and sucked them throughout the football games on those cold autumn Saturdays. At Berkeley we drank 90 proof lab alcohol cut with ice. Every so often, when the guys decided to throw a party and invite girls who might come across, they injected watermelons with the stuff, cut it up, and made it look, in its big round bowl, like punch with pretty little bites of pink fruit in it. The girls took to it like water and, not long after, ended up in the bathroom or, if they had a strong stomach and a weak brain, in a bed not their own. By this time I had a boyfriend who ingested the stuff as if it were water, and who much of the time ended up in my bed ranting incoherently, throwing up in my shoes, and eventually rendering himself comatose until the following noon. Sweetly apologetic then, he did it all over the next night. If I had stayed to get a PhD, I would have died early. As it happened, my boyfriend did: He died early, though not of drink but by his own hand.

It took me an embarrassingly long time and the women's move-ment to stop wishing I had been born a boy and, short of that, want-ing to hang out with boys. Boys, it seemed to me as I was growing up, took pleasure in being boys: They were unself-conscious about their bodies, they laughed and flung themselves about, they were bold and sometimes daring, initiating sexual encounters—or not—as they chose. Being a boy seemed far less complicated than being a girl, and a lot less scary. Had I been pressed to explain myself, I might have had to admit that I didn't really want to *be* a boy, but I wanted to be anything—a boy, a rabbit, a turnip—other than a girl. Girls were rejected, boys weren't. Girls had to be pretty, boys didn't. Girls agreed to be made love to by one boy, her husband; boys had sex whenever they felt like it with an infinite number of girls who were not nice.

Had I been forced to take a final exam on the differences be-tween boys and girls, I would have flunked, for of course lots of boys get rejected, make love to only one woman, are more success-ful in life if they're tall and handsome, and are just as complicated as women. But in the fifties in midwestern America there were no courses to sign up for, and the girls around me seemed very happy being girls, so how was I to find out anything? I certainly couldn't ask my mother. I was forced to fall back on what I knew: I wasn't pretty, so I had better behave as if I had no interest in making out or making love or getting married. I would be safe, then, from the rejection that surely would have befallen me otherwise, especially if I let a boy, even my husband, have his way with me and he found out I didn't have the slightest idea what to do. I knew from my reading of bodice rippers that a husband could order me to get un-dressed, and there I'd be, on my honeymoon, without a stitch on, and he would hate me. Being a girl was just too risky.

But dammit, no matter how short I cut my hair, how too-small I bought my bras, and how much I swore, I stayed a girl, not by choice but by default. And then when my boyfriend in Berkeley diddled me just before he threw up in my shoes, I out and out had to admit that I liked it, the diddling, that is. I liked his rough hands all over me and his tumescent member in me (I had read that somewhere, and knew that saying "penis" was bad); and, finally, I did what most girls of my generation did: I got married. To the wrong man, who taught me to be ashamed of my desire and who made it clear that he preferred the bathroom alone to bed with me. It would take psychoanalysis to rid me of shame, to convince me that desire was normal and that doing something about it was not evil. So I did something about it.

Except here I am, seventy-one and sober, most of the time, and all the people who used to pay attention to me on my birthday—my parents, my aunts and uncles, even most of my cousins—are dead. There are lots of ways to be unaccompanied: One of them is to live a long time and watch as, one by one, the people who made up your life fall by the wayside, leaving you standing in the middle of the road wondering where everybody went. So here I am: my own birthday girl. What fun. And where are the boys?

They are not far away, for the next day, Monday, will find one of them on my answering machine. "Please call Dr. Favor's office tomorrow morning between eight-thirty and eleven." Who? Instantly I conjure up a scene in a hospital emergency room, to which everyone I had ever loved had been taken following a massive accident. Why did I have to wait practically a whole day? And a sleepless night.

Eight-thirty A.M. sharp I phone. "Please hold." After what seems a lifetime, what sounds like a doctor's voice says, "Jane? Jane Juska? The author?" Oh, what is this? I sigh with relief; my loved ones are not dead after all. I answer yes, and Dr. Favor says, "What can I do to entice you to come to our book club?" Hell, a bunch of married couples who want to see what a septuagenarian sex maniac looks like. I mumble something about being very busy. He says, "Your book is our current selection." Holy cow, they didn't even wait for the paperback, they bought it in hardcover! My tone grows warmer, yet I continue to demur. "We're a group of men from different walks of life—lawyers, doctors, even a writer." All men? "We will do the cooking and ensure fine wines." Hey! When and where? "Thursday, seven-thirty, my house. I'll send a map."

Maybe, finally, I will get a date. That's really why I'm going. Maybe, even, I will do what my mother wanted me to do: marry a doctor. Or a lawyer. Or even a writer. Nah, not a writer. They don't make any money. Wonder how one even got into this group of rich guys. In my mind I have made them all rich and good-looking and single: Why else would they be reading *A Round-Heeled Woman*? They are probably younger than I am, everybody is, but they know my age and everything else about me, and so what, they're inviting me so I can look them over and pick out a couple for the future. It's about time. Dr. Favor e-mails me directions to his house, adding, "I thought I was the only person in the world who remembered the Weather Girls." He is referring to the mention I made in my book of one of their songs. Gosh, maybe Dr. Favor will be the one. Look what we have in common.

Thursday morning one of my eyes opened, the other one didn't. My head weighed at least fifty pounds, and when I got my eyelid unstuck from itself, I could see in the mirror that the eye itself was a fiery red. I went back to bed and at noon, no better, called Dr. Favor's office to apologize for my absence that evening. "Omigod," he said, "you've got to be kidding! You've got to come." I explained that I couldn't see out of one eye. He was not impressed. "You've got to come," he repeated. "There's a guy flying in from Nebraska just to meet you." I shared with him that my head was booming. "He's on the plane now!" I pressed: My eye was a flaming red. "I'm an ophthalmologist," he countered. "I'll bring drops."

So I went. I dragged myself into my red jacket and black pants and I went. Even through half an eye I could see that oh boy, we're in rich people's land now. No rentals in this neighborhood. The houses were big and set back on manicured lawns, and the house of Dr. Favor was old and big and once Victorian but made new and comfortable and charming by lots of money and good taste. So was Dr. Favor comfortable and charming and only twenty years younger than I and just as nice as he could be. In his kitchen eight or nine men cooked away while Dr. Favor dropped medicine into my eye, commenting as he did on the wonderful blue that my eye would become once again when the conjunctivitis—pinkeye— went away. "Surely you're wearing contacts," he said. "Your eyes are so beautifully blue." "Gee," I heard one of the men whisper, "and he's not even driving her home." I felt better.

Dinner—salmon, wild rice, chardonnay, spinach salad— around the table is very nice, about ten of us, including the guy from Nebraska. "We're not like women's book groups," they tell me. "We don't plan ahead, we don't assign dishes according to the first letter of your last name." Everyone laughs. "We just bring what we feel like cooking." This would explain the platter of spaghetti and meatballs that now appears in the center of the table. It is delicious, a perfect follow-up to the salmon and precursor to the brownies and lemon curd brought home from a recent visit to the British Isles.

For a time there is talk of skiing and second homes and children at Dartmouth or would it be Brown, and I am fading. My headache beats a tattoo inside my temporal lobes, my right eye is throbbing, and my pants are tight around my waist; of course, I ate all that food. I want to go home. Then they turn to my book. As it turns out, the man who flew in from Nebraska did not go to all this trouble just to meet me; he is here on business, had read the book back in Nebraska at the behest of his girlfriend, and thought how much he would enjoy telling her about our meeting. For a bit I am angry with the good Dr. Favor, but the good humor of everybody here is irresistible; almost everybody—the internist, the gynecologist, the attorney, the radiologist—has read the book and admired it. Then the surgeon says, "I have done a lot of work on transsexuals. Interestingly, many of them now in their fifties tell me they don't know what all the fuss was about when they first came to me, that all this interest in sex is overrated." He moves quickly to a rhetorical question: "Wouldn't you agree? Don't you think that desire decreases with age?" Well, here's one who hasn't read my book, that's for sure. I murmur something about "Not in my experience, though I can't speak for a large number of either men or women." On no evidence whatsoever I sense that he's talking about himself or perhaps his wife; or maybe he just wants to prove me wrong, his experience far outweighing mine. Maybe he wants to dispel the notion that I might have some expertise in a field in which I do not belong. I will never know because just then the specter of wifedom enters the room. Mrs. Favor, she is arrived.

Mrs. Favor, dressed all in black, pencil-thin, is right out of New York's East Eighties. I have seen her and her doubles walking up Madison Avenue, the initials of designers on bags and shoes and capes and umbrellas proclaiming their owners' fine taste and money, to make it come alive to those of us less fortunate who, really now, have no business being uptown anyway. Mrs. Favor, her face white, her lips bright red, her hair black and skimmed back into a chignon, seats herself at the far side of the enormous island that sits in the middle of this enormous kitchen. Although this is clearly her kitchen and the host her husband, no one says hello, no one acknowledges her presence. This must be an unwritten rule of this book club: Men Only. Mrs. Favor, in compliance, went somewhere and has come home early. From the look on her face, she has no use for this rule; either that or wherever she went was not kind to her. She looks mad.

Well, my eye is less puffy, I have been wined and dined by all these nice men; they have complimented me on my courage, agreed that often courage and foolishness go hand in hand, expressed their appreciation for my book and for my company, so Mrs. Favor does not intimidate me. She does not introduce herself to me and I don't introduce myself to her. Now we're even.

The evening is drawing to a close and I am downing lemon

curd like a native of Gloucestershire, when Dr. Favor says, "Before you go, will you read my favorite part of the book?" Oh god, he's going to make me read some sex part, with his wife sitting not ten yards away, looking like Morticia stepped out of a Charles Addams cartoon. I point lamely at my eye, but there's no fooling an ophthalmologist. "I'll put more drops in before you leave," he says. "I didn't bring my book," I say. He hands me my book open to the last page, where he has bracketed a paragraph, and in this very large and very quiet room, ten men and me around the table, Drusilla Vanilla on the far side of the moon, I read:

"Life just keeps coming at you. Make no mistake, it's out to get you, and in the end it will. But every so often, you can catch a piece of it and make it do what you want it to, at least for a little while. You've got to stay alert, though. Heads up so you won't get caught off base, though if you do, what the hell, it's not the ninth inning, until it is."

I gotta remember that.

I GREW UP in a family of surgeons. My father was a surgeon, as was his father and his father before him and his father's brother and his first cousin. I cannot imagine my father treating transsexuals or, even if he did, talking about it. But the aloofness, the confidence in his professional expertise, the cool rationality of tonight's surgeon were my father's, too, and my uncle's and my grandfather's. I imagine that cutting into someone's body requires all that; I certainly hope my own surgeon will be confident and a little bit superior and supremely rational; somebody else can do the bedside manner. Tonight's surgeon did not scare me as, too often, though always unintentionally, my father did. As with the other men present, tonight's surgeon was an improvement over the men of my generation, just as in some ways I am an improvement over myself as I was back then. Tonight's company of men saw me as a curiosity, I'm sure, but also as a specimen worth examining, and in the end, because I brought a bit of confidence and picked up on their good humor, we all got along happily, sitting around a big round table, laughing and drinking like pals.

So what if I went home alone.

the last lamplighter

It all seemed to me incredibly romantic and exciting.
Even the dingiest dive seemed magical to me.

—STEPHEN FOTHERGILL in his memoir, *The Last Lamplighter*

My friend Jo's house is for sale. It was a perfect house for her; it is a perfect house for me. I want to live there, not that I could fill her shoes let alone her house. But even without Jo it has a warmth and a comfort made just for me. I would have to learn to garden and I would, I would, so that all Jo's efforts would not rot out there in her very own fenced-in backyard, totally private, all hers. And her bookcases I could fill so quickly and with the books that Jo loved, the same books I love, and what does it matter if I don't have any furniture? I will give a housewarming party or a shower, and everybody will bring something to sit on or eat off or sleep in. Jo's house has a study and a real dining room and a dishwasher and a disposal in the big eat-in kitchen and—in the basement—a washer and a dryer. It's only a few blocks from where I live now, which means I could still walk to the movies and the library and the doctor's office and the drugstore. In addition it is one block away from the best grocery store in the entire world: The Star Market.

The Star has been where it is forever. One man owns it and op-

erates it with the help of a few high school kids whose faces are il-
luminated by high IQs and sunny dispositions. A few years ago
the Star hit tough times, and, as a money-saver, the owner turned
off the lights of the outdoor sign, which looks a bit like an art deco
movie marquee. Good heavens, could the Star actually go out of
business? Well, the neighborhood got together and put that sign
back to work, and the store got back on its feet and so did the
owner, and now, just as it was years and years ago, if you forget to
bring enough money, you can bring what you owe next time, or
you can charge the whole thing, and if you do, you make out the
charge slip.

One day another customer, a resident of the neighborhood, and
I stood on the sidewalk outside the Star. We were talking about—
guess what—real estate, and the man leaned down and said, "Just
remember, it's important not to move too far away from the Star."
Good advice, but advice is cheap, houses aren't. Maybe the neighborhood will get together and turn my lights back on, but no. As
prices of homes continue to rise, the people who live in them now
and have for twenty years could never afford to buy their own
homes. "We could sell and make many thousands of dollars, but
where would we go? We could move to Utah, we could afford
Wyoming, but then we'd have to live there." Our realtor neighbor
tells us that Berkeley is a niche market and our neighborhood a
niche neighborhood. Translation: Everybody wants to live here. I
hate the free market.

So how much will Jo's house cost? It hasn't gone on the market
yet; maybe it won't; maybe Jo's daughter will move into it, maybe
maybe maybe . . . And then I am called to London to publicize the
paperback edition of the book. My friends and neighbors, who are
sick to death of my constant lament over looking for a home—I
am sounding more and more like an Irish dirge, "*Find me a
hooome*"—will keep an eye on Jo's house as it gains a new owner.
Oh, let it be me!

My London publisher is trying to kill me. She has put me up at her club, which is very nice of her and which is even in the guide-book: the Groucho Club. It is in Soho, which is also in the guide-book. What is not in the guidebook is that my room is on the top floor (fourth) and there is no elevator. For the first time ever I feel like saying, Hey! I'm seventy-one years old! I can't climb all these stairs! But I do climb them, and I don't complain because, after all, I am here as a septuagenarian sex symbol.

I am sounding like my great-uncle, who described all his trav-els, every one of his many trips, according to accommodations—how good or bad they were—and if the trains were on time and whether or not he had an outside or an inside stateroom. The rest of the details he left to the thousands of photographs he took, all of them of flowers. No matter where he went, flowers were in bloom, though maybe he timed his travels to coincide with blos-som time. No matter, for always, because we were polite children, my brothers and sister and I, we sifted through all those pictures, exclaiming as we went: "Gee, Uncle Clarence, here's another red one!" And my brother would say, "Hey, here's a great big red one!" and then he'd laugh because he'd said something dirty, which none of the rest of us got.

I learned how *not* to travel from my great-uncle. I never com-plain about my accommodations (see above) or whether my flight is delayed, and I never ever take photographs of flowers; in fact, I almost always leave my camera at home; a very smart friend once pointed out that a camera interferes with the immediacy of things. Travel light and never make the kids back home look at your souvenirs.

I first went to London in 1955, the trip a graduation present from my parents, though my dad, stingy as ever, actually made me *get a job* the previous summer to help pay for it. Can you believe it? Each of us—five of my friends, not one of them having been forced untimely into the workplace by an adamantine parent—got to-gether one thousand dollars, an enormous sum, and off we went right after graduation to Europe, where we stayed until Thanksgiving—almost six months—when we got cold and hungry or when, in my case, I wrote my father asking for a little more money so I could stay a little longer, and received, by return mail, an airplane ticket. Honestly, Dad.

It being June when we first arrived, all six of us wore khaki Bermuda shorts, white shirts, and Wigwam socks in Keds. We must have looked like a troop of Boy Scouts. Likewise, we were all virgins. Or so it was assumed. We never talked about sex or boyfriends because here we were twenty-one years old and we didn't have any. We had each other, though, and we laughed and talked our way around Ireland and Scotland and the Continent and Scandinavia, hitchhiking sometimes, riding buses and trains, and all day every day loving what we saw and the people we met and each other.

We were a hit in London and in the rest of England, too, because we were Americans and women, and only ten years earlier Americans had helped win the war and now had as their president Dwight David Eisenhower, the hero who had helped to bring an end to the war. How times have changed. In 2004, Londoners avoided conversation with me about American braggadocio abroad and the swagger of the American president, who in only four short years had become the most dangerous man in the world. Just as well: I didn't want to talk about my government's criminal behavior, and I enjoyed London newspapers in large part because they relegated news of the United States to the inside pages.

In 1955 we stood at the side of the road—two of us, the other four hiding in the bushes—and stuck out our thumbs. When a lorry stopped—"Hallo there, girls, you're Yanks, are you?"—we ran, all six, and jumped onto the back of the truck or scrunched ourselves into those tiny cars and said, Yes, yes, we were Yanks and proud of it.

What we were after was getting laid, and at the same time we were terrified we might. One of us confessed that in high school she had let her steady get to second base (nipples), but aside from a kiss here and there, we were American innocents abroad. What delicious horrors might befall us in Paris or Rome or—decadence, here we come—Hamburg. First stop: London.

London on less than five dollars a day—our thousand dollars included boat and airfare—kept us busy finding a place to sleep; boys were of secondary importance. When we did find a youth hostel or a grungy little bed and breakfast—Oh god, I loved those breakfasts, everything fried up and greasy, even the tomato—we spent our evenings arguing over whether or not we needed to behave properly because we represented our country or whether free will was ours for the taking. Sarah said yes, we did have to behave; Pat said no, we represented ourselves. This was the closest any of us had yet gotten to an honest philosophical debate, and we kept it up until Pat got disgusted and left for Paris early, where, oh boy, she went all the way and more than once, too.

Those of us who remained in London and represented our country behaved properly, and as a result no boys were interested in us, probably because in our Bermuda shorts and Wigwams we looked more like boys than girls, probably because we were having such a good time with each other we weren't interested in them. This was before lesbianism was invented. Or, more accurately, before we ever knew there was such a thing, though Sarah's psychiatrist father, in a triumph of intelligence over ignorance, had given her *The Well of Loneliness* when Sarah was in high school, which was probably why it was Sarah who let her high school steady get to second base. In that novel, written by a woman named Radclyffe Hall, the heroine—named Stephen by her father, who wanted a boy—grows up on her rich father's country estate into a mannish adult. She is elegant-looking, prefers jodhpurs and boots to skirts and slippers, cuts her hair short, and lives all her life in a well of loneliness surrounded by people who stare at her and talk about her behind her back, forcing her, finally, to abandon the woman she loves. Even Stephen's father steers clear of her; could Sarah's father have intended the book as a warning? In 1928, the year of its publication, the book was banned in England because of its sympathetic portrayal of that kind of woman. So Sarah, growing up in the 1950s and having read what happens to girls like that, was determinedly heterosexual and, to prove it, in her sophomore year unhooked her bra in the backseat of Brad Morris's car. The power of words. When Samuel Goldwyn wanted to make a film out of *The Well of Loneliness,* someone questioned the tastefulness of such a project, and Goldwyn, never at a loss for words, many of them wrong, answered, "Where there's lesbians, we'll use Albanians."

When I wasn't giggling with my friends, I read banned books, books that were banned in America and in England, too, except I found them in little London bookshops. I knew what I was looking for: Henry Miller's *Tropic of Cancer* and *Tropic of Capricorn,* and when I finished them, I read all the books that being an English major at Michigan had left no time for. In London every book I had ever wanted to read was in Penguin paperback and cost an amazingly low two and six. Reading was affordable on under five dollars a day.

Now, fifty years later, books have brought me once again to London: This time it is my own book, from which I will be reading all over town. Gee, I might even get laid. This time I wouldn't be afraid, except if he were elderly and tried to climb the four flights of stairs to my room and his heart or knees or both gave out. Won't hurt to look, though, and off I go to do a little pub crawling. Maybe that's why my publisher put me up there—so I would stay put, behave properly, and represent my country as it should be represented: Shut up and remember your manners.

Soho is a rowdy place. Its history includes people like Dylan Thomas, Francis Bacon, and Louis MacNeice, artists and writers who frequented the pubs, got drunk, read their writing aloud, talked about art and life, and passed out. The French House is one of those pubs. It's even in the guidebook. I didn't know it was famous then; I just went in the direction the room clerk at my club pointed, and when I came to a pub overflowing with people who, drinks in hand, weaved right out onto the curb and into the street, I went in and stood at the bar. Champagne seemed the thing to order, some kind of celebration was surely in order. And everyone was very, very nice to me; nobody said, "You're a Yank, are you," and spat at my feet. They asked me how I came to visit this fair city, and when I told them I was a writer, they bought me more champagne and gave me cigarettes. I don't smoke anymore, so these cigarettes were utterly delicious, and nobody gave me bad looks—as they would have in America—when I blew a smoke ring right into the air above the barman's head. I had two cigarettes. What a night.

But it's not over. There at the end of the bar is a very old man, older even than I, older than anyone else in this pub. He is wearing a trench coat, like the ones John le Carré's spies wear, only this trench coat is very, very dirty, stains down the front, pockets and sleeves frayed at the edges; it looks as old as the man wearing it. The man is talking up a storm to a young couple, who are trying to look interested and failing. He is showing them a book, which I move closer to get a look at—I am very nosey when it comes to what people are reading. The old man turns to me, lanks of hair falling onto his forehead, and smiles, revealing that he has some but not all of his teeth. Beneath his coat he is very thin and, if he weren't stooped, would stand quite tall, maybe six feet. His name is Stephen Fothergill and he is selling his book. It is a memoir of times gone by, of places in Soho, the French House being one, in which writers and artists congregated and talked about their art. "I was a very young man then," he tells me, "and I was thrilled to be in the company of men who had made writing and painting and poetry their lives."

"What about women?" I ask. "Did women writers come here, too?"

"There weren't any women writers," Stephen answers, and at my look of disbelief adds, "at least none who came at night to Soho." He smiles. "The women who came to Soho at night were not your usual sort. Some were artists' models, some were the mistresses or girlfriends of artists and writers, some were prostitutes, some were all three. They had no independent lives of their own. Women writers?" The idea is new to him. "I suppose they minded home and hearth, no time to muck about with the poets and novelists who came here."

I tell him that I, too, have written a memoir, which makes me a woman writer who is here to muck about with the crowd. Times have changed, he agrees. More visitors than regulars descend on the French House these days, and on the weekends hordes of young suburbanites invade Soho. And my ears tell me that people in this pub are not talking about writing, not most of them. Most of them, somewhere in their thirties, are talking loudly back and forth about media, about public relations, about graphics, about software, about getting ahead, the implication being that they are ahead, just listen to how loud they can talk. Stephen and I shake our heads. "The world has gotten noisy, hasn't it?" His smile is rueful. "My hearing isn't what it used to be, and often I'm happy it isn't." Was the French House, in the days of his young manhood, quiet? "It was not like this," he answers. "People bent their heads over manuscripts or talked intensely but softly until the drink took hold, and then someone might raise his voice, fighting might ensue, though serious brawling was rare. But a constant din like this? No."

Stephen's memoir costs ten pounds. I buy a copy and promise to bring him a copy of my book the next night; every night Stephen travels an hour and a half from his home to Soho, hoping to sell his book, which he carries in the pocket of his coat. He offers to buy me a glass of champagne. "No, thank you, I've had quite enough." It's time for me to start climbing the stairs to my room at the top. I lean over and kiss Stephen on his paper-thin cheek. His skin is that velvet of a very old person. "Good night," he says. "Come tomorrow." Stephen's memoir is called *The Last Lamplighter*.

Unfortunately, I will have to disappoint Stephen because the next night I am impressed by my publisher into making an appearance at a bookstore. It is a wonderful evening, the audience is warm and welcoming, and—the bookstore has a wine bar! Hear this, you Puritan booksellers in the United States. In London people can buy a glass of wine if they wish; at the end of the evening, if they buy the book, they are refunded the price of the wine. This is creative merchandising.

But I must keep my appointment with Stephen. Two days later, book in hand, my book, I walk to the French House, once again overflowing with boisterous young people and more than a few tourists who have read about this place in their guidebooks. Stephen has buttonholed two of them and is peddling his memoir. He is pleased to see me, though he does not appear to have changed his clothes since our first meeting two days earlier. It comes to me that Stephen may have no clothes to change into, that my earlier suspicions are correct and that Stephen is not just old and eccentric but poor.

I hand him his memoir, the one I purchased from him on our first meeting, and ask him to sign it. He does. I hand him my memoir, he asks me to sign it "To Stephen" and I do. Then he tells me, "Of course, I will not be able to read it." Stephen is almost blind. "I have a very strong magnifying glass at home; perhaps that will help, but I think not enough." Damn, I have two copies of my book in large print sitting on my desk back home. Stephen says, "I will ask my home help to read it to me. I'm sure it's very interesting." Oh lord, all those sex parts. I can see this well-meaning woman flinging the book to the floor, refusing to continue. I can't blame her; I can't read those parts aloud either. And there, in my imagination, in Stephen's flat, a gas heater in one room, Stephen will sit until time to board the train again and find his way to the French House and perhaps another sale of his memoir.

No, I do not want to make love with this man. But I love him—and the champagne I am drinking. I want to clean him up, comb his hair, get those teeth brushed, take that trench coat to be cleaned, shine his shoes, and hope the home help hasn't quit for good so she can wash the underwear. I want to hold him; he is a valiant soul and so very much alone. I take his face in my hands and kiss him, this time on the mouth, a perfectly respectable kiss but as tender a kiss as I've ever given or received. "Thank you for your book," we say to each other. And off I go to the fourth floor and then British Air and then home.

There is no pub crawling to be done in Berkeley, not by the likes of me; and there is no cause for celebrating. While I was gone, Jo's house sold to the highest bidder: seven hundred seventy thousand dollars. Jo bought it in 1983 for sixty thousand. I wish she were here to enjoy the profit. And cook me roasted potatoes and chicken and little tomatoes, and pour me wine the way she used to, and talk sense to me when I need it and nonsense when I don't. I wish she were here to read with me.

the young one

Once while plaiting a wreath
I found Eros among the roses.
I grabbed him by the wings
And dipped him in the wine
And drank him down.
Now inside my limbs
He tickles me with his wings.

—ANAKREON, "The Rub of Love"

urry up, Graham, come back to me before I slip and fall in the shower or go blind like Stephen. I am empty without Graham. It is surprising, though it shouldn't be, how much time, interior time, I spend thinking about him, writing to him, waiting for him to write back or phone. He is gone. He is with his wife, he has a young life, maybe he will become a father, and what will he want with me then? Goddammit, he is my muse! He reads my stuff, tells me my transitions are lousy, tells me I verge on the profound and then back off (I'm lazy, he suggests). He tells me I'm funny and smart, and now he's traveling somewhere in Italy. Well, sure, she probably wanted to go to Italy and so they did. I miss him, and when I look real life squarely in the face, I have to admit his help with my writing has become something of a trickle. I may

be looking at past tense here. Hell. His absence is a huge emptiness in me. Oh, Graham, I remember when you came to see me
and stayed in my cottage, your feet dangling out over the futon
that was our bed, and afterward we walked around my neighborhood and you said, "This is wonderful. I could live happily here."

Well, so could I. Let's hope I am allowed. Because—uh-oh—in
the front yard of my landlord's house is a FOR SALE sign. I am on
the market again.

3 Bdrms, 2.5 Baths, Fireplace, Formal dining room, Eat-in kitchen, Bay
view from master suite, Separate in-law unit, $949,000.

What can happen to me is that the new owners can kick me out
if they claim my cottage is needed by an in-law or some other kind
of blood relative. If the new owners decide to keep me, they can
raise my rent—again. I say this to everybody, even strangers, because in a niche neighborhood of a niche market, word of mouth is
powerful. So everybody is listening and looking, and I am leaning
(gently) on the people two doors down, who live in a cottage
double the size of mine, for which I would pay much more than
it's worth. Sell me your home, I will make it worth your while. It's
easy. You buy my landlord's property, we just sort of exchange
houses. Why is it that good ideas like that rarely get heard by anybody who matters? I wish I could claim discrimination: racial or
gender or age. Guidelines abound, and then I might have a
chance. But no, it is the numbers that discriminate against me.
Banks won't lend me money, not because I'm a woman of a certain
age or color, but because my earning potential is not actuarially
high enough to allow so great a risk. I am really on my own here,
without a dad to guide me, and on my own doesn't get me much
in the way of desirable living quarters. At a time like this I wish
I had a husband, one with money. I know, today's woman pays
close attention to her financial independence, and bully for her, I
am a fan. But I am not a woman of today; I am a woman of yes-

terday, and all those yesterdays found me working hard, loving my teaching job, earning a steady salary, and saving nothing. I am a financial orphan. And it is storming out there.

A man would come in handy for two reasons: money and size. With a big rich man I would be safe and warm, far from the ravages of the outside world, in a house where, if he insisted, I suppose he could live, too. Would I give up my independence for him? Well, I'd certainly like the chance to consider it. So where is he?

Maybe in Walnut Creek. Walnut Creek is a town, small city, some forty miles inland from Berkeley, and tonight I am scheduled to read in their Barnes & Noble store and sign books afterward. It will be a distraction and, yes, indeedy, I could use one. I would not wish to live in Walnut Creek; it is hot out there, you would need air-conditioning, and while it has charming (expensive) neighborhoods, its downtown is full of stores for rich people: Tiffany, Armani, and also a bunch of stores for the young and soon-to-be affluent: Crate & Barrel, Banana Republic, Pottery Barn, though Pottery Barn just made it in, there being some discussion over whether or not it had polished its image to the brightness demanded by retailers in Walnut Creek. There are no stores in Walnut Creek for poor people: You have to go miles to find a Dollar Store or a Wal-Mart. Another reason I would not wish to live in Walnut Creek is that many people who do live there are white and retired and look like me. Different colors of people don't live in Walnut Creek; they don't even work there. I like my people all mixed up. A last and probably most important reason I would not live there is that I don't have enough money. It's pretty expensive in Walnut Creek, though I don't know if it's a niche market. Probably it is. Would I give up my reverse snobbery if someone bought me a house in Walnut Creek? Well, I'd certainly like the chance to consider it.

Barnes & Noble is full of people on all their floors. One of my favorite sights: people sitting on the floor between the aisles of books, turning pages, some reading to their children in the comfortable chairs Barnes & Noble is smart enough to pepper their stores with, still others standing in the aisles, deaf to the world around them, intent on the book they've opened. Reading is dead, some pundits proclaim, but in my experience stores like this and the libraries I visit and the cafés I frequent are filled with readers, people for whom the printed word provides a time out of mind, a refuge from the world's unsteadiness, and an appreciation for the permanence of print. For a time, we are out of touch, incommunicado, away from our desks, neither landing nor taking off. For a time, we are safe at home.

Lots of readers—let's hope they are also buyers of books—have come to hear me talk. Sometime during the evening I will say what, finally, I have become brave enough to say aloud. It is a response to the many members of the audience who say, "I borrowed this from my aunt" or "I loved your book, I loaned it to all my friends." I do not correct the grammar with, The verb is "to lend," past tense is "lent." Correcting grammar is not something you do if you're hoping for people to buy your book. What I say is, "Wait. The next time a friend asks to borrow your/my book, tell them this: 'Buy the book. I know the author, and she needs the money.'" "But your book is doing very well!" someone exclaims, and I say once again that I still live in three hundred fifty square feet and go to the laundromat every week. They nod and promise to do better.

Not long ago, at a reading nearby, I said this very thing. Afterward a young woman, her turn to ask for my autograph come round at last, said, "I feel terrible, just awful. I got your book from the library; I had no idea. So I want to give you this." She handed me a check she had made out to me for the full price of the hardcover. I tucked her check back into her hand and thanked her—I wanted to put my arms around her—and suggested she give the money to her local library. She seemed happy to be asked to do that and to believe that I was not as financially desperate as I may have implied.

I said it again in Saint Louis and got this response from a young woman: "I'm sorry, I would love to buy your book, but I can't. I am not of your persuasion." Huh? She explains, "I used to be of your persuasion, but I'm not anymore." She is all dolled up in good-looking small men's clothes: trousers well creased, shirt and tie, a camel hair jacket, and penny loafers. She looks good. She also looks moneyed enough to buy my book. She says, "Could we meet later for ice cream?" "No," I answer, and then, "Buy my book anyway, I need the money." She smiles and wanders off into her persuasion.

Tonight, as the line begins to form, a little birdlike woman rushes ahead of everyone, right up to the front of the line, where I am about to sign books. She pokes her face into mine and whispers, "Are you still seeing Graham?" I nod. She sighs as one sighs just before swooning, and says, "That's all I wanted to know. You've made my evening." And skitters off. Graham, whom my readers have dubbed The Young One, has become a favorite of many of them. They demand, "Tell us about The Young One" or ask, "How could you get undressed in front of The Young One?" He will become beloved among readers for his sexual prowess, his kindness, his intelligence, and his appreciation of me. "How does it feel to be so admired?" I asked him (before he went to Italy). "Odd, very odd."

The person at the end of the line tonight is not a man wanting a date. Damn. A man from Walnut Creek might just think sharing his money with me is a good idea. He might even buy me a house where air-conditioning is built right in. This kind of thinking brings back the memory of Barrett, my rich lover who couldn't, or wouldn't, back then buy me a house. I wonder if he could now. Maybe I should have tried harder, hung in there longer. It seems a lifetime ago that the two of us strolled about London and New York enjoying each other's company, though not in bed. All that happened during my Romantic period. Now I am in my postmodern period, form over function, façade over feeling. Forget the love stuff; I need a fucking house. So where is it? Not here, not now. Tonight's last person is a woman who strides forward, book in hand, an enormous grin on her face. "I waited until the end because I have a story to tell you."

Her name is Jody. She is fifty-four years old. Over the years her husband lost all interest in making love, and for a long time he has not touched her. In all other respects he has been a commendable companion and father. Except no touching anymore, no touching of any kind. "Sometimes I reached out to touch his cheek," she says, "but he brushed my hand away. I felt humiliated." When Jody turned fifty, her husband asked her what she wanted for her birthday. "I want you to make love to me," she said, and he replied, "We're beyond that" and bought her an expensive necklace, which lies in her drawer, unworn, to this day.

"I didn't want to leave my husband," she tells me. "He is a good man, we have many things in common, he is a good father to our kids, but I knew I could not live the rest of my life without physical intimacy. I needed to feel desirable. I needed the touch of a man, I needed to make love to a man. My skin burned sometimes, my throat would close up without warning, and one day I decided enough was enough. It was time to find a lover. And then I read your book. I thought I was alone, and here you came to keep me company." She stops and her eyes sparkle. "The surprise is that my lover is quite a bit younger than I am."

Jody is aglow. She stands before me tall and strong, her dark red hair springing up in little curls all over her head. "This has been the most wonderful year of my life," she says. Now, I could spend hours in Jody's force field; I feel energized by her, happy that she is happy. I don't even care to know why she is so happy, it is enough to catch some of her radiance. However, the bookstore is closing, and so Jody asks if she can write me and I say yes, and she strides back up the aisle, turns and says, "And I'm reading all of Trollope." Well, Trollope helped start off this new and incredible life of mine. Hers, too, apparently.

Weeks later an e-mail message appears on my screen. It is an invitation to go for a motorcycle ride. Jody has owned and driven bikes for years. I bet she looks fabulous in leather. So of course I say yes.

You have never seen the streets of San Francisco until you have seen them from the back of a motorcycle. At the start I saw them with my eyes tight shut; eventually I peered over Jody's fabulous black leather motorcycle jacket—which I clutched with all the strength left in my seventy-one-year-old fingers—and marveled at the power and the roar of this amazing machine. San Francisco is famous for its hills; we conquered every one of them, and by the end of our ride, I felt great, I felt strong, I felt tough, as in, Hey, man, don't mess with me, I'm a Harley babe. And I hadn't even done anything, just clung to Jody's leather midriff. Motorcycles are sexy beasts, all that throbbing beneath the seat that rises up right into your private parts. It's no wonder you feel more alive at the end of a ride than at the beginning.

I fell in love with motorcycles when I was in high school. A few of the boys in my senior class of thirty-two (biggest class to graduate from our school up to that time) owned and rode motorcycles. Dick was one of them, and every so often we would skip out of afternoon study hall and hop onto his motorcycle and roar off to Goll's Woods, where kids went to neck, except for me. I just wanted to ride on the back of Dick's bike. Then here came my dad who ruined it all, wouldn't you know.

One day—and mind you, my dad had never said one word about my accompanying Dick on his bike, though of course he knew; everybody in town knew everything about everybody—he called to me to come out to the backyard. I went, and there sat Roger Nafziger in a wheelchair. Roger was a year behind me in school and had been captain of the basketball team, and now, at sixteen, there he sat and would sit "for the rest of his life," said my dad, also Roger's doctor. "Roger, tell Jane"—by now some of the neighbors had gathered, among them my biker buddy Dick—

"tell everyone how you sustained your injuries." Well, we knew, we knew that Roger had been in an accident with his motorcycle and had missed practically the whole year of school. It was a really awful thing that happened to Roger, but what did it have to do with us? What was my dad trying to do here? Roger said, "I lost control of my bike, crashed it, bike fell on top of me, crushed my legs, cracked my spine . . ." His voice wandered off, and he looked suddenly old and worn out and terribly sad. "I guess," he said, "my advice would be not to ride motorcycles." Through it all my dad never took his eyes off me. He never said another word about it, and I never rode a motorcycle again until graduate school twenty-five hundred miles away from my dad, and only when Bob, who was getting his doctorate in physics, so how could he lose control of anything, beeped the horn of his bike and off we went. Riding a motorcycle is a thrill, nothing else like it. So I wondered if Jody's bike was a substitute for the thrill of the love-making her husband denied her. "It helps," she said, "but only a little."

Jody wants to talk, so we settle ourselves on a stone wall over-looking San Francisco Bay, and marvel at the cloudless blue sky, the Golden Gate Bridge, Alcatraz, and the absence of any fog, per-haps in this summer month the most unusual part of the day. It is as if no time at all had passed since our bookstore visit. "So I read your book. My god, you took a lot of chances to get what you wanted. And what you wanted was the same as what I wanted: touching, with good sex, too, if it happened, but most important was feeling a man's desire for me." I nod. "So I went on Craigslist."

Craigslist is an Internet bulletin board. It began in San Fran-cisco, now has sites in New York and other big cities. You can find everything on Craigslist: houses, cars, jobs, dates with men, dates with women, and it's free except for realtors who want to list prop-erties. Jody advertised thusly: *"I am a 52-year-old married woman who loves architecture, motorcycles, and chess. My husband has not touched me in years. I want to stay married but I can no longer live without intimacy and sexuality. Tell me why you would want a relationship with a married woman."*

She received more than seventy responses within a twenty-four-hour period. "I had to pull the ad. I was afraid I would be buried. And their letters, most of them, took my invitation seriously and wrote candidly about themselves. Some were married but most were single, some black, some white, men of sixty and men of twenty-six. It was a revelation. So many lonely men." And then there was Dan.

Dan was thirty and had just finished his Ph.D. in genetics. "Something about his response tugged at my heartstrings. He claimed to be the quintessential nerd, ignored by girls most of his life, and filled with the romantic longing most of us have abandoned by the age of twenty-one. The undercurrent of passion in his letters rocked me."

What the hell, she thought. So they met for coffee. Age must have improved him, because he showed no sign of the nerd; in fact, she couldn't take her eyes off him. It didn't mean anything would have to happen, and it didn't, and then they met for coffee again and the hours went by and they talked and talked and, well, it got dark and Jody's husband was traveling on business and Dan lived nearby and "How," says Jody, "could a young and beautiful man bear the sight of my scarred, overweight body? Wouldn't he take one look and shrink right back into his boxers?" He didn't; he said, "You are so beautiful and you don't even know it." And they fell in love. "Not something I planned for," she says. And so began "the most wonderful year of my life."

But she is on the edge of tears. "I was so happy, I began to exercise, lost twenty pounds, bought new clothes; I began to be proud of myself. My husband grew happier, my daughters were happy to see me when they came home from college, my friends marveled at my new self. With my husband away so often with friends or on business, Dan and I made love all the time, at his apartment, at my house, in the countryside where we traveled on my bike. Dan loved the fact that I rode a bike. I made gorgeous picnics and off we would go to the wine country, buy a pinot noir, and feast on pâté and sourdough bread and cornichons, and cookies I made myself. Afterward . . . He loved my spirit and my libido. I loved making love to him and with him. I was like a thirsty man in the desert; after all the years of not being wanted, I couldn't get enough of his passion for me." She is definitely crying now; she reminds me of Roger Nafziger sitting there in his wheelchair, knowing his life is over. "We ended a month ago."

I have not said anything for a long time but understand now that her offer of a ride through San Francisco was not just a thank-you for my book; her invitation came from a need to talk. She rushes on: "Nobody knows anything about this. I can't talk to anyone. I'm so bottled up. I'm sorry, I don't mean to burden you, I'm just so sad, I need someone who understands me."

I do. I know that there are many layers of the love between a younger man and an older woman. It's nothing new; in fact, it is encouraged in some cultures; for instance, there was and perhaps still is the custom in Italy of placing untried boys with skilled older women, not prostitutes, often women of good reputation, who instruct them in the art of love, the manners of lovemaking. We talk briefly about famous couples in which the woman was older than the man: Anne Hathaway, Elizabeth Barrett Browning, Susan Sarandon, and let us not forget Demi Moore. Jody looks at me, her tears stanched, and reminds me that seven years are all that separate these famous people, with the exception of Demi. "Not twenty!" she says, and I think but do not say, And not forty, the age difference between Graham and me. Jody tells me how the age difference worked to Dan's advantage. She was much more skilled than he. "Part of the pleasure," she says, "was his eagerness to learn. We practiced a lot. We laughed a lot. We even went shopping for sex toys! Neither of us had ever . . . No one had ever touched me like that, even my scars, my middle-aged belly, my toes, and a place he found at the back of my neck I never even knew was there. I felt so free. We were new together. And now . . . it's time for him to find a woman to carry his children, to grow old with." She is quiet and determined and in pain.

I murmur, "I know, I know." I would take her hand, but she still wears her motorcycle gloves; I would put my arm around her, except she's so much taller than I and it would be awkward and, well, of course, here in San Francisco passersby would assume we were a lesbian couple, which would not trouble either of us. I feel useless, and then she says, "You are the only person I can talk to and I've only met you twice, but in your book you wrote about Graham"—a bit of a smile here—"and so I thought you wouldn't make fun of me or scold me or judge me. I thought you would understand how you can love someone and let them go. God, I'm not sure if I feel sixty or sixteen." Although the sun is rapidly going down behind the Golden Gate Bridge, she puts her sunglasses over her eyes. "I'd forgotten how shitty sixteen can feel." She takes off her gloves and blows her nose. "He wants children," she says, "and I can't give them to him. All I can give him is the freedom to find someone who can. So here we are, you and me, and there he is . . ." She points down toward the marina.

"Letting go is hard," I say.

"And I haven't yet. But I will, I have to. Hop on."

Our ride back to the lot where I've left my car is subdued. The motorcycle purrs rather than roars, and I am hoping the ride eases Jody's pain. Because I can't help, I can only hope that my open ear and closed mouth helped a little. At the parking lot, she gives me a hug and I give her one back. "Wait!" she says. "We've gotta have a picture!" She hands her camera to a passerby and we stand before her Harley, she in all her leather beauty, I in my red shirt and New York Public Library baseball cap, tough women for tough times.

I feel pretty shitty myself, for I have not let go. I have not been as brave, as generous, as Jody. I have clung to whatever shred of himself Graham is willing to toss my way. I have berated him for his long silences between e-mails, I have written and sent midnight dui's that embarrass me in the morning, I have cried over his inaccessability when I'm in New York for fun and he's in Chicago on business. I have even hoped for bad luck to befall him in Italy. "The time Dan and I spent together," Jody had said, "was a year out of time. It was a year of growth for him and happiness for me. Now he will make the life he needs and wants, a life with children in it." Graham has made the life he wants. I should let him live it.

Next day, on my computer the photograph of the two of us arrives. There we stand, arms around each other's shoulders, grinning as if we were happy, the Harley gleaming behind us. Biker Babes Forever. That's us. Good thing my dad's not around. He'd kill me.

how reading can change your life

A reader's faith in literature is the truest form of assisted living.
—THOMAS MALLON in his review of
JULIAN BARNES'S *The Lemon Table*

n case you were wondering, when we came back from
Europe in 1955, we were still virgins, except for Pat, who
came back pregnant—though she didn't know it until some
weeks after she'd got home. She had an abortion, a bad one, an illegal one, a dangerous one, almost died, was disowned by her father and ignored by her mother for the rest of her life. Eventually
she married a nice man, had two kids, and spent holidays with her
in-laws.

Next to Pat, I came the closest of anyone in our little group to
Becoming a Woman. As travelers in foreign countries, each of us
had a job: translating the dollar into local currencies, reading the
map, finding a place to sleep—*"Haben sie Zimmer für sechs Perso-
nen?"* Now that we were abroad—on the Continent, ta-da—we
convinced ourselves that we were becoming more sophisticated
with each passing day, and so we felt free to be risqué, to unleash
the natural sexiness in ourselves, at least in words if not in deed.
With that in mind, I was given the job to discover, learn to speak,
and teach to others, in the language of the country in which we

found ourselves, the phrase "sexual intercourse." Germany was tough, and provided us with our least favorite word for "sexual intercouse": "Geschlechtsverkehr." "Rapporti sessuali," the language of lovers in Italy, was our favorite. We made a kind of Gregorian chant out of it: "Rapporti sessuali sit in perpetuum," which we sang up and down the streets of Florence and Rome, forgetting that our new language belonged to everybody who happened by and who smiled, mostly, at those American girls. We had such fun. Though one day, in Rome, as we sat in a café sipping red wine so cheap that our teeth were already dark brown—oh, yes, we were smoking Gauloises, too—we looked at each other and admitted that not one of us had been pinched.

Somewhere during our adolescent lives we had read that Italian men were outrageous, that they pinched wantonly every creature they believed to be female, that respectable girls and women had to be on the alert at all times; otherwise, a tweak, a bump, a pinch—how dare they! Now here we were in Rome, the capital of pinching, and not a rub. Maybe if we walked slower. One day we found ourselves on the city bus. It was very crowded. It was so crowded you just couldn't move. Annie, the tallest of us all, stood pinned between passengers in the middle of the bus. Suddenly she uttered a cry heard round the bus. And then she smiled. And we all smiled. She had been deflowered, lucky girl. If one is pinched, can the rest be far behind?

I had to wait till Paris, where I fell drunkenly in love with Gunnar, a hunk of a Swede who lived on welfare because when he listed his vocation at the welfare office, there wasn't any work for zither-stringers, which Gunnar insisted he was. So we drank a lot of red wine, danced on tabletops with Russians escaped from Stalin, drank some more wine—Encore! Encore!—until one night I was ready to *faire l'amour.* Gunnar and I had done a lot of kissing—*Embrasse moi, bébé*—even in public, which Paris allows couples to do, and it was time, it just was. So I answered yes to Gunnar's "Come *avec moi* to my *chez.*" I weaved with him to his pension, and there, blocking the stairs to his room, stood the concierge, broom held crossways against her bosom. "It is too late for young ladies to go upstairs. Shoo." She said it in French, of course, but no translation was necessary. Gunnar walked me back to the bistro, where I promised that when I got home to America I would get a job and send him money so he could get to Mexico and then sneak into America, which wouldn't let him in because he was a Communist. Wow! I'd never met a Communist before, and this one was soooo neat! However, I had the definite feeling my dad would not give me the money for Gunnar's emigration to America, and that I would have to go to actual work, but I was in love and an almost-woman in love is not to be denied. The job I was able to get—typing—paid me enough to rent a room with a hot plate. *Mon amour* didn't even send me a postcard. *Tant pis.*

Needless to say, none of the six of us who traveled to Europe in 1955 is a virgin now. We are divorced or we are widowed. Along with Communism, our men exist only in our memories. Except for me, who has been out on a sexual limb for the last four years, we have left romance and danger behind, and here we are, loving our grandchildren and knowing our book clubs aren't quite enough. Something like 85 percent of women who buy books belong to book clubs. Astounding, though not really, for we are great readers, our generation, and along the way of our lives we have learned to talk about what we read without the specter of professors shushing us and admonishing us to take notes. And so we gather.

Most of the people who come to my readings are women, most of those middle-aged, I suppose. Maybe it's young middle age. I have gotten confused by the changes in labeling. Now, at seventy-one, I think I am referred to by gerontologists as middle-old; before seventy I was young-old, and when I hit eighty, I'll be young-really-old, until ninety, when—there's just no getting around it—I'll be old, though by then someone will have come up with different labels. Actually, I have some: 20–30, Medieval;

30–40, Renaissance; 40–50, Baroque; 50–60, Neoclassical; 60–70, Surrealist; 70 until death, Masterpiece. I am, as you can see, early Masterpiece. I like that better than being postmodern.

Seattle, where I am reading tonight, seems like a good place in which to be whatever age one happens to be at the moment. It is beautiful, very beautiful: snowcapped mountains, lots of hills and water, blue sky, nice people, and good food. I am ready to move here; it is small enough to walk around in and big enough to have a stupendous new library, concert halls, terrific bookstores, and a good basketball team. However, I am advised by those who know that I must spend a winter in the rains of Seattle before I commit my financial resources to buying a house here, though—ha!—real estate prices here are almost as high as they are in Berkeley. Another niche market. Thank you, Bill Gates.

In the bookstore the man at the end of the line is accompanied by a woman. They introduce themselves to me. "I am Evelyn." "I am Arthur." They are smiling broadly, unusual in men and women in their later years—I would label them middle Masterpiece—grimness being too often an accompaniment of old age. "We waited until we could have a bit of time with you. We have a very special thank-you." Evelyn is pretty, and not just for middle Masterpiece. It is possible to be pretty long after child-rearing and menopause, right up to death. It is even possible to be prettier than you were at twenty-one, though Evelyn strikes me as having been pretty her entire life, one of those girls who dated seniors when she was only a freshman. Arthur, nice-looking, a bit shy, stands just behind Evelyn's left shoulder. "Tell her," he whispers to Evelyn, nudging her gently.

Evelyn leans forward and explains, smiling all the while. "You see, we are both widowed and we have been seeing each other now for quite a few months." Arthur ducks his head and moves farther behind Evelyn. Evelyn says, "And then I read your book. I loved it, just loved it."

Over Evelyn's shoulder, Arthur whispers, "Go on."

"So one day I put the book in the center of the kitchen table, the day I knew Arthur was coming over."

Arthur says, "You can't miss it, that cover. Wow."

"So he picked it up and asked, 'What's this?' And I told him about your book and he looked surprised, and I just rushed right ahead and said, 'Arthur, do you think you and I could ever be intimate?'"

No longer shy, Arthur steps forward, smiling broadly, "And I said, 'How about now?'"

The two of them are radiant. They offer their very special thanks and leave hand in hand, a beautiful couple if ever there was one.

It has been a long night. Back at my hotel I drink a solitary scotch, climb into bed, and wonder how I might go about finding an Arthur who does not live three thousand miles away. I think kind thoughts about the man from Modesto; maybe I should have stopped him, asked to buy him a cup of coffee, tackled him at the knees before he could get out the door, offered to . . . to . . . Christ, I need a pickup line.

I remember all too well searching the hardware stores for men, where I figured older men hung out, men who knew how to do stuff. I was right: There they were fingering belts, measuring wire, putting nails into paper sacks, comparing screws to each other. They were busy. Their lives had purpose and meaning. They were going to fix things, to make things, to build things. Do it to *me*! Peering through the shelves opposite some unsuspecting man I had stalked into the nuts and bolts section, I thought, Now what? What should I say? What's a nice guy like you doing in a place like this? What time do you get off work? Women of my generation didn't own pickup lines; those belonged to the men they would turn down. So in the hardware store I turned myself down before I could make a bigger fool of myself, and left.

But what *does* one say? Do you tell the truth—I want to lie down next to you, maybe? Of course not. What if it turns out you don't? Or do? How do you not scare a live man away? How do you protect yourself from rejection? Men have been running these risks forever, and maybe they get used to rejection. But boy, it's scary. Takes balls. We women are supposed to have them now that we're equal, but, after all, they don't grow overnight. Look how long it took me and look what I had to do! And look where I am now! Manless for all practical purposes, potentially homeless, and without a pickup line to call my own.

All this, of course, I keep under wraps at readings so as not to spoil my readers' illusion that I knew what I wanted and got it. Well, I did know what I wanted, but getting it doesn't mean you stop wanting, and maybe, oh fickle creatures that we are, what you want changes into something you don't have, and then oh boy, the restlessness of the human spirit begins its work, shooing content-ment out of its way to make room for yet another ride on the roller coaster.

Back home, in my post office box, there is a letter. From Bryan. I do not know Bryan, but he writes, *"I found your book on the table of an older woman (I am 40, she 64) whom I was visiting for purposes of business. I enjoyed the book enormously and feel compelled to write our gratitude to you. Your book served us well. Thank you. Please extend our thanks to Graham."*

Whaddya know. My book has become a pickup line.

So when Barbara, a complete stranger, calls me on the tele-phone from her home in San Mateo and breathes, "I've just fin-ished reading your book, and I know I have a lot of nerve calling you," I don't hang up. She continues, "I'm fifty-three, divorced for ten years . . ." And she invites me to the next meeting of her book club, where *A Round-Heeled Woman* will be discussed. "Some of the older members," she says, "will have trouble talking about the sex parts, so if you could come and just sort of facilitate things. You have been so brave." And then her confession, tears in her voice, "My goodness, I just . . . can't even . . . get a date!"

If I were there or she here, I would hug her. I would try to comfort her, to tell her that . . . I don't know what to tell her. When I began these readings, in June of 2003, I would leave burdened with the responsibility of having opened a great big kettle of fish. Women whispered their longings, their sins, their failures, their hopes for a better future. What had I done? But by the time of Barbara's call, I have become, if not hardened, at least more sensible. Books, if they're worth anything at all, let the readers take from them what the readers need to have. Apparently my book did that. If that something is hope, well, there's little enough of it around, so have at it. To Barbara? Oh, in the absence of truly sound advice, I'd probably tell her to go online. And I do. And she answers, "But what would I say?" My heart goes out to her.

So, Barbara, I'm thinking of doing something sort of like what Evelyn did: I'm thinking of making T-shirts with the cover of the book on the front and the message, in big bold letters, **Ask Me About This Book**. If you get shy, you can always wear it inside out.

CHAPTER 22

reunions

Plus ça change, plus c'est la même chose.

I f hardware stores or online dating services are not for you, go to a reunion. Reunions are all over the place. High school reunions are the best because so many people there are widowed.

Julia, a friend of mine for many years, went to her fortieth reunion and hers is a different story. Julia lived in a big old 1826 wonderful house, peaked roof, white clapboard, and green shutters. I used to envy Julia her house and many of the things in it, things she had inherited from her mother, things that belonged to ladies, like candle snuffers (six), and silver tea services (two). I did not envy Julia's life; she didn't like it much, either. A bad and short marriage, a daughter she adored forever, and a longtime love affair with Herbert, a man she loved but who couldn't marry her because his sisters wouldn't hear of it. Herbert was a good, if somewhat timid, man who loved Julia very much, so much that he paid off the mortgage to her house. So there she sat in her big old wonderful fully paid-for house, loving Herbert for twelve fine years, when news of his death from a heart attack came to her. Julia was fifty-five and would never recover. Herbert's sizable estate was claimed by his sisters, the evil twins, so it's a good thing Julia had free lodging for the rest of her life. Even so, she grew bitter.

She hated her job and the people who worked with her. She stopped going to movies or plays; she refused to travel except to the library across the street, where she read just about everything in it. Reading was her drug, though not strong enough to dull forever the need for company. So one spring, at her daughter's behest, she drove the few short miles to her high school reunion. And there he was, her high school boyfriend, cute as ever, recovering from colon cancer, and married. They talked and talked, exchanged phone numbers and from that day on spoke every single day on the telephone. "Come to Austin this weekend; I'll be there for a meeting," he urged. "I'll come to see you next month," he offered. No, no, said Julia, no men, no sex, it was just good to hear a man's voice telling her that she was smart and pretty and sexy. Julia *was* smart: no involvement with a married man, no falling in love and spending the rest of her holidays alone, and no participation in adultery. Julia's ideals remained untarnished, unless you count the hours of foreplay on the telephone.

If Julia got one thing right in her life, it was Frannie, Julia's daughter and best friend for life. Frannie grew into a smart, funny, loving, and lovable woman. Frannie married a loving and lovable man, and together they gave Julia two grandsons, whom she loved almost as much as she loved Frannie. Frannie knew about Julia's phone affair and sometimes urged her mother to go ahead and meet this man, but Julia was adamant, and Frannie stopped counseling her mother and went back to simply loving her.

Julia retired early from the job she hated and took up drinking. She had always enjoyed a drink; now she drank in earnest. Unfortunately, drinking and reading were incompatible, so when it came time for her to choose, she chose drinking. Frannie worried about her but not terribly, because Julia was always in control of herself in the presence of her grandsons. Besides, what could Frannie do? She went back to her children and her garden and her husband.

One Wednesday, Frannie got sick. She complained of a terrible headache, vomited, and frightened her husband so that he rushed her to the emergency room, where she was diagnosed with meningitis. What? Julia was unbelieving and rushed to her bedside, where, on Friday, Frannie died. She was thirty-five.

Julia returned home, sedated by a doctor's prescription and as much merlot as she could carry. After that she gave up eating in favor of drinking full-time. Not many months later her liver gave out, she was taken to the hospital, tried to walk to the bathroom, fell, and died. She was sixty-four.

All her life, in addition to Frannie, Julia had loved the Boston Red Sox. If only she had lived a few more months to see them win the World Series, their first in eighty-six years, her world might have brightened a bit, might have given her a reason to persist.

This may be the saddest story I know. Without a doubt, Julia's house is the saddest house I have ever known.

BUT LET US not despair, for Carol, back in my hometown in Ohio, put together a fine celebration for *her* fiftieth reunion, and here came Jim, retired, wealthy, ever so nice, and widowed. They were married last summer and, between them, have three houses, all of them happy. Likewise Carolyn and Bob in Upper Michigan, who met again at their fortieth high school reunion, and all those couples in Sunday's *New York Times*'s wedding section who unite or reunite in later life.

People are getting married all over the place without, in some cases, the blessings of their expectant heirs, but what the heck, time's a-wasting. What is the lure of this ritual? At such a late age? One would think that, after suffering through a wretched marriage or a painful illness or both, people would abjure marriage. Why don't they just live together? Lots of older people do when they find out that their Social Security benefits will drop if they marry. But many men and women go right ahead and do it all over again. Of course, men and women whose marriages were good ones want to repeat them; then, too, there is the urge to repeat an experience in order to correct it: "I'm going to do this until I get it right." I suppose that once in the fold one yearns to stay. The fold offers convention, and convention offers protection and social security of a sort that has nothing to do with money. The fold provides us a respectable face so that we can look the world in the eye without shame or embarrassment. The fold provides a comfort unavailable to existentialists like me, stuck as we are with the belief in the void. I'd just as soon believe in something else; the void is dark and cold, but faith in it, faith I never asked for, got me here and isn't letting loose. To ease matters, great literature and my long life have provided me a belief in the indomitability of the human spirit, the human capacity for reason and choice, and I take comfort in that. But often, especially when Carol sends me photographs of her marriage to Jim, and Carolyn sends me a wedding invitation, I long for a partner, someone who will keep me warm, light a lamp. I marry; therefore, I am: the credo of blessed partners everywhere. Marrying is easier than thinking, but then, almost anything is.

However, not everyone looks immediately for commitment and the promise of marriage. There is Susan, who came to my reading in Virginia. She is seventy-eight and is, as she will write to me, "a testament to the miracle of endurance, blessed to be still standing, in love again, and eager to proclaim: It's not over 'til it's over." The real reason she came to my reading was to get the name and address of my agent. Susan has written a memoir, just like me. Her life is much like mine. She wants my good fortunes to be hers. I like her. She is full of life, small and bouncy, and cute as a button. She looks happy. Not only that, she brings the hardcover, the expensive edition, to me to be signed. Of course, I like her. And then, too, she grew up in a small town in Ohio, just like me. She married a cad and a bounder, got divorced, made another life, like me. So, given all that, we are practically best friends. We're kind of having our own very small reunion right here in the bookstore. As at any good reunion, we are reminded of the past we shared and are delighted in the presence of each other.

Well, she tells me, there he was, at their sixtieth high school reunion, standing at the punch bowl—alone—and still a hunk. A BMOC sixty years ago, he was still a big man, now a lawyer (ret.), father of four, grandfather of eight, and widowed. Oh, how they talked and talked, and exchanged e-mail addresses, and one year later, Warren came to visit.

Now, Susan had made for herself a complete and satisfying life; her exhumed friendship with Warren was just that, a friendship. In their e-mailing he had informed her of his impotence and had written, "Consider me a friend if you like." And so she did.

On his first visit, Susan put him in the guest room, kissed him goodnight on the cheek, and repaired to her own bed, door closed. In came Warren: "Would you like me to hold you?" After three nights of incomplete but wildly arousing lovemaking, Susan was smitten, and she worried that her feelings had gotten out of hand. There was, after all, the fact of Warren's steel heart valve. And so off she marched to Warren's room, where she blurted, "I have become besotted with you. And it is—inappropriate."

And Warren said, "I'm sorry if I have caused you pain."

Dear reader, allow me to pause in this narrative to wonder about Susan and this Warren fellow. The day after Susan confessed her "inappropriate" feelings, she and Warren discussed, in her words, her "strange affliction, I rueful, he commiserating. We agreed lovemaking had probably been an unwise decision." Why, Susan, do you consider your passion inappropriate? Why do you call it a "strange affliction"? Of course, you would worry about his heart valve, but after all, Warren is a doctor and undoubtedly aware of the dangers lurking within. And surely, the two of you could discuss all this and then the two of you could . . . Do you think, Susan, you are too old to feel such passion? You're not. Do you think that your passion was greater than Warren's? Now, that's possible; it always is. And maybe you called it an "afflic-tion," that is, something beyond your control, in order to avoid your own judgment, your own responsibility for your feelings. And finally, perhaps you wanted to spare Warren, to make this "strange affliction" *your* problem, to take the blame, to assume the guilt, to exonerate Warren from all of the above. How womanly of you! Oh, how things stay the same!

And now, Warren, if I may be so bold, who do you think you are to commiserate with poor dear Susan for her "inappropriate" feel-ings? Why should she feel rueful, apologetic? For what? I am hop-ing you convinced her that her feelings, intense as they were, did not repulse you, that they were natural; and I hope you said some-thing like, "Well, I started the whole thing." Because, of course, you did. What did you think would happen if she said yes to your "Would you like me to hold you?" Being sorry if you caused her pain is fine and dandy, but it doesn't get you out of anything. How often have we women heard that? It's supposed to make every-thing all right again, it's so you can slip out of our lives with only the tiniest regret, gone by the time you hit the freeway. If you'd thought about it, Warren, you'd have known this is how it would be from the minute you stepped off that airplane. But no, a little cuddling, a little conversation about the old high school gang, free room and board for you, and a lot of screwing up a woman who's been waiting for you forever and well, gosh, "I'm sorry if I caused you pain." Good but not good enough. Is it possible your whole heart is steel? Okay, I presume too much.

But hold on: Here comes Helen. Yes, Warren, you mentioned Helen early on, didn't you, a woman you sometimes traveled with, "just a friend," you assured Susan. And Susan, well, god, at seventy-eight she's as dumb as we all were at sixteen and seem to remain. Okay, we think, so there's this Helen person and we certainly can-not demand exclusivity at our age! In fact, we can't demand any-thing, all we can do is take what we can get and be grateful. Warren, of course, gets both Susan and Helen to diddle with as he pleases, casting crumbs to the besotted as he does. He takes Helen to France; he takes Susan on a cruise, and in between is relieved that Susan refuses cunnilingus, because, she says, it would be unfair since only she would receive the pleasure. Oh, please. Susan is content now, she says, to enjoy whatever intimacies Warren chooses to provide her. She is grateful that the various medications necessary to a healthy life at age seventy-eight do, mercifully, dull the libido—a bit.

But wait! Who would ever think *Time* magazine would rise to the occasion and become the hero of the day? And lo, there cometh upon the plain of darkness enlightenment, and its name was Testosterone. Susan sends the issue on sexuality to Warren. A coupla shots and Warren is up and running. Warren's back and Susan's got him! And so has Helen, apparently, for the two of them are off to Paris. Helen has found out about Susan, has accused Warren of betraying her but, says Susan, "I guess she's like me and accepts whatever." And Warren? He must be one happy guy.

So I'm not sorry to have missed my fiftieth high school reunion back there in Ohio. It happened the week after 9/11, so I flew to New York instead of to Toledo. I heard that my classmates had a very nice time. And everybody who got married is still married and hardly anyone has died, so lord knows what pain awaited me there. New York was safer.

staying in touch

"What really knocks me out is a book that, when you're all done reading it, you wish the author that wrote it was a terrific friend of yours and you could call him up on the phone whenever you felt like it."

—HOLDEN CAULFIELD in *The Catcher in the Rye*

My phone rings a lot these days, even though I am supposed to be unlisted. "Hah!" one caller chortles. "You thought you could hide! I went to the library! Gotcha!" Not long ago my phone rang at five-thirty in the morning. I stumbled to answer it, and a deep, slow southern voice said, "Hey, Jane"—the kind of voice, only deeper, that said, "Hey, Boo" in *To Kill a Mockingbird*— "I just wanted to hear your sleepy-time voice." I hung up. The phone rang at seven-thirty. "Hey, Jane, just want to apologize for waking you. Loved your book, and if you're ever in—" Clunk. There are nice phone calls, too, from John in Mississippi, a lawyer who read the book at the insistence of his wife, and who wants to thank me for "showing them the way." I do not know what I wrote that would show them the way, but if they found one, maybe they can write a book and show the rest of us. Len, who lives in the Bronx, phones every other week, "just to see how things are going, make sure you're all right." Len tells me about his job that bores

him and his Japanese girlfriend who doesn't, about his mother
and her dementia that frightens him, about his dream of hiking
the Appalachian Trail. He is a nice man. Then, too, there is a man
named Phil who loves New York, "just like you," and who wants
"to walk the length of Manhattan" on me. I'm not sure how he
planned to do that, because I hung up fairly quickly. A man in
Quebec calls every so often, in that seductive French—okay, French
Canadian—accent, to tell me that he has read the book many
times and . . . Oh my, this man is very needy. After forty years of
work in the government, he moved back to Quebec and bought
his childhood home, and now he lives alone, except when he goes
to the library—I hasten to end the call without being rude.

Who do men talk to?! Sometimes, during these calls, I want to
reach out and touch them, hold them, and tell them—*What?*
That everything will be all right? Because the certainty grows—as
I listen to men from every state in the union and beyond—that
nobody holds them, that nobody listens to them, and that, probably as a result, or maybe because of their own silence, they don't
talk to anyone—not about boring jobs or spending time in the library when kids get there from school just to be near some kind of
life or . . . I have been told by men that when they get together,
they talk about golf and skiing and sometimes politics and sports
and their jobs and moving and buying houses or fixing them up—
Sheetrock and shingling seem big in the conversation of men—so
I wonder, do they ever talk about sadness or joy? I know, feelings.
Who was it who gave feelings a bad name? Who was it who said
to men, Feelings are not on the docket, they are off-topic, they are
outsourced—to women? So now here are these men saying to me,
"My sister died six months ago and I lived with her and now I was
wondering if you and I could go for a cup of coffee" and "New
Mexico is beautiful this time of year, I would love to show you this
part of the country, my wife died in June" and "Are you still taking applications?" Maybe I'm a mom to these men. Maybe I'm
someone to unburden themselves to and then, if they're lucky, set

up a sleepover with. The whole oedipal thing resolved in a single phone call. Whatever you call it—loneliness, despair, alienation—whether its explanation is Freudian or neurohormonal or god, my telephone trembles with it.

One day a woman calls. Her voice is low, with the hint of a Southern accent. She introduces herself this way: "I've never done this before and I don't want to bother you, but my husband and I so loved your book I just had to tell you right away." This is nice to hear. She continues: "We are coming to your city to celebrate our anniversary and would love to take you to dinner." I don't want to do this. Who are these people? But wait: She sounds nice, she sounds interesting, she sounds as if she will pay for my dinner. What's to keep me home? I go.

Her name is Emily and her husband's name is Alan. They have been married for four years. Emily at eighty is truly lovely to look at. She is tall, slim, with no pouch of a tummy I can distinguish— She wears her sweater tucked in! and a belt!—and her eyes are big and brown, cataract surgery having rid her of the necessity of wearing glasses. Her hair is brown, streaked here and there with white. She is an elegant woman. Alan has my favorite look: Slim in khakis and a button-down shirt bedizened by a rep tie and covered by a V-necked sweater, he is New England softened by Lands' End. His hair is white and thick, and his smile is of very high wattage. He is eighty-two.

At the end of a very fine dinner with fine conversation, Alan invites me to visit them in Oregon. "We mustn't let this evening be our last." I agree, and some months later I go. During the course of my visit they tell me the stories of their lives. The lives of Alan and Emily are the stuff of dreams, of fairy tales, of nightmares and miracles.

In a photograph of the two of them, taken in 1943 on Emily's porch swing in Saint Louis, Emily is lying in Alan's arms, her dark hair falling back onto his shoulder, his head bent to her face, which smiles happily and confidently into the camera. The photograph doesn't show Alan's face, only his hair, a bright blond cap that would stand him in good stead when he went off to Harvard. They promised to be true to each other.

Alas, Harvard was very far away, and Emily met a boy who lived nearby, a boy who was tall and dark and handsome in a Heathcliff sort of way. Emily's mother warned her. "He is a wild boy," she said, "and dangerous, too." But Emily was captivated by that very wildness, and one night, in the midst of winter sleet, she ran away with her wild boy to a land of sun and water, where fruit trees dropped oranges into their laps, and where, for the first time, Emily gave herself to a boy she swore to love forever.

On the far East Coast, Alan grew to handsomeness, and on a weekend in New York City, in the bar at the Biltmore, where at nineteen Alan could drink legally, a very beautiful woman, clearly older than Alan, perhaps even as old as thirty, smoothed herself onto the bar stool next to him. For a brief moment Alan feared she was a lady of the evening, and while Alan's father was rich, Alan himself was not, and was at the moment without the means to avail himself of such a woman.

"My husband is an officer stationed in France," said the woman, "and on occasion I come here for company and the chance to dress in the lovely clothes he bought me before the war." Alan looked at the satin of her gown and the satin of her shoulders and the dark sheen of her hair and determined to be good company. Two manhattans later she said, "Come with me; I live nearby."

The woman, without her gown, was satin from top to toe, although Alan in his youthful eagerness took no time to notice. Afterward, he was ashamed. The woman shushed him: "Do not despair; time is on our side." Sure enough, only minutes later, her mouth and hands in all the right places, Alan made love to this wonderful creature. And again. And all night long.

Far away, in the land of sun and water, the wild boy grew angry with Emily. "You told me you were a virgin! Why didn't you bleed?!" Emily curled herself into a very small ball of misery and soon after hurried home. The wild boy, having decided that a demi-virgin was better than no virgin at all, followed her, and on Emily's mother and father's porch the police met him. Emily never saw him again.

In New York City, in the early morning light, the woman kissed Alan. "You are a lovely man," she said. Despite several trips to New York and more than a little time in the bar at the Biltmore, Alan never saw the woman again.

And so ended the fairy tale of their young lives. It didn't come out right, did it? If it had, Alan would have returned to Emily, they would have married and lived happily ever after. But they didn't, and so real life took over.

Like ordinary people Alan and Emily did the ordinary things. They got married, though not to each other, and had children, who—if children have a purpose at all now that the world has enough people in it—serve to notify parents that life is not a fairy tale. The children grew and some of them prospered, some of them didn't. The marriages of Alan and Emily did not prosper, yet somehow, even though they were on opposite sides of the country, they felt the presence of each other. They wrote each other polite notes at Christmas and on birthdays, always correct, never romantic, just notices to each other that they had not forgotten and would not forget, just to stay in touch.

On a few occasions in the wintertime, at Alan's invitation, Emily and her first husband flew to Vermont, where Alan and his wife had a cabin. Emily's husband knew of the long friendship between his wife and Alan; he knew nothing of their early love for each other. For her part Emily believed herself to be grown up, responsible, capable of friendship without a rekindling of feelings from so many years before. One stormy winter evening, the four of them warming themselves before the fire, a thought, completely unbidden, came to Emily: Oh, why don't they leave us, why don't they go and leave Alan and me alone? She knew then she shouldn't have come. Watching Alan in the firelight, skiing with him down the powdery trail, standing next to him in the kitchen or on the porch or in the hall or in the driveway, anywhere at all, her heart leapt and she fell in love all over again. For his part Alan couldn't take his eyes off Emily, who seemed to have grown lovelier over the years. The time they spent in each other's company was not enough, not enough at all, and his heart ached with wanting her. But what could they do? There were children on both sides who needed them. Losing a child—and both Alan and Emily did—retards, and sometimes destroys, the lives of the parents. It is the most unfair and most catastrophic event in an unfair and catastrophic universe, and for a long time Alan and Emily, along with their spouses, removed themselves from life. Only their remaining children gave them reason to resume living.

And then one fall Saturday, Emily, on her way with her husband to France, stopped in New York, and there, in the Egyptian room at the Metropolitan Museum, she came upon Alan and his new and second wife, Laura. The four of them exchanged introductions and a few pleasantries, then Laura and Emily's husband wandered off to view the pyramid, and Alan and Emily were, for a few minutes, alone. In an instant the world grew both larger and smaller; colors were brighter, sounds clearer, and all the people disappeared; there were no people at all, just the two of them standing there close to each other. Suddenly Emily leaned over and whispered, "Somehow, someday, I think we will be together." How bold! Emily hardly dared look at Alan, but when she did, he was smiling. And then they parted.

When Emily was fifty and those children who hadn't died early had grown, she divorced her husband, a philanderer and, worse, boring. Early in the marriage, in addition to other women he had taken up the cello, one of Emily's favorite instruments until he began to play it, though once she got used to the screech and scratch of it she became fond of the time he spent with it. She was a cello widow and quite content to be so.

Alan's second wife was a termagant, and why he married her no one could understand, Alan being the gentle soul that he was. Wife number two made a good deal of money in her career in finance high above Wall Street, where being a termagant seemed appropriate. But there came a time when Alan had had enough and decided to divorce her. He went to Vermont, to his ski house, to think things over.

Emily, enjoying the freedom afforded her by her own divorce, flew to Boston to visit an old friend. From the city she called Alan in Vermont just to say hello. "Come ski with me," he said, but Emily, unaware of Alan's plans for divorce, declined his invitation, knowing that the two of them alone would spell trouble for his family life. She tried to explain, but her voice, filled with tears, trembled so that Alan determined to stop thinking about divorce and make plans to do it; and then a terrible thing happened. In New York City, Alan's wife was robbed and beaten; she sustained severe and irremediable brain damage; she would be an invalid for the rest of her life. Divorce was out of the question.

Emily married again, not Alan but a man named Roger, who at first seemed fond of Emily but who in fact loved the acres on which she lived. Christmas cards and an occasional valentine continued their trips between Alan and Emily; their messages remained polite and informative, never hopeful of what might yet be, but never despairing of what could not.

Unlike Alan's marriage, filled completely with caring for his wife, Emily's marriage was typical of many. Emily and Roger were polite to each other; she cooked the right food for him; she saw to it that he had a clean shirt to wear every day. She invented a sort of social life for the two of them, though Roger had little interest in the riches of their local museum or in the books Emily adored or—well, he did go to the movies every so often, railing against subtitles, accusing Emily of undermining him when he found himself, against his will, watching a foreign film. Roger watched a lot of television and spent hours channel surfing, after his workday at the bank. Where Emily's first husband had sawed at the cello in the studio across the meadow from Emily's house, Roger watched ESPN. Roger was the first of their acquaintances to get a dish, which he positioned atop the studio, thus blocking the view of the Pacific—but providing him access to new favorites, such as professional wrestling, monster truck rallies, and porn whenever he felt that having sex with his wife was too much trouble. At times the two of them went out to dinner and were that couple you have seen many times in restaurants—middle-aged and silent, staring at their food—two people whose interest in each other has died long ago, perhaps as soon as it began, a husband and wife who have simply run out of things to say.

Why had they married? Surely not out of passion, absent even in the beginning of their marriage. The custom of the country—in this case, marriage—is a powerful one; two seemed safer than one. After the divorce Emily did not miss her first husband, but she did not know how to live without one; she felt useless to herself now that the children were gone; what good was she, she wondered; she was lonely. Roger, who began courting Emily only months after his first wife's death, had no idea of how to live alone either; he never had. He had done what he was supposed to: He had made money, quite a bit in fact, worked hard, and been taken care of until his first wife died. Now there was no one to iron his shirts or feed him or change the sheets on the bed where he had claimed his conjugal rights whenever he was moved to do so. There was, however, an increasing number of widows, women in their sixties, like Emily, who were accustomed to doing all those things and who, like Roger, were unaccustomed to living alone. So they teamed up, you might say, in the hope of providing a small fire by which to warm themselves against the coming of the night. The fire turned to ashes before their very eyes, and custom—a man and a woman married to each other—resumed its preeminence in their lives, providing no warmth whatsoever, simply habit.

Ten years of a marriage of that sort is a long time, and when Emily turned seventy, she decided that, Roger's needs notwithstanding, she wanted to travel. She cooked two weeks of meals and froze them; she drew a map to the laundry in town, where Roger could take his shirts to be washed and ironed; she renewed his subscription to *TV Guide* and said good-bye. But before she left, she wrote Alan this note: *"I plan to visit Boston the last week of this month. I will be staying at the Ritz-Carlton. If you happen to be in the area, perhaps we could have dinner. It has been a long time."*

Alan, a resident of New York, had not planned to be in the area, but lickety-split he was, and on a gentle spring evening, in the hotel dining room, Emily reached across the table, took his hand, and said, "Unless you need to get back to New York, we might have breakfast tomorrow." Alan looked down at his napkin, and Emily grew afraid.

Aging brings with it illness, infirmities, collapses, debilities, plain old exhaustion. Alan, seventy-seven and a survivor of prostate cancer quieted for the time being by surgery, was even more afraid. The years spent caring for his invalid wife had been sexless, and Alan had been too worn out to look for companionship elsewhere. What the hell was he doing here, he wondered. He hadn't made love to a woman—for that's what being with Emily would be—in fifteen years; his prostate was whacked; the chances of performing at all were minimal. Humiliation waited just upstairs.

Emily, for her part, had lousy knees: Going downstairs hurt like hell. Her elbows ached even at rest—What if she had to get on top?—and her lower back had acquired the habit of going out without giving notice. Like Alan, she had not made love in many years. Though her husband had had sex with her when he felt like it, those occurrences had diminished in number until finally, supplanted by Extreme Sports on ESPN2, they had ceased altogether. Dried by age and disuse, Emily doubted she could provide the necessary slippage necessary for Alan to make love within her.

Perhaps there have never been two braver people in the world. How easy to lead troops into battle! How inconsequential to swim stormy seas, to fly into a hurricane, to climb the highest mountain! Making love at any age takes nerve—there is so much to be lost—and when the lovers are old in body, courage had better show up. Show up it did, and shored up by love it took a stand and made everything work just fine. So said Alan and Emily to each other the next morning over the breakfast tray: "Everything worked just fine." And they decided then and there that, adulterers both, they would be together whenever they could wherever they could. They shared a past and would make a future somehow. "Somehow, we will be together."

And this is what they said to me as the three of us sat on the patio overlooking the acres of paradise they had bought together after the deaths of their spouses. Alan and Emily, husband and wife for four years, are very much in love.

"My mother told me, when I was very young," says Emily, "that the first love is the best love because it never ends." She looks at her husband and smiles. Alan nods his head in agreement and says, "We have been very lucky, Emily and I, though I would add that our determination to stay in touch had much to do with our happy ending."

In their dream life, which they spend happy hours planning, they will move to a vineyard where they will drink wine and raise animals, and in the fall and perhaps in the spring they will visit their pied-à-terre in New York on East Eighty-first Street, near the Metropolitan Museum. For now they live happily in a peaceable kingdom by the sea.

In the photograph I take of the two of them, the Pacific sparkling behind them, Emily stands tall next to Alan—she has two new knees—her brown hair streaked with white, her face alight with happiness and confidence. Alan does not look at the camera but at Emily, his first and endless love.

On the way home I decide to call the phone company and get myself listed again. Think what we would have missed had Emily not been able to get in touch.

CHAPTER 24

a gentleman caller

Most people know more as they get older:
I give all that the cold shoulder.

—PHILIP LARKIN, "Winter Palace"

will be on the West Coast around the time of your birthday. May
I take you out for dinner?"

Graham has been alive to me in my imagination and, with
less frequency, in my e-mail. And so, just as I was the very first
time we met, I am alarmed and excited, terrified and eager, to see
him. Since he has not given me enough advance notice so that I
can shed fifteen pounds, I prepare for his visit by drinking in the
afternoon.

What will I wear? All that is loose and dark around my midriff.
My extra pounds seem to have gathered there, making me a prime
candidate for stroke or heart attack. I pray to the god of medicine
to keep me upright and ambulatory until after he leaves. It is,
after all, going to be my seventy-second birthday, and I have my
dignity to consider.

Will we make love? Where? Oh, on my futon, where we made
love before. But will he want to or will he insist on remaining
above the carnal as he did when last we met in New York? Will he
turn his back and run should I advance? My dignity already in

shreds, I see myself blocking my French doors, barring him from escape. I see myself hiding my only chair, thus forcing him to sit in the only other place available—on the futon next to me. My bed still looks too small for two, although with fifteen pounds less of me, it might do—or have done. Too late now.

Here's what I plan to do: clean until the bathroom sparkles. Seeing my medicine cabinet through new eyes—his—I will hide my blood pressure pills behind my Purely Silk Body Lotion, my calcium supplement and baby aspirin behind my Lubriderm and vitamin C chewables. Medicine cabinet stuffed to the gunnels, I will throw into a sack my Metamucil, flaxseed, and milk of magnesia, and the sack into a kitchen cupboard way back where he wouldn't think to look. But I don't do it. Graham is not the least interested in medicine cabinets, mine or anyone else's. Besides, he knows exactly how old I am, plus I'm sure he knows flaxseed is good for ages ten to one hundred. So I pour myself a(nother) glass of wine.

In the living room I think about replacing *Vanity Fair* with *The American Scholar, Time* with *The Atlantic, People* with *The New Yorker,* all magazines at hand. But I don't do it. Graham is an intellectual but not a snob. Besides, he knows *what* I read; what he likes is *that* I read—widely and a lot, just as he does. So I leave the magazines where they are: scattered all over my cottage. I consider replacing my CD of Benny Goodman's *Carnegie Hall Jazz Concert* with Bach's *The Goldberg Variations.* But I don't. He might want to dance, and Bach, though sometimes a toe-tapper, doesn't encourage partner dancing. However, I do do this: Right next to the futon, on the table, I put the *Collected Poems* of Philip Larkin, his favorite poet and one of mine.

Food! He's always hungry! So I actually do this: I put down my glass of wine and I bake cookies. I have not made cookies, not even for my granddaughter, since Graham and I, three years ago, in our picnic *à deux* atop Nob Hill in San Francisco, consumed little chicken legs, Brie, and a baguette, sipped champagne, and, for dessert, nibbled daintily on my homemade chocolate chip cookies. Actually, he devoured them. "Women today," he announced, "don't do this sort of thing." Right, I wanted to say but didn't, women of *my* generation do! So what if he and I have committed gross generalizations. Generalizations have their place, serve a purpose. They're like a giant exhale; they clear your head of the mess all those particularities made of it.

Tea! He drinks tea! So okay, he didn't sip the champagne on our picnic; I did. He drank some kind of Odwalla, weird. How is it that not one man I have met during these years of adventure drinks, except for one who was an alcoholic? Graham has never touched alcohol or dope—"Never felt a need for either." He doesn't even drink coffee! Now, in my kitchen I have no tea. Well, I have tea: Earl Grey. What if he doesn't like it? Cookies out of the oven, the smell of them turning my cottage into a real home, I race to the store and get green tea, English breakfast tea, incredibly expensive lemon ginger iced tea in a pretty bottle in case the weather—It is March, and you never know, the warm sun of April might show up early—Good god, should it be caffeinated or not?! I buy some of each.

IT IS NOW two o'clock in the afternoon and I have put in a good eight-hour day. I slip into all black, pour just a little glass of wine, and listen for the phone. Listening for the phone has got to be one of the more painful demands of life. It asks for what most of us do not have: patience. Patience asks that we occupy ourselves with something useful—crewel, for instance—and think of others while we wait. It asks us to put ourselves on the back burner, stand at the end of the line, weigh ourselves once a month instead of once an hour, call sweetly to our dilatory children, keep our screams to a minimum. Waiting for the phone to ring is its own kind of torment. If we are bold—and have his number—we can call him and give him hell: "It's four o'clock and you said you'd call at three, and goddammit, I have better things to do than sit here and wait for the fucking phone to ring!" And he says, "I love it when you talk dirty." If we are medium bold or upper-middle shy and we have his number, we sit on our hands to keep them from tapping the telephone keys, we sit on our cell phones, anything to make it impossible for us to call, because what would we say? "Are you dead? I feared you were in an accident when you didn't call, so this is all about you and how much I care for your safety." No man past thirty will believe this. Our pride crumbles before the phone.

He calls. "I'm sorry I'm late, got held up, will call you from the train when I get there." Although it will take the train forty minutes to get here, I leap into action. I knock back a shot of Scope and head for my car, certain that I'd better get to the station early, because what if I have a flat tire on the way or my battery dies or there are no parking spaces? I would be late and, finding no one at the bottom of the escalator, he would simply turn his back and go away forever; he probably wouldn't even wonder if I was dead. Ten minutes later I am parked at the station, near the bottom of the escalator, cell phone at the ready, unprotected by anything to read—In my haste I forgot to bring a book, what is happening to me!—and I stare miserably into the approaching evening, waiting for the phone to ring. Only thirty minutes to go. I should've asked my doctor for a defibrillator; my heart is hammering in triple time. Jesus, I'll be dead before he gets here. Maybe it's for the better.

He's beautiful. He bounds down the stairs as he did four years ago, way back when we met for the first time in New York. A brief hug of welcome and we are off for cookies and tea. At my cottage he sits in the chair, leaving the entire futon to me; he chooses Earl Grey and devours cookies. We talk about our reading: old Thucydides for him, new Pamuk for me. We meet somewhere in the middle with Kafka and speculate on whether or not he was serious when he ordered his papers to be burned after his death, or whether or not it matters.

I cannot take my eyes off him—Graham, not Kafka. His oval face, green eyes, full lips, and long limber body make it hard for me to join him in a discussion of anything. It's not that I want to leap on him, I don't, it would spoil everything; it's that he is so splendid to look upon. He resembles Sir Thomas Lawrence's portrait of the Duke of Wellington in London's Victoria & Albert Museum: same oval face and eyes, full mouth, the hint of a receding hairline. Dress Graham up in red coat, black collar, gold braid over his shoulder, and you couldn't tell one from the other. Graham has a regal bearing—okay, I'm exaggerating a little just to give you the idea. And of course, beneath his khakis he's hung like a moose. No exaggeration. Memory fails me all too often, but the memory of Graham sans clothes remains as vivid as anything I have ever experienced, and will stay with me forever. Which is good, because it looks as if that's what we are working on here: old memory, not a new experience.

He refuses a ninth cookie, and we're off for dinner. The wine (mine) is lovely, the food is good, the restaurant is crowded, and would that I could tell you what we talked about but I can't. Somewhere near the end of dinner I feel a tremendous urge to flee, to get out, to go. I must have begun rattling my silverware because Graham asks, "What's the matter?" I answer, "I don't know, let's go." So we do.

In fact I do know, but I choose not to tell him. The truth is that I have felt this panic every time I've been with him, here or in New York. Will he ask me to sleep with him? Will I ask him? Do I really want to? What will I say? What if he says nothing? And, far more seriously, will I ever see him again? Is this the last time? Will I have to imagine my life without him? All these unknowns eat away at whatever equanimity I have managed to conjure, and finally I get up and leave, hoping by my action to precipitate the answer to the question, What will happen next?

In silence I drive him through the night streets of town to the station. He gives me a juicy kiss and says, "I'm free tomorrow.

Shall we meet here around eleven?" I give him a juicy kiss back and say, "See you then."

So my question is answered. Tonight isn't the last time. Tomorrow will bring him back along with the same questions. I'm not sure how much more of this I can stand.

MORNING'S AT ELEVEN and all's right with the world. He's there and so am I, and off we go up the coast to a little town that Graham has read is home to a salvage shop nonpareil. I have never heard of this place, but the sun is bright, the sky is blue, the air is warm, and below us the wide Pacific sparkles.

Graham is aware of my home search. He's gotten enough e-mails from me, lord knows, and besides, he himself may be moving out of New York, which, should he actually go, will answer one question, Will I ever see him again? For, as much as I love him, I'm not spending money to get to Topeka or Ashtabula, no matter how torrid the tryst. In addition, there's his wife. A seventy-two-year-old tryster is kind of hard to hide in a town the size of Topeka. Maybe he'll go to London. Now, there's something to stir up dreams.

"Slow down," he says, pointing to a sign. "There's an estate sale." Graham loves to rummage in dead people's stuff. "Come on," he says, "the house must be for sale. Let's take a look." Thirty-six-year-old men walk really fast, so I trail behind him, having long ago stopped trying to keep up with him, and ignoring the lesson implicit as I do. Inside the house—the view of the ocean is breathtaking—I demur: "It's like walking on the dead." "It's fascinating," he says, "one can reconstruct the people who lived here from what they leave behind."

Dutifully I follow him downstairs, where the hallway and the bedrooms are lined with books. I am beginning to like this dead person. "A Jewish doctor lived here," Graham pronounces. He points to a bookcase that contains medical texts. He points to an-

other that holds books about Israel. I wander over to the bookcase
that holds Thoreau and Hemingway and Sinclair Lewis. Graham
joins me and says, suddenly, "Look." There, Saul Bellow on one
side and John Updike on the other, the pink spine of my very own
book shines forth: *A Round-Heeled Woman.* Graham and I are both
silent, ruminating on the two of us somehow having been a part of
this man's life on this California coast, a dead Jewish doctor who
knew both of us when he was still alive. Otherworldly, miraculous. What good company I am in: Updike, Bellow, a well-read
physician, and Graham. Doesn't get much better than that. I am
humbled.

Outside, Graham tells me about some law of physics that
claims that, contrary to popular belief, "miracles" happen often,
about once a month. "So this might not be quite so miraculous as
you think." But it is, and we are quiet on the drive home. "I prefer
books to people, you know," he says, interrupting the silence.
"Most people bore me after an hour. You are different. We have
been together a long time, haven't we, and not a jot of boredom
anywhere." I smile in agreement, and for the first time feel myself
relax. I like being with this man, and vice versa is good enough
for me.

Somewhere along the coast, not far north of San Francisco, the
highway allows us to pull off, to stop the car and gaze at the sun,
which is disappearing far too rapidly but beautifully into the
ocean. I turn to him and say, "Graham, tell me your wife's name."
He does. It is the loveliest name I have ever heard. I tell him that,
and he says, "Yes, and she's . . ." I finish it for him in my mind,
"the loveliest girl." I have never before seen that look on his face—
he has been graced by love—and I am overcome with the sweetness of it.

No, we will not sleep together now or ever again. And, most
likely, we will never see each other again. Somewhere between despair and relief, I fill the vacancy of him with a certainty that he
will not disappear entirely from my life, no matter the geography

of his whereabouts or the claims of his family life. He will write to me and I will write back.

Sure enough, next week he's there on my screen. *"Places in the heart get dusty, even though we throw sheets over the furniture, hoping for future ecstatic unveilings. This is sanity. We have built a long wall with a wide chink. This is wisdom."*

My place in his heart has gotten dusty, I guess, yet I take courage in the long wall he says we have built—with a wide chink where anything might get through. Finally, in his desire to console and amuse me, he ends with, *"Minus the painful excisions, we feel a bit like Heloise and Abelard. And you could do a lot worse than that."*

Yes, indeed. And yet, I end this chapter of my life in tears.

gimme shelter

Prosperity is not without many fears and distastes; and adversity is not without comforts and hopes.

—Francis Bacon

oving Graham all this time has been a little bit like renting: You know you don't have many rights, know you could be ousted at any time, and that the cost of living in this place you like could rise beyond your means without warning. But because you love your place and the pleasure it offers, and because leaving it behind frightens you—Where will you be without it?—you hang on past the time when you should be looking for something more suitable, more stable, more dependable, more your age.

Of course, life itself is a great big rental: We can pretend we own something, like a house or a husband or a child, but we don't; they are ours for only a while; then they go and it's time for us to vacate the premises and make room for the new tenants. Graham never offered a washer and dryer, let alone a place to put them, nor did I ever consider that his responsibility. Neither did I expect a homecoming from John or Robert or Sidney, though I will admit that every so often I wondered what I would do if one of them offered. With my single state in mind, I know it's time for me to find a space to fit me. I want to own no matter how short-lived my tenancy may be.

Leonard, my homeless friend who waits for me and my dollar in front of the post office, would say to me about my travails, "God loves you anyway." But I remain unconvinced and continue to wonder at Leonard's faith in a god who gives him nightly shelter behind the shrubs of a Bank of America parking lot. God loves in mysterious ways.

Leonard has made me appreciate my cottage, which I do not believe is a gift from god, unless god has assumed human form: the people who will buy the property next and who hold my future in their hands. So I clean my cottage, put flowers on the bookcase, and hope that new owners will believe in my excellence as a tenant. For Sunday is Open House, the day people will troop in and out of my landlady/lord's house and my cottage with spying eyes and bulging wallets. Let's do the math: Two years ago the house sold for $800,000; now the asking price is $949,000. Let's see, that will give them $149,000, a 19 percent profit. Not bad for two years.

One hundred and fifty-eight people came to the open house. The realtor counted. I recall those halcyon days of yore when a seller offered his/her house for a price, the buyer offered something less, and eventually the buyer and seller reached a compromise somewhere in between. Perhaps this civilized transfer of property still exists. But not here and not now. The bidding war, the feeding frenzy, in this town is fierce and on fire; it seems as if everybody wants to live here. I know, in Cambridge and New York City and in Miami, too, people are willing to mortgage their lives, their livelihoods, indeed their souls, to become homeowners. So I should not have been surprised when my landlady, twenty-two pounds of baby at her breast, tapped on my door with the news that she and her husband had accepted a bid for $1,800,000, a 125 percent profit. Benvenue is the name of my street, sort of a misspelling of bienvenue, which means "welcome." I guess so, though

Rue des Rêves—Street of Dreams—would be more like it. People who have lived on this block for thirty or more years stand on the curb, look back at their houses, and think: "We're living in a million-dollar house! Let's sell! And take our 125 percent profit and go . . . ?" So far not one of the longtime residents has cashed out and left.

So. Will I ever own a home? Not here, not on this street, not on this block, probably not in this town. The best I can do for now is be grateful that my new landlords want to keep me without raising the rent. So I will hunker down and appreciate what I have, cultivate my landlord's garden, and hope that it will all work out in the end and that everything happens for a reason. I don't believe any of that. I believe that much of life works out for the worst and not just in the end; that faith is what we use to armor ourselves against the fear that everything is random. But, given that randomness, life offers joy as well as tears, love as well as hate, pleasure as well as pain, along with everything in between. What we want and don't want is there for the asking, although not always for the taking. It is a rich life we lead.

"Happiness was but the occasional episode in a general drama of pain." I first read this last line of Hardy's *The Mayor of Casterbridge* in my twentieth year and, as yet pain-free, proclaimed it false. Since then my long life has aligned me more closely with Mr. Hardy. Yet, while he describes the dolor of our lives, he does not answer the question, "How shall we live them?" A. E. Housman is helpful: "Our business here is not to live, but to live happily . . . We must make up our minds to risk something." Yogi Berra said it differently: "When you come to a fork in the road . . . take it."

Not long ago the man with the great ass came back. He stood at the end of the line of people waiting for me to sign my book. When it was his turn, he handed me his copy and said, "Will you write, 'To a man I like'?" He was tall and big across the chest and looked as if he could give me shelter without any trouble at all. I looked up at him in surprise and said, "I don't even know you!"

He smiled and said, "Just your name then." I signed, returned the book to him, and stared at the dimple in his chin.

Oh dear, I seem to have reached another fork in the road. But I am determined not to race pell-mell down either one or both. I am like one of Schopenhauer's porcupines: Having suffered enough pricks from enough quills, when all I was after was a little warmth on a cold day, I am seeking a bit of distance, a zone, however small, of safety. Indeed, living alone has its advantages. It's nice not to listen for the phone, check my e-mail every twenty minutes, ride herd on the mailman, all in the hope of shoring up my life with the voices of my men friends. On the other hand—Curse the other hand!—memories of closeness, of touch or talk, rumple my sleep and pursue me during the day.

Today images of hard bodies assault us on the beach, on the television screen, in magazines and movies, even on the street. The celebration of youth—of tone and sheen—is loud and everywhere at hand as boys and girls, as young men and women, go at it in a display of healthy animalism. Everyone, it seems, is Doing It—in the halls of middle schools and on into the surrealism of reality TV—but without tenderness, without patience, without empathy or longing, without kindness or the generosity that comes with age when the coupling of man and woman is mutual in regard and ends in a contentment inaccessible to the young.

It takes years to learn how to be grateful and at the same time gracious. It takes years before patience is ours to command; but when it comes, we understand that there is a civility to making love, that lust need not be frantic, that kindness ameliorates the urgency of desire. The sweetness of bodies that yield, that fold in on each other, comes with age and in private. It is a fine thing, to be sought after and cherished when it is ours.

So, at the same time as I celebrate my single self, I recollect the touch of a man's hand on my thigh, my cheek, my breast, and I want it all again. Yet, memory serves me well. For now it is enough.

acknowledgments

My thanks to my editor, Susanna Porter, who refused to accept less when she knew I could do more.

To Johanna Bowman for her guidance and good manners.

To Mary, whose intelligence and patience helped me to clarify my thinking and gather my courage.

To D., whose careful reading of the manuscript kept me honest.

To J., whose encouragement once again made this book possible.

To Carl and Ryan of Vino, who listened to my kvetching and never once refused to sell me a bottle of wine.

about the author

Born in Ann Arbor, Michigan, in 1933, JANE JUSKA grew up in Archbold, Ohio. In 1955 she moved to California, where she has lived, with brief intermissions, ever since. She has taught English for more than forty years in high school, in college, and in prison. Many of the articles she has written about teaching and students have appeared in professional journals. She lives in Berkeley, California. *Unaccompanied Women* is her second book.

about the type

This book was set in Garamond No. 3, a variation of the classic Garamond typeface originally designed by the Parisian type cutter Claude Garamond (1480–1561).

Claude Garamond's distinguished romans and italics first appeared in *Opera Ciceronis* in 1543–44. The Garamond types are clear, open, and elegant.